To Ren

Best wishes

Blossoms Of Bloomo

An autobiography

from

Bernice Kozlowski

Blossoms Of Bloomo

An autobiography

BERNICE KOZLOWSKI

Matador
5 Weir Road
Kibworth Beauchamp
Leicester LE8 0LQ, UK
Tel: (+44) 116 279 2299
Fax: (+44) 116 279 2277
Email: books@troubador.co.uk
Web: www.troubador.co.uk/matador

ISBN 978 1848764 187

British Library Cataloguing in Publication Data.
A catalogue record for this book is available from the British Library.

Typeset in Palatino by Troubador Publishing Ltd, Leicester, UK

Matador is an imprint of Troubador Publishing Ltd

Printed in Great Britain by the MPG Books Group,
Bodmin and King's Lynn

This book I dedicate to the young. May their friends, provide them with as many happy memories, as The Blossoms of Bloomo did for me.

My heartfelt gratitude, to my Daughter Elzbieta and dear departed Son in law Ric. Who urged me on to record these memories. To my Granddaughters Alicya and Amelia, who still patiently show interest in Nana's endless stories.
To my husband, my grateful thanks for the countless cups of tea you provided .These on so many occasions helped revive my flagging spirit.

To:
Members of the Nottingham Writers Club, I acknowledge the interest they have shown in my book. I also extend thanks for the advice given me by the WRITERS WORKSHOP Oxfordshire.

Finally my appreciations to Adam and Stephanie of 13 Souls Nottingham, for the expert restoration work they carried out on my tattered old photographs.

Introduction

The unexpected call came late at night. The persistent ringing of the telephone disturbed my sleep, and barely awake I slowly clambered out of bed and reached over to pick up the receiver.

Without any introduction, I heard a voice convey an urgent message.

"Maureen has been admitted to the intensive care unit."

Sounding deeply anxious, the breathless person continued speaking.

"An ambulance has transported her to the Queens Medical Centre. The doctors here say her condition is critical."

I gasped as the caller, her voice now trembling with emotion, abruptly added, "I have to go; there are others to contact. Get here as quickly as you can."

Dazed, I replaced the receiver and briefly began to analyze the message; disturbed by the call an icy fear engulfed me as the message began to sink in. Glancing down at the recumbent figure beside me, I turned towards him, shaking him and shouting out "Get up! Get dressed!"

The sleeping figure, oblivious to the unfolding drama, did not respond. My anxiety was by now increasing to fever pitch; I continued shaking the reluctant riser and shouted even louder.

"Wake up; we have to go to the hospital, something has happened to Maureen."

The bewildered occupant of the warm bed now slowly began to stir; blearily he opened his eyes and glanced around the room. Noticing I was getting dressed, he appeared startled. But, without asking any questions, he threw back the blankets and jumped out of bed. As I tossed him a jumper from the wardrobe, I urged, "Get dressed!"

Within minutes – and now suitably attired – we were both in the car speeding towards Nottingham's University Hospital. As we approached the large impressive building, a feeling of utter disbelief overwhelmed me: had I imagined the distressing phone conversation? Was this a dream? What disaster had so swiftly struck down my childhood friend? A voice in my head began repeating the same questions over again like a worn out record. What could have happened? Has she had an accident? Is she seriously injured?

As the late night caller had provided no clues I was puzzled, and the caller's urgent words began echoing in my mind.

"Come quickly," they had said.

In record time, we reached our destination. Jumping from the car, I glanced towards the hospital. Now anxious to reach the building I hurried towards an entrance door. Feeling confident that it would be unlocked, I approached a doorway I had entered many times before. However, this time everything around me felt strangely unreal.

It occurred to me that if the medical staff had advised the family urgently to travel to the hospital then this indicated a major crisis. Yet receiving such dramatic message seemed unbelievable.

Only a few shorts hours ago, Maureen had celebrated the wedding anniversary of our close friends Jean and Ken along with a happy crowd of friends.

I was there, and Maureen, in top form, had sparkled – for on special occasions she loved holding court, especially when surrounded by her beloved family and friends. She livened up the gathering by laughing talking and teasing, as only Maureen could do. During the evening, she circulated around the room, making a special effort to talk to everyone. I noted her urging reluctant dancers on to the dance floor; moments later, they happily whirled around the room. In short Maureen, a few brief hours ago, was at her glittering best: she was the life and soul of the party, making people smile.

My husband and I made our way into the vast hospital. The night porter watched as we entered. I had no need to ask him directions, I knew the multi-story building well. Anxiously I hurried to summon the lift, my bewildered husband hurrying to keep me in sight. He did not speak until we had entered the lift.

"Are you sure we are going to the right ward?" he anxiously asked.

I nodded and briefly replied, "Yes, Maureen has been admitted to intensive care, the unit is housed in this wing."

There was no answer; he just continued looking anxious and continued to trail silently behind me.

The corridors, busy during the day, now lacked the familiar daytime bustle; this intensified my anxiety, as everything seemed uncanny and still. The lift doors clanged open and as we stepped onto another deserted corridor. The sound of our footsteps eerily echoed around us. With apprehension we continued heading towards our destination, wondering what we were about to discover.

Looming up was a notice board, it stated a designated place had been set aside where visitors could sit and wait for news.

I surged towards the sound of familiar voices. Waiting in the room were several people. Maureen's sister-in-law was the first to greet me. Immediately she explained that a member of the medical staff had informed the family that Maureen was critically ill. They also indicated that Maureen appeared to have suffered a catastrophic stroke. Her husband and Maureen's daughter Beverley, on hearing the tragic news, had entered the inner room to sit by her bedside.

Anxiously I listened as earlier events of the day were recounted – of how Maureen and her husband, accompanied by their work colleague Joan, visited Jean and Ken at their home, conveniently located just steps away. Maureen had gone to congratulate the couple on the success of last night's celebration. Then, having accepted an invitation to stay there for a meal, shortly afterwards Maureen stated she wanted to go home. Jean and Ken were perplexed by her sudden announcement – for, despite Maureen having for years battled chronic illness, it was totally out of character for her to let anything interfere with her social life. Within moments of reaching her own home, Maureen collapsed. Jean, urgently summoned, immediately went to Maureen's home. Once there she swiftly called for medical help; with sirens blaring, an ambulance raced towards Queens Medical Centre. Maureen Sylvia was hurriedly then admitted to a high dependency ward.

On a professional level I was accustomed to dealing with medical emergencies; now, hearing the distressing news, I felt overwhelmed with shock. In the past, I had many times offered support and advice to others in similar situations. Yet I felt inadequate to offer comfort to the people gathered around me, folk I knew so well. I wavered and at that moment desperately felt myself in need of an understanding nurse's support.

I struggled to regain composure as a distraught family member approached me. I listened as anxiously they asked my advice on Maureen's prognosis. In response to the questions, I promised to seek further information. Realizing how worried relatives often became confused and unable to comprehend what has happened to their loved ones, I prayed the outcome was not as grave as they suspected.

I stepped forwards towards the door of the intensive care unit. There was a strict policy on the numbers of visitors permitted at the bedside of patients in this unit. However, they waved at me to enter when they recognised me as a staff member. As I entered the inner room, the sound that attracted me first was the respirator rhythmically pumping. I noted that it was attached to the unconscious patient; surrounded by equipment, she lay motionless in the bed.

The bed, situated close to the nurse's desk, had two unoccupied visitor's chairs conveniently placed close by. I recognized the grave faced young doctor standing nearby; he glanced in my direction, and nodded to acknowledge me. Two anxious people were standing at his side, listening intently as he spoke. They were Maureen's husband and daughter; they looked up and beckoned me to join them. The doctor continued, gently explaining the reason Maureen was on a respirator. Finally he promised to speak to the other family members who were waiting in the outer room. The doctor slowly walked away, leaving three silent people reflecting on what he had said.

I reviewed the situation, and my concern mounted for Maureen's heavily pregnant daughter. Beverley looked pale and bewildered. Slowly she walked towards the bed and blankly stared at the respirator, unaware it seemed that I was by her side – yet moments before she had acknowledged me. I guided her towards a chair, she uttering a bitter sigh of anguish as she sat down; reaching across the bed, she grasped hold of her unconscious mother's hand. Gripping it tightly as if she hoped for a response, to her dismay there was none.

Maureen's husband now walked across the room and returned holding a chair. Placing it at the side of the bed, he beckoned me sit down. Now three desolate people, deeply wrapped in their own thoughts, sat close to Maureen Sylvia and began keeping vigil throughout a long unforgettable night. Stunned into painful silence, we huddled together, devastated and forlorn. The only sound heard was the clicking of the respirator, as hour after hour we worried and wondered.

As time slowly passed and morning approached the machine rhythmically continued pumping air into the motionless figure. Increasingly everything seemed unreal. The identification bracelet on the wrist of the motionless figure bore a name I recognized. I knew it so well, it belonged to my eccentric childhood friend, a larger than life friend with an unusual character. She bubbled with joy, for Maureen Sylvia was a laughter-maker who promoted many adventures and shared many happy times with me.

Illogically I reasoned the motionless figure, firmly secured by tubes and wires, could not be my friend Maureen Sylvia, for this pale sombre figure was silent and still. The deepest despair now overwhelmed me, followed swiftly by panic.

How could my friend have vanished so suddenly and taken the sunshine and unique sound of her laughter with her?

I felt lost, wondering how to cope, having bathed in the glow and warmth of her friendship for so long. Her optimism and spirit encouraged others. Her flamboyant personality and enthusiastic zest for life had also strengthened me in the past. I felt aware how deeply I would miss her.

Her unconventional actions met sometimes with disapproval, yet despite her unconventional character she appeared to achieve so much. I gazed again at the still form before me and while acknowledging it bore an armband bearing my friend's name, I wanted to deny it was the same person who had amazed folk in the past. She had the reputation of beating the odds. A miracle survivor with the tenacity to cling to life, despite the odds being stacked against her. Time after time, she had bounced back from the brink.

For a brief moment, my back turned on the reality before me, I prayed.

"Let her win this battle."

For Radford's Victor Ludorum was a winner who never was willing to lose a race. So despite the fact that the active pumps surrounding her were now – chillingly – silent, for one sweet moment I sensed her presence and felt she was close by and aware of my distress. Her voice, it seemed, was calling my name and bidding me farewell.

"Bernice why be upset?" she seemed to be saying. "You have always known it was my destiny to cross the final hurdle ahead of you."

Tearfully I realised the Radford champion was right; she had always led the way.

I watched silently as the hospital staff discreetly dismantled the respirator. Concern for Beverley mounted as silently she sat slumped in a chair, looking exhausted. I felt anxious for her well-being yet unable to offer worthwhile verbal support. Putting out my hand I simply touched her arm, hugged her and wondered how she would ever cope with such a tragic loss; then, uttering a few inadequate words, I bid her farewell.

The same lift that a few hours ago transported me to the tragic scene now carried me back to ground level. In a daze, I walked down the wide corridors, now bustling with people. Despite their presence, everything felt strangely empty. It was difficult to accept anything now was normal, for I believed that Maureen Sylvia had been invincible!

Willing helpers now appeared, urging me towards a waiting vehicle.

As the car headed home, approaching Radford recreation ground, vivid memories flooded into my mind of the time we had spent here. For at this spot so many childhood adventures had occurred. I clearly recalled sunny hours spent there with Maureen and tears began to flow. She had gone. Yet look – I see her standing beyond the old tree, waving and happily smiling. The scene alters, now I hear her, giggling and talking with friends. See how wildly she is dancing at the local youth club. The scene changes at the sound of her voice harmoniously singing with the school choir. Flooding in now was the brightest image of all. Of a girl who could run like the wind and victoriously hold aloft her champion's trophy with pride.

Maureen Sylvia, the brightest of the Bloomsgrove Blossoms. She surged ahead, ignoring poor health, and entertained us until the very end.

Chapter 1

The hearse carrying the brightest Blossom of Bloomo made its dignified way through the grey back streets of Nottingham. Everything appeared to be happening in slow motion. Saying goodbye to Maureen Sylvia, the most flamboyant of the Blossoms, seemed unreal.

Her death stunned everyone, including the group of friends who long ago were known as the Blossoms of Bloomo. They would now be waiting at the cemetery for the hearse to arrive –

Mavis, Rita and Pearl – all as shocked as I was to realise the most energetic zany Blossom in the group had suddenly left us.

I sat silently in the back of the limousine. Through the windows, I could clearly see the hearse; red and white flowers in abundance surrounded the coffin. Maureen Sylvia would have approved the choice of colours, for she had always worn red and white outfits at every football game she attended and would have laughed at the image of being carried on her last journey in such a distinguished style.

Remembering her distinctive laugh provoked bittersweet memories. Now quietly I sobbed, for the deep sense of loss felt tangible. Huddled together the accompanying limousines carried Maureen Sylvia's three brothers, united by grief.

My concern for Maureen Sylvia's daughter intensified, for I knew how distressed Beverley, being heavily pregnant, would be – especially as at this time she would need her mother the most. The loss would be a dreadful blow.

Slowly the funeral cortège wound its way up the hill.

So many people now were arriving. It seemed the chapel would not accommodate so many. All who had braved cold winds to pay their respect on such a depressing November day. So many hearts, it seemed, were crying out: "Maureen Sylvia, how will we ever replace you?"

You were a flamboyant eccentric who stood out in a crowd, whose outrageous behaviour shocked and yet amused people. Folk would smile as they shook their heads at your antics, for they realised you would never change.

Known for your exuberance and outspoken personality, people loved to hear of your adventures and exploits. Be it how you protested at the pomposity of dignitaries attending an event, or the way you spontaneously began to sing along loudly to operatic arias, thus causing an interruption, knowing your outrageous action would bring a drawn out long evening to a swifter end. You loved to shock, wildly revelling, especially when attempting to push aside restrictive social barriers.

Diagnosed with a life threatening illness at an early age did not prevent you living life to the full. You chose instead to burn the candle of your life at both ends – and created, as you did, the brightest and most glittering light. Known and loved by many but fully understood by few. You were wife, mother, grandmother and sister and friend, work colleague, football supporter, opera lover. A highly intelligent human being, yet at times, it seemed, as mad as a March hare. Often I witnessed how, without a word spoken, you could enter a room and your presence like a magnet attracted everyone's attention. At your final appearance, true to form, you did the same.

The light created by your prolific spirit illuminated the lives of so many folk in your hometown and people united by their loss now began to realise how much they would miss you.

More vehicles joined the funeral cortege as the hearse diverted from its usual route. The cortege slowly began winding towards the small chapel, making its way through narrow back streets, bought to a halt at times as the drivers became aware of the groups of people gathered by the roadside. Patiently they were waiting in the cold biting wind, anxious to pay their respect on that bleak November morning.

In dignified silence, as the hearse approached, some bowed their heads, while others stared straight ahead. I noted some clutching red and white scarves and using them to wipe their eyes as they noticed the colour of the flowers. Who was this individual known and loved by so many?

To me she was a true Blossom of Bloomo, my friend Maureen Sylvia the unconventional mad cap, a live wire who did and said many things that astounded conventional folk. On one occasion after Maureen had carried out a particular flamboyant act, I asked her, "Why do you do such outrageous things?"

For a brief moment Maureen Sylvia hesitated, then she smilingly confessed that she had no idea what made her so impulsive. Then, unwilling or unable to give me an answer, she put out her hand, pointed towards a mirror, and said, "Look, life is too short to be bothered by convention, enjoy yourself and don't try be everything others expect of you; all that ends up doing is giving you wrinkles."

Then, with a flourish, she pointed to my reflection and thrust a jar of anti-wrinkle cream into my hand, as the sound of her infectious laughter filled the room.

I smiled ironically as I realised it was the closest I would get to a serious answer from Maureen Sylvia, for she didn't do serious, although seeking out truth and fair play was high on her agenda. For like a preverbal bloodhound sniffing for clues, on many occasions she would hunt with fanatic determination to solve a problem.

Among her favourite pastimes, reading mystery stories was highly rated. Halfway through a book, she often outraged me by announcing, "I have already solved this mystery; I know who the murderer is."

I would cry out, "Maureen, discuss your conclusion later, after I have had chance to read the book myself."

My plea rarely stopped her; she would just ramble on explaining her theory, while feebly I attempted to prevent her divulging her verdict.

On one memorable occasion her curiosity drove her into solving a real mystery story. With little information available but great determination, she attempted to solve a missing gap in her family tree. The quest took her to London, where she hoped to find information to the missing piece that would complete a puzzle. She hunted through old records and documents. The trail eventually led to Old London Town. It was there she searched and seeing a name etched on a worn out old tombstone, she placed a few pebbles on the grave of her ancestors. Satisfied her journey had been worth the effort, instinctively she felt what she had done was right and that finally a past injustice was forgiven. For to Maureen Sylvia her blood ties meant far more than bigotry. The unexplainable bond that strongly had drawn her to this previous unknown branch of the family, that in the past had been lost due to cultural and religious divisions

As the hearse approached its destination, I was reminded of Maureen's search and how proud her ancestors would have been at her achievements, for so many were gathered shivering in the cold weather to pay her their respects.

The ushers threw open the doors and as the chief mourners entered the chapel I glanced around the crowd, all gathered there to say farewell to a woman who at every opportunity had proudly revealed how she was reared in a backstreet of a poor area of Nottingham. She lived life to the full, yet as a child she had not been expected to survive, and for years had amazed medics and lay-folk alike with the energy and enthusiasm she displayed.

Just a few days previous I had enjoyed her company along with others, as together we gathered at a celebration. There amid bright lights and music, Maureen attracted attention by flitting around like an early summer butterfly. Laughing, teasing and chattering, at the end of the evening she had embraced everyone. Strange, for now somehow it felt she had been making peace with us all as she said goodbye. For her death came so swiftly afterwards. We were left stunned. Her brilliant light now extinguished, we were unable to accept the warmth we had received from her glow was gone.

Many now began expressing gratitude for those last memorable hours spent with her. Remembering the words she last had spoken to them, eventually these words provided comfort. Maureen Sylvia, I wonder if you realised how many folk were going to miss you.

4

Forest stalwart Maureen dies

NOTTINGHAM Forest have lost one of their most ardent fans and fund-raisers with the sudden death of Mrs Maureen Sylvia Smith, at her home in Girton Road, Sherwood. She was 51.

For many years Mrs Smith was the secretary of the Forest supporters' club, in which role she organised raffles and other fund-raising events.

She travelled to most of Forest's games at home and abroad and was one of their most ardent supporters.

Clerical officer

She worked as a clerical officer at the DHSS in David Lane, Basford, up until her death.

The funeral is to be held at Bulwell Cemetery, on Monday, at 12 noon, and ex-Forest chairman Geoffrey Macpherson will represent the Forest board of directors.

Mrs Smith leaves a husband, Colin, daughter Beverley and grand-daughter Kelly.

Forest stalwart Maureen dies

shareholder of the club, was a committee member of the Supporters' Club and a former secretary.

Paying tribute, club chairman Maurice Roworth, said : "She had so many friends not only in football but anyone knowing Maureen would realise exactly why because she was such a popular person.

"She spent hours working for the good of the club without any reward for herself and it is a tremendous understatement to say that she will be very badly missed."

TRIBUTES TO A DEDICATED FOREST FOOTBALL SUPPORTER

"I would like to say a sincere thank you to everyone at the club, directors, staff and players alike, and to the many friends in the Supporters' Club who gave such kind and loving tributes to my dear wife Maureen following her recent and sudden death.

"Maureen devoted her life to her beloved Forest and I hope her everlasting memory will guide the club she loved so much to continued success. Through me her cherished commitment will live on".

You helped lighten my own spirit so often and your outrageous bold actions caused me to gasp at your audacity.

You were a free spirit who refused to be contained and charging through life would break stuffy conventional rules.

Triumphantly you succeeding in bridging gaps between so many people. Frowning on class distinction, you refused to be looked on as a second-class citizen and attacked all pomposity with the distain it deserved.

As a child often you attempted to break down unreasonable barriers and where conventional methods failed, your unorthodox plans often succeeded

Fair play both on and off a football field became your war cry. You excelled at using charm and fluttering eyelashes if the occasion warranted it. Yet you never hesitated to jump in feet first and stride across a room – as if a builder's mate – to confront a perpetrator you considered had rudely ignored you.

Often you stated, "Everyone has the right to be heard." So being heard is what you strived to achieve.

We will never know how many people you befriended, or the impact you made on their life. For the path you choose to walk was varied. Sometimes you travelled alone; as my friend, thankfully, you often chose to walk beside me.

I witnessed many of your outrageous exploits as we travelled through the various stages of life together. To others we must have appeared very different characters as I often disapproved of your methods of solving problems. I was however grateful that from the earliest days of childhood we had remained closes friends.

Outrageous and outspoken, you were a larger than life personality – and I realise my own journey through life would have been poorer without you. For you helped me negotiate the many steep hills of life I encountered as a child.

At your funeral, through tears, I watched as Jews and Gentiles, Catholics and Protestants, people from many faiths and others who lacked faith, stood together, side by side. They were rich and poor, honest folk and others who sailed close to the wind. Shoulder to shoulder, educated dons and simple folk. Well recognised sports

Radford class meets after 50 years

Bernice, Pearl, Maureen and Rita in 1985

personalities along with their supporters; tinkers; tailors; so many people from different backgrounds – on this occasion all united by the same deep sense of loss.

Such was the power and mystery of Maureen Sylvia.

People in the past would sometimes smile hearing of her adventures and say, "Maureen Sylvia, one day some one will write a book on the antics you get up to."

Well folks, they were right – and here it is. I decided to write of the early treasured childhood days, especially the memorable moments I spent with Maureen Sylvia and my other friends, the unforgettable Blossoms of Bloomo.

Sharing these stories with you I hope will explain how important early friendships can be to vulnerable young children, especially those facing obstacles that seem difficult to conquer. Despite adversity, the group of Blossoms emerged from those early years able to laugh at the things we experienced and draw lessons from the tears and frustration we suffered. As an adult I realise how fortunate I was to be befriended by Maureen Sylvia and my unforgettable friends, the Blossoms of Bloomo.

Chapter 2

*M*aureen Sylvia was born in 1936. The birth of this little girl brought changes.

From the beginning it seemed dramatic arrivals was to be Maureen Sylvia's trademark.

Times were difficult in the 1930s and unemployment was rife. The poor struggled to survive, with many health problems caused by inadequate diet and lack of good medical care. For a free National Health Service and welfare benefits were not yet available. Having to live in dismal poor and unsanitary conditions, infections were difficult to contain and contagious diseases were rife – a dangerous situation, especially for the young.

It was fate decided the time and place where Maureen Silvia was born. But, given the choice, would she have chosen the same poor street in Radford as her birthplace?

Problems burdened her family who, having an older sick child, had little money to spare. How would they cope, having another child to rear?

Maureen Sylvia's arrival surprisingly was a blessing. For the birth of a daughter brought her mother joy, and gave her reason to celebrate.

Little Mabel, Maureens Sylvias mother was affectionately given her nickname by a group of friends, the same folk who willingly offered assistance to the midwife who attended Maureen Sylvia's birth These friends, being good Samaritans, were used to helping woman in labour and proved a great asset to busy midwifes. For drawing from their own personal experience, they understood the pitfalls of delivering children under harsh conditions.

For so many problems lurked in the backstreet Radford homes, as few amenities were available. The women gallantly struggled to provide hot bathing water and soothing drinks, as well as supervising inquisitive junior members of the labouring women's family.

The fathers by tradition remained conspicuously absence – for the tradition in the 1930s was for men to stay away from home on delivery day.

Primitive unsanitary conditions in the terrace houses affected the health of both the young and old. Little aid was available, for life-saving drugs, antibiotics, free school milk, cod liver oil and orange juice had not yet arrived. These were benefits awaiting tomorrow's children.

So many families lived in these overcrowded deprived areas. The children played in narrow unlit alleys and dingy cobbled backyards. The facilities were primitive and unsanitary, with outside communal toilets; many residents obtained drinking water from a single tap sited in overcrowded backyards. Survival was sometimes a gamble for the stoic women of 1930s, who risked contacting life-threatening infections when they delivered their babies. They accepted and viewed their situation as the price you pay for marriage and motherhood.

Little Mabel did not complain yet had reason to feel concerned. For one of her sons was in a poor state of health. The arrival of another child placed extra responsibility on her shoulders, yet she welcomed her only daughter with joy. For Maureen Sylvia, a round-faced pretty child, bought laughter and joy into the home. However, the year she was born, Maureen Sylvia's parents would experience both bitter and sweet memories. For shortly after celebrating the birth of their little girl came a period of deepest grief – for Fred and Little Mabel would mourn the death of a young son.

Friends, who had joined the family in welcoming the arrival of a baby girl, now rallied to comfort them in their sorrow. For Little Mabel was well-loved – a personality who possessed a giant size heart (unlike her height, for she stood barely four feet ten inches tall – hence her nick-name suited her well). Exuberance of spirit, combined with a generous nature, made her a staunch and vibrant friend. Strangers who judged Little Mabel by stature alone, would be surprised to discover how resilient she could be. This was something neighbours had witnessed in the past, for when hell bent on defending an unfortunate underdog, Little Mabel was a formidable force to behold. Transformed by determination into a fierce opponent, she faced the mightiest of foes; measured by bravery, she stood majestically tall.

Fred Booth, Maureen Sylvia's father, was a jolly man. Tall and well built, he plodded through life enjoying the simplest of pleasures. He demanded little, was grateful to be earning a meagre day's pay, and content after a long working day to go home and there be served his modest dinner. If funds allowed, later he wandered down to the local inn and there joined his friends. Clutching a pint of the local brew, he gathered with other men in endless discussions that frequently centred on the latest world events. For in the 1930s life was unsettled and becoming more alarming, as political troubles began casting long gloomy shadows across Europe.

a friend means more than words can say

Maureen

Chapter 3

The unsettled times of the thirties intensified and by the end of the decade Britain was at war.

People's lives began to change. Some women, performing tasks that previously they would never have considered undertaking, grew confident – while others became depressed and frightened after they had waved their khaki- or navy-clad loved ones off to war. They worried about coping alone, much later discovering hidden strength, as increasing numbers of men donned uniforms. So many loved ones were now ordered to depart and make their way towards designated military units. In droves, they packed bags and headed for Nottingham's main line station. Husbands, sons and brothers, conscripted to fight for their country, obeyed the command and rallied round the flag – unaware a long tough battle for survival lay ahead.

Until the men departed, the war appeared to have little effect on the daily events and life in Radford, but things rapidly began to change. Little Mabel carried extra burdens that caused her great worry. Doctors informed her that Maureen Sylvia was suffering from serious health problems. This troubled her; Little Mabel recalled times in the past where she listened to doctors' words and took their advice. Now, she was reluctant to do so.

Loudly she declared, "The advice they gave me last time did not save my son."

Her anxiety caused her to cosset and indulge Maureen Sylvia. Her young daughter, being unaware of the sacrifices her mother was making, lapped up the attention. Little Mabel continued trying to

Bloomsgrove Street, 1946

provide her daughter with everything she desired and young Maureen Sylvia, oblivious to the sacrifices made, soaked up the attention. On good days she looked as fit as a fiddle; at other times, her childish features appeared puffy and pale.

Doctors continued explaining to her parents that their daughter had suffered renal damage. Her mother listened suspiciously to their dismal prognosis, then, feeling the need for moral support, often rushed away to seek reassurance from friends and neighbours. Thus, Maureen Sylvia became her mother's main topic of conversation. Pointing to her young daughter, Little Mabel would ask friends, "Don't you think she is looking better today?"

They would glance at the child and hesitate to reply. Little Mabel, anxious for a response, urgently continued, "Some doctors think they are God and know all the answers."

Neighbours silently listened as Little Mabel nervously rambled on. "See how well she looks? Who would think a few weeks ago she was at deaths door. It was a waste of money my visiting the doctors; I would have been better going to Alfreton Road and paying the herbalist."

The neighbours continued to listen, but made no response. Agitated at their silence, Little Mabel exclaimed, "Just fancy the buggers telling me she will never recover."

The neighbours nodded and noted her distress, realising the death of her son had made her cynical of accepting any doctor's opinion. The reason was, she was afraid another tragedy might occur. This fear caused her to ignore medical advice and continue to indulge her daughter. However, despite her mother's constant care, there were worrying days when her daughter again became pale and listless, and other times when to her relief Maureen Sylvia appeared fit and lively. It was then that Little Mabel triumphantly would exclaim, "Fancy the doctors saying her kidneys are not working, look at her she is full of beans."

Then fiercely she added, "She is better staying at home with me. I am going to keep her away from that bloody hospital. She was kept on that ward and nearly died despite all their treatment."

Well-wishers understood her anxiety, for being residents of the little terrace houses in Radford they had become friends, confidants, advisors and fellow survivors. Young ailing Maureen Sylvia, surrounded by this army of well-wishers, often listened to the women gossiping and heard the good-hearted neighbours invite her mother to pay them a visit: "Come and join us Mabel, I will put the kettle on and mash some tea." "No use you sitting alone and worrying, it will not do you a bit of good."

Then as their children played together, the little band of stoic woman huddled around a small coal fire, sipping tea, chattering together, willingly providing each other with good advice and counselling. Their knowledge was acquired not from impressive university degrees, but the personal experience they amassed by being hardy survivors who lived in difficult backstreet conditions.

Maureen's Grandparents, above is her great grandfather, Mr. Davis

Far right is Maureen's paternal grandmother, with friend

Maureen's Distant Cousin

Maureen Sylvia's parents

Maureen Sylvia aged 2½ years

Maureen's Family
From left: Little Mabel/Maureen/Baby Kelly/Ruth Beverley

Maureen's brother Arthur and Joan

Ron, Maureen's brother

Chapter 4

*A*s she became older Little Mabel's girl became increasingly strong-willed, and signs of her being hard to handle were already evident.

Her mother, when reprimanding her daughter, did so in a light-hearted way – and Maureen Sylvia, aware that her "Mam" never carried out her threats, simply ignored them and carried on doing everything exactly the way Maureen Sylvia wanted it to be.

Shaking their head, neighbours pointed towards the little girl and sighed: "Little Mabel has got her work cut out controlling that one!"

Then sympathetically they would offer Little Mabel help, especially if she seemed stressed. However, neighbours sometimes had problems of their own to solve, especially on a busy washday. It was on such a day, unable to offer her assistance, Little Mabel was confronted with a mountain of dirty clothes and no one available to mind the "Wild One". In sheer desperation she made a drastic and hasty decision. She decided to go to the local washhouse and take her lively daughter with her.

Gathering together a large bar of coarse laundry soap, a bag of dolly blue and her favourite washing aide (soda crystals), she proceeded to get her cumbersome old pram. Then, gathering up two large bundles of soiled clothing, she placed them into the bottom of her worn out old pram determined to wash them. Maureen Sylvia watched with delight. She relished any kind of adventure and giggled as she was lifted up with due ceremony and placed on top of the two bundles of clothes.

Little Mabel had a well thought out and cunning plan. Although she also felt apprehensive, the mounting pile of soiled clothes urgently needed to be washed – so, having little choice, bravely she set off with Maureen Sylvia to visit the local washhouse.

She knew it was courting trouble sneaking into the local washhouse with a child. Getting past the bossy boots who managed the washhouse meant taking a risk. Little Mabel, being a plucky little battler, was willing to accept the challenge. Being a Radford woman, she was determined. Small in statue as she was, she possessed the spirit of ancient David – and, when necessary, she was ready to take on any Goliath.

Having decided on a plan of action, she began to make her way towards the washhouse. On the journey, she repeated a list of instructions to her strong-willed daughter, hoping Maureen Sylvia would obey. The most important instruction given was that on entering the washhouse her young daughter must remain quiet.

Maureen Sylvia agreed to do so – but having no fear of retribution from her mother, there was no guarantee the strong-willed child would comply. Being young, she was unaware of the reason she was so indulged, and happily accepted all the attention she received. This was a state of affairs noted with dismay by her older brothers, who sometimes protested at the favours she received. When their little sister was unwell, however, they also tended to indulge her – a habit they continued even when Maureen Sylvia grew older.

By the time Little Mabel reached the local washhouse, she had repeated her list of instructions several times to her daughter. Hoping to secure a successful outcome, she came armed with a few distractions. Reaching into the pram, she produced a brown paper bag; it contained a comic book and a slice of bread and dripping. As she handed them to a delighted Maureen Sylvia, she instructed her to stay hidden under the pram cover and remain so until they had safely passed the window of the occupied office. For there, ever alert, sat "Bossy Boots", keen to apprehend anyone who looked at all suspicious of flouting the rules.

This ruthless council official who ruled her domain with a rod of iron would never tolerate any attempt made to sneak children into the premises. Anyone attempting to violate these rules she *swiftly would deal with*. No pleas of hardship were considered, and nothing would deter this dictatorial official from firmly saying, "It's council rules." One unfortunate woman, who had dared violate the rules, was apprehended sneaking her child inside the premises. When threatened with eviction, she thrust her pathetic bundle of clothing, still unwashed, at Bossy Boots, and frantically declared, "I have the right to stay. My old man's been fighting a war for you and the bloody council." Her words fell on unsympathetic ears, for Bossy Boots refused to bend an inch.

"Rules are rules," she said, and smugly added, "no exceptions are made for anyone who breaks the rules."

On noting the harsh words spoken to her so arrogantly, the distraught woman became frantic. For she urgently needed to wash her babies clothing, especially the meagre supply of nappies, as she had no way of obtaining more. Just how did Bossy Boots imagine a stressed mother would manage to clothe her baby on such a wet miserable day?

Living in their small backstreet terrace houses and devoid of laundry facilities, these women struggled to safely rear young babies. For these were the days before disposable nappies, detergents, dishwashers and microwave ovens. These women day by day fought a tough battle for survival. Standing on the front line, they waged constant battles against poverty and poor health. They struggled to protect their young against unsanitary conditions and received no accolades or medals for the efforts they made.

Other courageous women in the past had also been prepared to run the gauntlet at Radford washhouse, knowing of the severe penalty they risked if caught by Bossy Boots. For this officious worker would loudly declare, "You know the penalty for flouting the rules. You are permanently banned from using this washhouse."

Knowing the risk, brave Little Mabel went ahead, hoping her gift of the comic book would work. Realizing Maureen Sylvia loved reading, and books being a rare treat in the Booth household, her mother placed her trust in providing her with such a treasure. She hoped it would quietly occupy her daughter and the plan would run smoothly. With her mountain of dirty clothes she approached the building, gripping the handle of the pram and firmly manoeuvring it forward. Opening the heavy wooden door, she stepped inside and made her way towards the entrance desk.

The assistant was busy chatting to a customer; the woman rudely glanced at Little Mabel but did not acknowledge her. She is as stuck up as the snobs from The Groves, thought Little Mabel – bet she gets stuff on the black market. Still, luckily she was diverting Bossy Boots attention, and unintentionally helping get her through the first hurdle.

So far so good, now move safely on to the next challenge.

Glancing up she noted displayed on the office window a clear warning: "ALL UNLOADED PRAMS ARE TO BE PLACED IN THE STORAGE AREA. NO PRAMS ALLOWED NEAR ANY WASH STALLS AT THIS WASH HOUSE."

Hoping her old pram with its large cover and hood remained hidden at the back of the storage bay, she proceeded to unload the washing. Reminding Maureen Sylvia to stay very quiet, Little Mabel handed her a paper bag containing a sandwich. Praying the food and comic would keep her daughter occupied, she hurried away towards the washing stalls.

The far end of the bay was unseen from where Bossy Boots sat. If she approached the storage area then Maureen Sylvia had received instructions to hide under the large pram hood and remain out of sight. Everything was going to order and with the washing drying on the large heated racks, Little Mabel headed back to the storage bay. She was desperate to have a cup of tea, even if the tea these days was as weak as water. She held the cup tightly as she bent over the pram and whispered to Maureen, "It will not be long now. The clothes are on the drying rack."

Then, patting the pram cover that was so effectively hiding Maureen from view, she fondly whispered, "You are being a good girl, reading your comic."

Slowly unwrapping her own thinly meat spread sandwich, she broke off a piece of bread and gave it to Maureen, who by now had already eaten her own sandwich; she happily accepted more, however, and proceeded to munch the bonus she had received.

Shortly afterwards Maureen noticed the cup her mother was holding.

"I want a drink, Mam."

Little Mabel hesitated; due to her diseased kidneys Maureen Sylvia often needed to us the lavatory after drinking hot fluids. Realizing the entrance to the lavatory facilities lay directly in front of the office window, Little Mabel hesitated.

Maureen spoke again.

"MAM, I WANT A DRINK."

Little Mabel whispered, "Shush, I will buy you some pop on the way home."

"NO, WANT IT NOW," Maureen said loudly.

Little Mabel anxiously looked around, hoping no one had heard the little piping voice. Then reluctantly, she said, "Here, have a little sup of my tea."

Maureen Sylvia grabbed the cup and took a big gulp. Her mam urgently pulled the cup away. "A bloody sup, I said." Pulling the now empty cup away, she realized now it was going to be a race against time. In a great hurry, she scurried off, hoping her washing was dry; for her daughter needed to go home right now. The washing was still slightly damp but Little Mabel hurriedly packed it in the pram, intending to drape it on her clotheshorse once she reached home. Afraid to risk staying longer, she made her way hurriedly towards the storeroom door. As she started to open it young Maureen's voice clearly rang out, "Mam want to wee."

Mabel in a panic urged her, "Hush, you must wait until you get home."

Maureen Sylvia wailed, "Can't wait Mam, I will pee my knickers."

Little Mabel ignoring the warning, scooped her protesting daughter up and proceeded to sit her on top of the clean pile of clothes. Pulling up the pram cover, she drew a deep breath and pushed the pram out of the storeroom. Fingers crossed, once she passed the office window she would be safe.   Gripping the pram handle, she moved forward. Above the humming of the industrial, spin dryers. She heard a voice address her. With mounting panic, she recognized who was speaking to her. It was Bossy Boots.

"Finished early today Mabel, all dry."

Keeping her head down, she replied, "Yes, I am just off."

It was then, from under the pram covers, a small voice began muttering, "I have pee on my knickers."

Bossy Boots, hearing the muffled voice, looked up with surprise. "What did you say?"

Above the noise of the spinner, sharp thinking Little Mabel replied, "I spilt a cup of tea, wet me right through to my bloody knickers. Looks like I'll be coming back tomorrow with another load to wash."

Then, before Bossy Boots had chance to reply, Little Mabel pushed open the door and stepped out side. Heaving a sigh of relief, she headed towards home. Maureen Sylvia, looking relaxed, peeped out from beneath the pram cover. No longer desperate for the lavatory, she ignored her sopping wet knickers and happily sat contaminating the pile of freshly washed clothes. Little Mabel by then had almost reached home and as she approached the local shop Maureen Sylvia shouted, "Mam, don't forget to buy the pop."

"I'll give you bloody pop," her stressed mother replied, thinking of the fresh clothing Maureen Sylvia had already soiled. Then, ignoring the sounds of protest, she continued heading home with the heavy pram, by now worrying that Bossy Boots may be pondering about the odd explanation she had given regards spilt tea and wet knickers. The rain continued to drizzle down as she sped by the little shop and headed home. No need to search for a door key, she had left the door unlocked. Living in the humble back streets, she rarely worried about a burglar: that was something rich folk spent time worry about. For the residents who lived in this area had few valuables worth stealing – especially on washdays when the majority of items they did possess had been transported to the local washhouse to be scrubbed.

Chapter 5

The road to school was usually busy when I set out that morning. Some children were making their way up the hill carrying little cases that held gas masks, something all schoolchildren were instructed to do. For they had attended regular fire and evacuation drills at school. We became experts at putting gas masks on correctly. At first, a flurry of excitement occurred doing so, but the novelty of carrying a cumbersome gas mask wore off and, given the chance, we intentionally often chose not to bring it to school. On a drill day that was not a sensible thing to do.

Situated on the rise of the hill the grey stone building that loomed ahead dominated the skyline. It housed the Douglas and Sealy Road Infant Junior School. For local children the early years spent in this building played a major role in their formative development.

The school, situated in Radford, was within walking distance of Canning Circus and close to Nottingham's town centre. In peacetime within the boundary wall of the school the chimes of Little John, the town clock – which was situated on the front of Council House – could be heard. The sound of bells calling worshippers to the parish church were also heard.

Due to Great Britain now being at war, these sounds were absent and unknown to the younger children who attended the school. Many years would pass before these children experienced the sounds once frequently heard by their parents. Deprived of many things, these children would listen in awe to tales of how once it used to be. Yet despite everything, they proved to be tough little survivors.

The school on the hill was not the only place where Radford children received their education, but it was there the opportunity of forming lasting friendships often began.

I became a Douglas Road pupil at a tender young age, and was enrolled as my older sister was before me. With so many mothers now working in local factories, it had become necessary to attend school at the earliest opportunity – so much so that and arrangements were made for younger children to be cared for by providing canvas beds, as many youngsters still needed an afternoon sleep.

Mothers often discovered going out to work caused dramatic changes and would often change their lives forever.

Maureen Sylvia was slightly delayed in first attending Douglas Road School. This was due to poor health and by the time our paths crossed, I had already settled down to school life.

Maureen Sylvia however soon became an eager pupil and lost no time in reaching the expected educational standard. A bright quick learner, she soaked up academic knowledge as if a sponge, determined from the very beginning to lead the way.

Inside the school building even on the brightest of days, the classrooms were dark and dismal. The inner walls painted in a dull shade of grey or green that did little to brighten the classrooms. These were colours frequently chosen to paint public buildings and the classrooms stood unadorned. Of solid construction with the floors well brushed, the entrance door stood close by a wire-caged cloakroom that was equipped with long wooden benches and rows of iron pegs fixed to the wall.

The youngest children, as directed, dutifully hung up their outdoor clothes. For at Douglas Road School strict rules were set by the teachers that all pupils were instructed to obey. Away from the building, our life may have been chaotic, but once a pupil stepped into school, everything ran like clockwork.

However, there were times when some children became sorely tempted. Especially curious children who discovered an unexpected activity was occurring. One such occasion was when a group of pupils sighted workers arriving at the school and ripples of excitement occurred. A flurry of activity commenced as inspection of the building began and strategically marked spots were placed on the walls. The children watched the men in amazement as they proceeded to drill holes and the task of fitting solid metal hooks in the marked areas began.

The children, pre-warned that sand filled buckets were to be hung on the hooks, were advised on the importance of them only being moved in the event of a fire occurring. The large sand buckets, having duly arrived, were securely placed on the hooks. Everything it seemed was now ship shape and ready for any emergency.

The children attending the next assembly were then sternly reminded, "No pupils are allowed to touch or interfere with the fire buckets or their contents."

For children who owned few toys and little chance of visiting a beach, the chance of dipping their hands into the buckets to experience the texture of golden sand became a great temptation. However, disciplined children heeded the stern warning, knowing as they did that committing rebellious acts would result in fearful consequences. For any child foolish enough to try committing such an offence risked severe punishment. Stern instructions would be given to the ones who disobeyed: "Come and stand at the front of the room. Hold out your hand."

The culprit, with no chance of escaping, would make their way slowly to the front of the assembly hall. As their classmates nervously watched, the harsh punishment commenced. The sound of a leather strap bought forcibly down on to a small-outstretched hand often caused their classmates to wince – and, being young, some cried out in fear or sympathy. However, the children's parents rarely complained about their off-spring being given such a punishment – for discipline was considered important, especially when living in such dangerous times. The maintenance of fire bucket being so important, most thought such a punishment was warranted.

Methods of discipline were rigid, as was learning the three Rs by rote. This was considered the normal method of teaching young children, for these were the days before modern technology and child psychology became fashionable. Eye-catching bright colours, interesting pictures and hanging mobiles were not yet in vogue. These

My grandparents Edith and Charles

Grandmother at Woodville Place, Bloomsgrove Street 1952

Dad on duty

Dad 1932

benefits to stimulate the young were joys enjoyed by future generations.

Children in the early 1940s were expected to leave junior school able to read write and recite their times tables. Due to the dedication of their teachers, who worked under the difficult conditions that existing at that time, the majority of pupils did reach that goal.

Education for many Radford children did not cease, however, when the school bell rang. For at the end of each busy school day they continued their education by osmosis, soaking up other kinds of information once they had left the confines of the school playground.

Children roaming the streets now recorded a catalogue of new experiences as torrents of strange sights and sounds drew their attention. Often, they witnessed unusual events occurring in the dark corners of the little back streets. For so many mothers were now combining home duties with factory work and would leave their children unsupervised; this gave their off-spring the freedom to wander unsupervised around the area.

Lost strangers sometimes spoke to the children playing in the streets, approaching them to ask directions. Many spoke in unusual accents and wore unfamiliar clothing and uniforms. These encounters at first bewildered the naïve youngsters. Gradually these meetings became a common occurrence. The civilian and military personnel they encountered in a strange way helped educated them by adding a new dimensions to their lives.

The motley of people daily streaming in to Nottingham also created trade for the innkeepers and some local woman benefited and enjoyed male company, in some cases even meeting their future partners.

The strangers would provide an interesting diversion for older children by talking to them. The children began asking the strangers questions; they heard true life stories about places and people that previously they had only read about in geography books.

Americans, Canadians, South Africans Poles and Czechs – all nationalities it seemed came to visit Nottingham, encouraged it was rumoured by the story that the friendliest girls in England lived there. The town buzzed with excitement, especially at the weekend as eager young servicemen came and went. For having enjoyed their brief stay, many of the men would return to their Lincolnshire bases with happy memories of their time spent in Nottingham. Waving farewell to the girls, they vowed to return very soon, often unaware that plans had been set in motion for their units to depart the English bases and fly away to dangerous war zones. So many young brave soldiers that departed sadly were fated never to return to Nottingham or even to see their own homeland again.

Some strangers did stay for longer. Among them were the young evacuee children, many barely school age, who were boarded out to be cared for with local families. In later years evacuees would return; now adults, they made nostalgic visits to Nottingham, hoping to contact the honouree aunts and uncles who long ago welcomed and sheltered the homesick little children. Many evacuees had at first encountered difficulty settling down and making friends. This was partly due to their failure to understand the pronounced Radford accent. The communication difficulties however disappeared eventually – and once acclimatised the little newcomers became accustomed at being addressed as "Mey duck". In addition, they even began adopting the local dialect; their original accents faded away and friendships began to form. When the evacuees eventually were able to return home, their loving parents were shocked to discover their children spoke in strong Radford accents.

Parents also discovered other reasons to be concerned, when some young children began relating dubious memories of the war years spent in Nottingham, for as naïve youngsters they had failed to understand the significance of what they had witnessed had sometimes taken place in the dark alleys of Radford . However, as adults they reflected on these memories realising their youthful innocence had hidden many disturbing facts and with dismay understanding now what they had witnessed, they shook their heads and asked each other,

"Was that really our finest hour?"

1939/40

Bernice with Mother and sister Mavis

Bernice 1938

Chapter 6

Another school day and children were once more gathering in groups in the schoolyard, some congregating at a popular spot close to an undercover playground area. This spot was usually out of bounds except on rainy days. A permanent feature was a long wooden bench firmly anchored to a brick wall. A plank of fencing timber balanced at an angle across the back of the bench, placed there for the caretaker to collect later in the day.

I watched in fascination as a round-faced girl with thick dark auburn hair stood up .She began waving her arms about to attract attention and shouting, "Watch this". The children turned to watch as the girl waved again to acknowledge her captive audience.

Climbing onto the plank, she spread out her arms in an attempt to maintain her balance, then wobbling along she proceeded moving across the plank. Reaching the highest level and feeling confident, she wildly attempted to tap dance on the narrow plank. Amazingly, she managed to maintain her balance. Then, to my astonishment, she began with great confidence to sing a popular chorus from a Shirley Temple film.

Although forbidden to climb on the bench and the girl clearly was breaking rules, she made no effort to hide. The plank precariously wobbled as recklessly she hopped up and down, relishing every moment of having an audience. More children gathered to listen and the louder she sang. It seemed there was no stopping her. On and on she performed, singing and dancing until she reached the end of the plank – and then suddenly she tumbled off. As she scrambled to her feet, the loud voice of a teacher boomed out: "Maureen Sylvia, just what are you doing? Trying to break your leg and land up in the hospital again?"

Maureen Sylvia, now standing upright, glared at the teacher and began to mutter under her breath. "Silly bugger, I wasn't in hospital with a broken leg."

I was stunned. It was the first time I had heard a child be rude to a teacher and a real shock hearing a child say bugger. To my relief, the teacher appeared not to have heard and proceeded to blow the whistle. The class began to get form a line, getting ready for the order to march into the school. Scuttling into place, to my surprise the auburn haired girl stepped up beside me. Smiling broadly, she asked, "What's your name?"

"Bernice," I replied.

Drawing closer she stared at my face and said, "I have never heard that funny name before, are you an evacuee?"

"No," I protested. "I was born in Radford."

The teacher, hearing voices, turned around. Grabbing the sleeve of my coat, she began furiously shouting: "Bernice, you were talking in line. You will get the strap if I hear you again."

I was shocked at the teacher issuing such a warning – and little did I realise they were words I was destined to hear more frequently. For from the moment Maureen Sylvia decided to become my friend, never again would my world be mundane.

Chapter 7

Quickly running into the schoolyard, I looked for my friends. Maureen Sylvia waved as I rushed to join her. Barbara and Maria patiently also stood in line, waiting for the order to march into school. Shuffling forwards, I noticed two friends approaching: Rita and Pearl, who were on their way towards a different classroom. Happily waving to them, I indicated we would meet again later in the day. For these friends had lived on Bloomsgrove Street since early childhood. Our lives were closely interwoven, growing up as we did in a tight knit community. With the country being at war we shared many activities – bathing, sharing beds, meals and hiding together in underground air raid shelters. I was surprise when older to discover that outsiders viewed our familiarity as odd. For as a youngster I assumed every child experienced the same closeness with their neighbours.

Maureen Sylvia, Barbara and Maria lived on different terrace streets but also developed bonds with their neighbours. For in those days, limited access to phones and so few people owning cars meant that people depended on a safety net of friendly, trustworthy neighbours who willingly offered each other aid, especially in difficult times.

Not that disputes among close neighbours were unknown. For battles did erupt in communal back yards, particularly when someone happened to light an ill-timed bonfire. For if foul smoke drifted onto a line of fresh washing, it caused great friction. However, like the offending smoke, trouble of that nature had a habit of simply blowing away. For wise peacemakers often intervened by saying, "Come on you lot, what's the good of fighting each other? With this war dragging on we have enough bloody enemies to battle with."

Soon common sense reigned and disputes would end; the freshly filled kettle would be put on the fire to boil, and neighbours could be heard happily shouting to each other, "I've just mashed, do you want one?" For the strong bonds of backstreet friendships were not easy to tear apart.

For the children who played on these overcrowded streets and knew the local people by sight, it all felt like being part of an extended family. Fondly they often identified each other by the name of their shared street.

The youngsters played together, feeling proud to be part of the Bloomo mob. However, sometimes mocking outsiders taunted us by sneering and shouting, "Look at that a kid from Bloomo." When sarcastically spat out, most often it was by a resident who lived across the great divide and enjoyed the privilege of living in a big house situated on the Grove.

I was never in doubt which side of the road I belonged, being a fully-fledged Bloomo girl, born at No. 16 Bloomsgrove Street where I lived in a neglected house. Standing three storeys high, it was situated at the lower end of the old street. There were two rows of these brick-built terrace houses, all having entries that led into straggly back yards.

Long ago, the taller dwellings had housed busy outworkers, who helped produce the famous Nottingham lace. These buildings originally served a duel purpose, as both homes and lace factories. The street was converted years ago and now boasted three shops, two public houses and a noisy bottling factory that belonged to Hart's Brewery Company.

Due to the popularity of local brews, frequent deliveries of home brewed ale were to be seen arriving at the street. These were destined for consumption at two public houses and a licensed *beer-off*, all sited on the street. One splendid sight to be witnessed was when, with a clatter of hoofs and rumbling sound of heavy wheels, the arrival of the Shipstone's Brewery horses were heralded in.

Pulling their huge drays over the cobbled surface, these majestic shires made their entrance, skilfully manoeuvring along the narrow

A Shipstone Brewery horse team, Alfreton Road, Radford

street. I would be among the first to run alongside them. Waving to the driver, with mounting excitement I watched as the beautiful groomed horses proudly trotted up the cobbled street.

The drivers of these immaculate Shipstone Brewery carts would proudly deliver the eagerly awaited large casks of ale; they would come even during the freezing weather, when horses sometimes struggled to remain upright on the icy surface. If their hoofs began slipping, fearing they were loosing their footing, their wide-eyed expression would reflect their fear. Children would gather to watch the caring drivers bravely reassuring their charges. Kneeling on the frozen ground, their heads bent within touching distance of massive hoofs, they whispered instructions to frightened animals. The concerned drivers would place sack cloths under the horse's mighty feet, in the hope the frightened animal would gain a firmer grip on the dangerous surface. Observing the trust displayed between the man and his horses proved a heart-warming experience.

Maureen Sylvia lived not far away from my home, in a little terrace house on Alfred Street. Due to the streets name, one young local wit shouted out to her in jest one day, "Hey Alfred did yer burn yer buns today?"

Maureen Sylvia, who knew the legend of the king who carelessly burnt cakes, laughed and enjoyed the moment. However, if the remark had sounded sarcastic, she would have quickly responded by making a wittier reply. For Maureen Sylvia from a young age never tolerated put-down remarks, and fiercely resisted hints of class distinction.

As she got older she remained proud and conscious of her working class background – to the extent that when she met people from other social backgrounds she would often promote discussions on the poor conditions she experienced when younger. Forthright and confident she firmly expressed her opinion: "Being born poor should never prevent a person entering the upper levels of society. Lack of wealth or failing to have a posh accent is no judge of a person's ability. Upper class family connection should never automatically pave the way to the top. Nor should less fortunate individuals be discouraged from achieving their own personal dreams. Obtaining success by birthright is immoral and unjust."

Maureen, having attracted a listener's attention, would continue loudly exclaiming: "People should be treated with equal rights. Judging them by a measure of where they were born and raised is wrong. No barriers should hinder a man, woman or child from reaching their full potential."

After Maureen Sylvia delivered speeches like these, people from privileged backgrounds – hearing the outburst – sometimes pondered on their own rise to fame. For Maureen Sylvia had cast doubt in their minds by indicating that by climbing the ladder of success by your own efforts, you could achieve more from life than reaching the top because of others.

Often her outbursts concluded by stating: "Success gained by ones own efforts creates a spectacular euphoria. An experience individuals placed at the top by dubious methods will never feel."

Maureen Sylvia's own competitive spirit never allowed her to be placed anywhere by the efforts of others. Striving to reach her own goals gave her great joy. She revelled in challenge; the tougher the opponent the more victorious she felt. Even as a young child she stood her ground, especially when someone doubted her ability to win.

It seemed even then that proving doubters wrong was always her aim.

Chapter 8

I travelled alone along a deserted street, as I walked up the hill towards school. It was almost Christmas and it had been a damp cold week. Until recently my sister had accompanied me on this regular journey up the hill, for she was also a pupil at the same school I attended. My tendency to dawdle however now greatly annoyed her. For after arriving late at school, both of us were reprimanded by the teacher. My sister decided she now preferred to walk to school alone, unwittingly giving me further opportunity to tarry and chance to stop at a spot on route I knew was out of bounds.

The place I focused on lingering was a spot situated directly opposite my school. It was there I was tempted to misbehave. The sturdy old wall captured my attention. The wall that fascinated me stood on hallowed ground and formed part of the boundary wall situated on land that belonged to the local parish church. I knew this place well, for each morning I had the opportunity of a clear view of the churchyard as I gazed down on it from the window of the bedroom where I had been born. Pressing my nose on the pane afforded me a bird's eye view of the old graveyard, situated just yards away. It was a sombre sight to view in winter, with its ornate old tombs, life-sized statues and rows of moss-covered head stones. In winter, often covered with sparkling snow, it looked suitably seasonal; however in summer it was a different story, for it was then unruly children could be spotted bouncing a ball back and forth off the old church wall or swinging like monkeys from the ropes they had suspended from the tall old trees. They played happily, unaware the daughter of their local special constable was standing at a window observing their activity. They had little reason however to fear my observation, as I longed to join them myself, despite my grandmother reminding me frequently of the wickedness of children who violated consecrated ground.

Until recently I had resisted the temptation, but now the lure of adventure had begun tempting me into trespassing on these sacred grounds. I was intrigued with the idea of walking atop the old uneven walls surrounding the churchyard. My ambition was to balance the whole length of the boundary wall. I discovered it was no easy task, for the wall was uneven and in wet weather slippery. At first I walked with my arms outstretched, but I soon lost my balance. Not to be defeated, over and over I tried, for I was determined to conquer this self-made challenge. Imitating a tight rope artist I became desperate, as I longed to walk unaided on top of the full length of the wall's narrow surface. Oblivious to the risk I continued trying – and this despite the wall being a dangerous height for an eight-year-old to take a tumble.

Eventually I gave up as I noticed the road leading towards the school was bustling with children making their way up the hill. Some pupils continued to carry little cases containing gas masks, something every schoolchild was supposed to do. For we had been instructed to be prepared for action, and regular fire and evacuation drills were conducted at the school. Demonstrations on correctly putting on our gas masks were taught. At first this caused a flurry of excitement but the novelty of practicing and carrying a cumbersome bag soon wore off; given the chance we chose to forget our case – never a good idea on drill day.

Mavis was nowhere in sight as I dawdled along. Lost in my own thoughts it was awhile before I became aware there were no signs of other children heading towards the school. Realizing it must be getting late, I began to hurry. It must have taken me longer than usual to practice wall balancing, and I was worried that the bell was ringing already. As I entered the schoolyard, I attempted to creep into the line, but the teacher noticed me enter.

"Late again Bernice. It's the third time this week. You can report to

Rita and brothers – 1940

the office and explain why."

I sighed: balancing on walls had once more landed me in trouble. I was fast reaching the advanced class of recognising the bite of a teacher's strap. However my skill at balancing on walls still remained at an amateur level, especially compared with Maureen Sylvia's skill and ability.

Inevitably, my paternal grandmother discovered my lack of respect for hallowed ground. Dismayed at my being seen misbehaving on church property, she questioned me at length.

"Just where have you picked up such an unholy habit?"

I began offering an explanation. However, she refused to consider my excuse was valid, especially when I loudly protested, "But Grandma, I was only practicing walking along the top of the stone wall; I didn't stand on any old tomb stones". Grandmother silently looked down at me. Frantically I continued to explain: "It's a difficult problem walking on that wall, it's very wonky, I have to keep practising balancing. I want to be as good as Maureen Sylvia. She knows how to balance the whole way round the church."

Grandma sighed, and said: "If you keep copying the bad example of unruly children, eventually wonky walls will not be the only thing that cause you big problems."

Then sternly she proceeded to inform me that a member of the Church Women's Association had reported my action to her. I blanched for I had a good idea who the informant might be! Grandma knew many ladies at the association, but one member was particularly righteous; this person lived just a stones throw away. Yet geographically her home, although situated close to mine, seemed a world apart. For this particular lady lived in an area populated by people who seemed more affluent and educated than the residents who dwelt in the humble backstreet where I lived. The dreamers of Bloomsgrove Street sometimes contemplated how it would be to live across the road in a big house. Achieving that goal for some would seem a gigantic leap up the social ladder. For living on the Grove somehow indicated you were someone of great importance – at least so it appeared to my grandmother, who treated the residents with deference.

However, I personally found it strange that these *"somebodies"* used the same public transport system, shops, schools and facilities that I did yet acted aloof, as if they came from an entirely different species. Fraternization between "them" and "us" was rare, and as an underling and one of the Bloomo mob, it was not a comfortable feeling to realise I had been spied on by a particularly snooty Grove dweller, who I suspected reported me to Grandmother.

My birthplace I confess, although having a pretty name, bore no resemblance to a flowering grove. For soft green-blossomed trees were not seen there. Ironically, there was little evidence of them growing outside the Grove dwellers houses, either. Their pavements however were wider, cleaner and better maintained than ours. It was also rare to see children playing outside the large impressive homes.

Rita at Woodville – back yard wall

I would hesitate to cross over the narrow divide, much less play there. For doing so might have led to encountering the folk who lived in such grand houses. Dominantly positioned, the dwellings stood proudly displaying their fine entrance halls and polished doorknobs, well-furnished sitting rooms and indoor bathroom facilities.

I imagined the ladies who lived there used lace tablecloths, sat in elegant dining rooms, and hosted Christmas parties that the vicar would attend. Their invited guests would confidently walk up the pathway and ring the heavy ornate doorbell, to be welcomed in through the large impressive front door. Unlike the reception I received on the occasions Grandmother directed me to deliver a package to the occupant of a grand home. Having received instructions from Grandmother to perform such a task, she would always remind me: "You must never go to the front door; always make your way around to the back of the house. Knock gently and do not forget to mind your manners."

I never questioned the instructions when young. For Grandmother from early childhood had advised me, "Bernice, remember you must keep your place."

I was older when I was to become more forthright and as Maureen

Sylvia did I and started asking probing questions.

"Grandma," I would ask, "who was it allocated me my place?"

For Maureen Sylvia had made me realise that acknowledging one's place was something I should question. Being forthright given the slightest excuse, she took great delight in walking up to the front door of a large house. There, boldly standing in the porch, she would firmly ring the big iron doorbell. I watched her from a distance, however, never waiting long enough to see who opened the door. By the time the door opened I had run swiftly away to hide, hoping to remain invisible. For my deepest fear was that the house she had daringly approached, might by chance be the very one occupied by the person Grandmother so admired.

Chapter 9

The weather becoming warmer, we again played for hours outdoors. Maureen Sylvia declined to join us, for she was busy studying a set of cards. These cigarette cards originally donated by a local shopkeeper to Liitle Mabel and Maureen Sylvia was lucky as her Mother decided she should receive them, desperately hopin that the cards would keep her daughter occupied.

Wanting to show me the whole collection of cards she had obtained, Maureen Sylvia invited me to visit her modest home. It was the first time I had been there and cautiously I approached and knocked on the back door. Suddenly it flew open: "Come in, Mam's gone to the washhouse, I have to stay in and keep our Kenny company."

Maureen Sylvia's young brother Kenny was sitting at the table and busy rolling a marble around an old tray; he did not look up or seem to notice I was there.

When Maureen Sylvia went upstairs to collect her precious card collection I glanced around the small living room. Situated close to an old fireplace was a door that led to a flight of ascending stairs, on the opposite side of the room another door, slightly ajar, revealed a dark alcove and a flight of descending steps leading to the cellar. Situated at the top of the cellar steps was an old stone sink; it was the only washing facility available in the house. It soon became obvious that with a large family, Little Mabel would need to visit the communal washhouse frequently.

Maureen Sylvia came back into the room carrying a paper bag in one hand and a piece of loose string in the other.

"Kenny," she yelled and frantically continued shouting. "Have you touched my cards?"

Kenny glanced up, refraining to answer as Maureen tipped the contents of the bag onto the table and started to count. Kenny, noticing his sister's actions, got up and started heading towards the back door. Maureen Sylvia continued counting the number of cards in the bag. Suddenly she yelled even louder.

"Our Kenny, if one of my cards is missing, I'm going to thump you."

Kenny by then had opened the door. Maureen Sylvia continued counting, and discovered that a number of cards were missing. At that precise moment Kenny swiftly disappeared out of the door. Maureen Sylvia jumped up, now shouting loudly enough to be mistaken for a town crier. She took off in swift pursuit of young Kenny. Furiously yelling at her terrified brother, I heard, "YOU LITTLE SOD, GIVE IT BACK!"

Kenny, hearing the fury in her voice, ran away even faster. I sat alone in the house feeling bewildered, wondering how long it would be before she returned. Suddenly the door opened. A small dark-haired woman, almost hidden by a huge bundle of clothes, came into the room. She put the bundle down. Then, coming closer, she stared at me and said, "Who are you then?"

Before I could answer, she continued, "What's our Maureen Sylvia up to this time?"

By then there was the sound of Maureen Sylvia shouting furiously. Kenny was yelling so loudly for his mam all the folk in Radford could probably hear him.

Their mother looked at me wearily and said, "That pair can't be left alone for five minutes. I bet you never give your mam a hard time."

"Haven't got a Mam," I said. "She left me. I live with my Dad."
Little Mabel shook her head.

"You must be the one from Bloomsgrove Street then."

"Yes," I replied. "My Dad works on the Forest."

Just then, her daughter and young Kenny returned. Before either of them had time to speak or explain the reason for their actions, Little

Mabel spoke. "Aye Maureen Sylvia gets that kettle on and mash a cup of tea for me and this little bugger, fancy you deserting her as well."

Maureen Sylvia opened her mouth to protest, but seemed too surprised to reply, having just witnessed her mother take a cake tin out of the cupboard, open up the lid and offer me a nice bit of cake. Tiny as she was, Little Mabel's actions clearly demonstrated her heart was big enough to mother and care for any one she decided needed mothering. It was obvious from that moment she had decided to mother me. Something she continued doing, for even when I was tall enough to tower over her, whenever the need arose, miraculously it seemed she always appeared.

Chapter 10

It had been had been a stressful arithmetic lesson. The subject was one I never enjoyed, for often during the lesson some unfortunate pupil received instructions to come and stand at the front of the room. The teacher would grab the chalk, write out a sum on the blackboard then loudly say "WORK OUT THE ANSWER".

For a nervous child, the action often led to humiliation. For if unable to oblige, they sometimes became the victim of ridicule when their classmates nervously giggled at their discomfort.

I was always glad when the lesson ended, especially if such an incident occurred. It was only when we were back playing in the schoolyard I could relax. There I would play with my skipping rope – this made from an old piece of washing line, as nothing was ever wasted. I had found it in Grandmother's backyard, sited at "Woodville" as it was named. The area was my treasure trove; there I would hunt and find odds and ends to play with. For like many young children at that time I had learnt to utilise. I acquired the ability to make playthings out of oddments and imagination and was always active.

I could never complain of being bored, as I made dolls from wooden pegs and turned smooth pebbles into snobs. At certain seasons, the local children had an abundance of choice – acorns, conkers and pinecones gathered from the park. Everything fired our imagination, for with youthful enthusiasm we changed odd bits into playthings that provided endless entertainment.

Girls played dolly parties using grass and leaves; converting the leaves into a tiny cabbage, accompanied by acorn pie this made a fine dollies dinner – and a safe one, providing we didn't eat any.

Out in the school playground I often recruited Maureen and Barbara and to join me in skipping games, but one particular day Maureen declined the invitation to join in. As Barbara turned the rope, I chanted a ditty: "All in a bottle of gin, all out a bottle of stout."

Maureen, being very competitive at sport, would usually skip the fastest and sing the loudest; on this particular day, however, she was unsettled. Not appearing her usual energetic self, she had been unsettled all week and had not been playing in the school ground. Instead, she chose to sit on the floor in the playground and read her book. Engrossed as she was, she did not notice the school bell was ringing. I ran to inform her and reluctantly she made her way into school. Maureen had recently acquired a treasured book. Maureen, who treated all books with great respect, felt that owning a new book was a special treat.

When the teacher entered the classroom, she directed a child on the front row to share out our reading books. A lesson was about to commence and as not enough books were available, we usually sat in groups of three or four and shared one book between us.

We in turn began to read passages of the book out. I was sitting at the front of the class and my turn came quickly. I enjoyed reading and felt comfortable reading to the class. One by one, everyone in the class had to read aloud. Soon it was Maureen's turn and, being an avid reader, she was able to finish a passage in record time. She passed the book to the next in line; the girl slowly began to read, stumbling over the words. Maureen began getting bored. I noticed her slide her own new book out from under the desk. She was anxiously wanted to read the next chapter and was too impatient to wait until the lesson ended. Deeply engrossed in reading, she was startled hearing a voice suddenly bellow, "MAUREEN, WHAT ARE YOU DOING? BRING THAT BOOK TO ME AT ONCE."

Maureen stopped mid-track. One moment in the Land of Oz with Dorothy and the Tin Man, and the next pulled sharply back to reality by the loud voice of an angry teacher.

Maureen hung on to the book.

"It's mine," she protested.

"GIVE IT TO ME," said the teacher.

Maureen hung on to the book. The teacher wrenched it out of her hand.

Maureen let out a yell. "GIVE IT BACK YOU BUGGER. MY MAM BOUGHT IT ME."

The teacher grasped the precious book in one hand. Holding it high in the air, she grabbed Maureen's arm with her other hand and dragged a now furious child out of the classroom. The rest of the class silently looked at each other. We well knew where Maureen was to be taken: *THE HEAD TEACHER'S OFFICE.*

What happened inside the office caused discussion later and great speculation among the children, for it resulted in being unable to see or play at school with Maureen for a long time. For on reaching the head teacher's office and being told to "Hold *out your hand*", Maureen, having witnessed her treasured book being roughly handled and tossed in a cupboard, became furious. Then, noting a leather strap being produced, she refused to hold out her hand. Instead, in her fury, she pulled the strap out of the head teacher's hand and struck out.

It took some time to control the situation. Finally, summoned to come to school, Little Mabel was informed that her daughter was to be escorted off the premises. Young Maureen Sylvia was being expelled, and it was a long time before she was able to continue her formal education.

With so many other problems to worry her, Little Mabel regarded Maureen's expulsion as a mere incident in Maureen's life. For compared to the concern she felt about her only daughter's survival, it hardly rated Little Mabel losing any sleep over. Many years passed before Little Mabel felt confident her daughter would survive. By then it seemed too late to bring Maureen into line, and so as she grew older her behaviour continued to be outlandish. The folk who knew her well simply acknowledged that Maureen would always be different!

Chapter 11

It was Mavis and Grandmother who assumed, from an early age, instilling discipline into my life. When younger I never questioned why they needed to shoulder the responsibility, or the reason it became necessary. For being young when my mother deserted her children, I had grown up with no recollection of events and was unable even to remember my mother's face. This was unlike my sister, who could recall many distressing memories of the past; Mavis, however, rarely mentioned them. It became obvious with the passing of time that our mother's actions in so many different ways caused heartache and grief for both of us.

In the early days, Mavis spent a lot of her time at our paternal grandparents home, because our father worked long unsocial hours and was often away from home. I spent hours unsupervised. Being young I failed to understand the reason for this. As I became older and was able to analyze the early formative years, I realized what a difficult task my grandmother had shouldered. This was something I failed to appreciate when younger.

I did, however, have many other childhood memories, especially events that occurred at Douglas Road School. During the war air raid drills would be arranged, and orders given to the children to line up in the schoolyard. Groups of giggling girls, each wearing their smelly rubber gasmasks, marched in crocodile fashion towards a windowless brick building.

After the first exciting exercise the class became used to

abandoning the school building.

With the familiar routine re-established, and little to distract our lessons along with my classmates I was fully occupied absorbing the vital three Rs. The days and weeks passed by, until my sister informed me the school nurse was due to pay a visit. For the nurse had already visited Mavis's class and completed their annual check. Several children it seemed had been noted to have head lice and been sent home with an official letter. These letters instructed parents that their child must have a strong potent smelling chemical applied to their hair, to be followed by vigorously combing, using a metal toothcomb. I had never yet suffered the indignity of taking home a school letter, although I frequently had experienced being thoroughly doused and fine tooth combed. Having thick unruly hair it was an uncomfortable experience, though one to be endured if you wished to prevent taking home a nurses letter. So willingly I submitted to being dowsed in lotion and combed, for I had no desire for the visiting nurse to hand me a *nit letter*. For to receive a letter so publicly could result in disaster, as others in the past discovered to their dismay. One nasty incident involved a parent arriving at school and angrily insisting the receiver of a nit letter be prevented from sitting near her *Grove child*. Recalling the event witnessed by classmates and the embarrassment

Early photograph of Douglas Road School

of the child being ostracised I felt uneasy. I began imagining what might happen if I received such a dreaded letter. Especially if the particular resident Grandmother admired discovered the news. I felt the lady would attempt to stop me attending any forthcoming church festival.

On Monday, the day scheduled for the school nurse to visit, I was aware she would check my teeth, and so applied salt to my finger and rubbed inside my mouth. She also checked for other health problems. For often this would be the only time a child received any a medical check up. It was by undergoing the examination it was discovered I needed medical treatment for flat feet and enlarged tonsils. So wondering what other problems would be discovered, I entered the schoolyard that morning feeling nervous.

The bell sounded and we all marched in. As I entered the cloakroom, I noticed a familiar figure standing in the corridor. The head teacher was saying goodbye to a small dark haired woman. The familiar figure waved, and I waved back. It was Little Mabel. She had escorted Maureen Sylvia back to school, as she also was to be examined by the school nurse.

Knowing Maureen was on the premises changed everything. Suddenly the lady from the Grove no longer seemed such a threat. For I felt certain she knew my friend Maureen Sylvia was back at school; once more I had a champion alert and rearing for action and – just like her mother – ready to defend an underdog, and if necessary battle Goliath. Even one as powerful as Mrs Farcuarson from Todd Hill.

Chapter 12

Maureen Sylvia had settled back at school. Her preceding school years had been interrupted due to poor health and her requiring admission to the local hospital. In addition, there was the incident when her unruly behaviour caused a lengthy absence from school. This had lost Maureen Sylvia months of educational opportunities. The exclusion had little effect, however, on altering her behaviour, for young Maureen Sylvia resisted any attempt to restrain her.

Holding a grudge, however, was never her way and if speaking her mind offended others, she seemed astonished that people failed to share her opinion. Shrugging her shoulders, she would out-stare anyone who objected to an issue she believed was right. Eventually her unorthodox way of thinking led both of us into conflict with my sister. Mavis was feeling annoyed because my bad behaviour had created problems for her. She decided to challenge Maureen Sylvia about our latest escapade. My sister, having no luck convincing Maureen Sylvia our actions had been wrong, flew into a rage as Maureen Sylvia calmly related the story of our encounter with the school fire bucket.

It all started following an interesting history lesson, when the teacher vividly described a device invented long ago for measuring time. The story stirred our imagination and before long, we decided to test this ancient method for ourselves; a plan was set to build a sand-timer for ourselves. The only problem we encountered was how to obtain the sand, for we lived miles from the coast.

Mablethorpe 1947

Mavis' grandmother and Bernice

Following a lengthy discussion, Maureen and I came to the conclusion that as God had provided sand free, he intended it for everyone to use – and being unable to collect it from a beach ourselves, he had provided so that we could sneak a handful from the school fire bucket. For if God had no objection, why should a teacher? We decided it was better not to ask prior permission, as we planned after trying out our experiment to return the sand. We were confident no one would notice its absence; however, things did not run smoothly and the headmaster punished us.

Mavis reprimanded us and had been warned to "Keep a better watch on your sister and curb her bad behaviour."

It seems a shame our plan failed to run smoothly; if we had stuck to our original idea of making a small egg-timer it probably would have worked. For the sand required would then have been a mere handful. But Maureen Sylvia, being an ambitious character, decided it would be more impressive to make a far bigger sand *clock-timer*. With her ambitious aim in mind, we energetically sprang into action.

At first everything went as planned. We managed to scoop up handfuls of sand each time we passed a fire bucket. As the brown paper bag containing our spoils filled, we became aware it was barely adequate to hold the sand we were collecting, so we decided to get a bigger bag. Maureen Sylvia acquired a worn out pillowcase from her mother's bedroom cupboard and hid it inside a deep store box situated on the school corridor. At the end of the day, we planned to sneak the pillowcase of sand out of the school. During the dinner break, we continued to collect sand by the handful, not realizing how heavy the bag was becoming. Maureen Sylvia was delayed, due to being instructed to report after her lessons to explain the reason another adventure had ended in disaster. Being anxious, I raced down the corridor to carry on with the illegal removal of the sand from school premises. Seeing the coast clear, I reached deep inside the store box, planning to hoist the bag up and swiftly carry it out of the school gate. Gripping the old worn out pillowcase, I attempted to hoist it up. It felt as if it weighed a ton. Giving an almighty tug I tried again; like a cork flying out of a bottle it moved. Suddenly I became aware of the sound of cloth tearing – and fluttering in my hand were shreds of material; with an ominous trickling the sound sand of sand discharging from the torn pillowcase faintly could be heard. Unaware then that the sand was widely spreading itself over blankets stored inside the storage box, I looked up at the end of the corridor. A door had suddenly opened and, in a panic,

I noticed the school caretaker arriving. Glancing straight towards me, he noticed that the lid on the storage box was open. Terrified at being caught red handed I froze on the spot. Just then, Maureen Sylvia came hurrying down the corridor to join me. Spotting her arrival, in a loud voice the caretaker shouted, "Ay put that lid down; you two know you're not allowed to look in there".

I failed to answer and neither did Maureen Sylvia as we both crept into the nearby cloakroom. Once there I confessed our plan had not worked, for the sand was still in the box. With the caretaker still on duty, unable to solve the problem, reluctantly we went home and discussed plans to remove the evidence the following day. Unfortunately, the caretaker early the following morning requested to collect a blanket from the store, and discovered the spilt sand. Guessing who was responsible, the whole saga ended with both of us receiving a sharp flick of the strap.

Mavis, hearing of my unruly behaviour, was outraged and feared Grandmother would be informed. Luckily, the sand saga never reached Grandmother's ears. However, Maureen Sylvia's mother did eventually work out the mystery of her disappearing old pillowcase.

Maureen Sylvia took the whole incident in her stride. She had settled with ease back into her old ways, and I was willing to join her in her mad escapades.

Chapter 13

My sister, having finished junior school education, was feeling important and had settled in at Radford Boulevard Senior School. She firmly informed me she expected me to be better behaved, as in the near future I would be attending the same school as she.

Mavis along with Grandmother often attempted to be the stern female influence in my life. I had never questioned why Mavis assumed the role, or even attempted to broach the subject of why Mother deserted us. At that time, I just accepted that it had happened long ago – when I had been so young that now I was unable to remember my mother's face. My sister, however, recalled distressing memories of scenes from the past; she had stored them away but rarely mentioned them. With the passing of time it became obvious that our mother's actions had caused both of us heartache and grief in so many ways. In the early days, Mavis and I spent a lot of time at our grandparents home. Our father, having to work long unsocial hours, was often away from home. Being a young child I failed to understand the sacrifices made on my behalf, but as I matured I began to recall and analyze my early formative years. I realized then what a difficult task they had taken on, something I did not appreciate when younger.

So many memories of childhood flooded back, for the war created many problems for grown ups and had disrupted children's lives. One day a flurry of activity interrupted lessons. Given instructions to hurry away from the school building, our teachers frantically escorted us towards emergency classrooms. Commandeered and conveniently situated on Ilkeston Road, several temporary classrooms were in the large private homes that stood on the hill. Feeling excited at the prospect of viewing the wonders hidden behind the impressive front doors of these dwellings, to my dismay I discovered there was little chance of inspecting the homes in depth. For we were ushered in at great speed to a large dining room, there we received instructions to begin a written test. The harassed teacher then hurried away to check the progress of other pupils, who were situated at another property further along the street. The adventure didn't last long and to my disappointment the emergency was soon over and we were transported back to the familiar dark painted classrooms on Douglas Road

Another memorable moment was the day each pupil received a gift. For each child was given a small tin box. Inside was a treasure trove of goodies: barley sugar, Horlick's tablets, a bag of glucose powder and a few sweets, whose smell reminded me of cough syrup. With sweets on ration, we all appreciated this unexpected gift. Tasting the creamy Horlick's tablets was a joy. The class willingly sent thank you letters to the members of a local air force base, who donated the tins. Another time we received a gift that caused rather more problems. It all began when instructions were given to every child to bring an empty cup to school. We obeyed and lined up eagerly to watch with interest as our teacher place a large tin on her desk. Drawing close we noted it was full to the brim with a light brown coloured powder. Impatiently we lined up as directed, holding our cups out before us. The teacher now slowly scooped up a large spoonful of the powder and deposited the sweet smelling product into our cups. We soon discovered that the treasure, which we had received from an American army unit, was sweetened chocolate milk powder. The order was given that it had to be transported home and given to our parents, along with the printed instructions of how to mix the powder into a nourishing warm drink.

Deprived of such a luxury, eager children given the task of carrying such treasure home found it difficult to resist dipping their fingers into the cup. By the time they reached home, some children had little powder left to hand over. I was one of them. Fortunately, Dad seemed to find it amusing, and the incident was recalled often with great mirth. Yes, there were fun times to recall – although also there were some unforgettable and sad times.

Due to the poor living conditions and lack of modern medical aide at that time, some terrible hardship occurred. Tragedy struck some grieving families who were to mourn departed loved ones – and to discover a few years later that drugs had been discovered that could have saved their loved ones was a difficult fact for them to accept.

One such local family suffered the fate of losing two young daughters. I had often visited their youngest child who suffered from tuberculosis. On the day before her funeral, I, being instructed to visit her home to bid her farewell, crossed the street. Entering her Bloomsgrove Street home I noticed a small coffin placed on a table that stood in the middle of the room. Her mother had requested that her daughter's friends call to bid her goodbye. I arrived at the same time as a neighbour, who accompanied her own child reluctantly through the door. Clutching a bunch of wild flowers, they beckoned me be the first to enter.

The room was dark, the curtains tightly drawn across the window; a heavy chenille cloth covered the table. Instructed to step forward I hesitated. I was encouraged to "come closer". Standing on tiptoes I gazed into the small coffin. Being so young I had no idea what to expect, nor did I realize the finality of death. Inside the coffin lay my small friend. Her head supported on a lace edged pillow, she rested, dressed in a white gown with her hands folded together, holding a small cross. She looked like a pale wax-sleeping doll. I was not afraid – death to me then was just a word. A long time passed before I fully was able to understand that in this life, I would never see her again.

Chapter 14

The door flew open: in tumbled a daintily dressed small girl wearing a large pink bow in her dark hair. Highly exited she started to speak, the words tumbling at a rapid speed from her mouth: "I'm going to Skeggy," she said.

I stared at her in astonishment; then stammering I replied, "Skeggy, who are you going with?"

"Me, Mam and Pat – and Sandra's coming as well." Her sparkling blue eyes grew wider and rapidly she began to blink, a habit of hers when excited. "My mam's buying me new bathers from Clays. I'm going to stay at Skeggy for five days," she said. I looked at her in stunned silence, speechless and unable to speak – not because she was to have brand new bathers, or new clothes. It was the information Rita was going on holiday to Skeggy that stunned me into silence. For kids who lived on Bloomsgrove Street, it seemed, had an ultimate dream of visiting that particular fantasyland by the sea.

My imagination began to soar. How many times in the past had I heard my friend's weary parents say: "If you behave yerself, when my ship comes in I will take you to Skeggy."

Skegness: the prime destination talked about, thought about and promised as a reward for good behaviour. During the long years of war, little opportunity existed for local children to visit the seaside – but they dreamt that one day their parent's ship would arrive and sail them away from the shabby back street of Radford and take them to paradise. It seemed an endless wait, however. Especially for children who had heard the stories of joys available just eighty-five miles away. The fairytale destination spoken of may just as well have been on the moon – as it must have seemed for their parents, especially the ones who themselves had never had chance to visit the coast. Yet incredibly, these parents were the ones best able to conjure up wonderful descriptions of unseen places. Verbally they painted colourful scenes and created vistas. Realistic visions that the children who listened to stories now in dreams could picture. They heard the sound of mighty waves crashing onto sandy shores and circling noisy seagulls loudly calling to each other overhead. All created by their parents creating such beautiful scenes. It was amazing, considering the contrast to the life that their parents lived. Yet planning a wonderful seaside holiday was part of the fun – for it produced a glimmer of hope that one day the happy adventure would come true. All one needed was a magic carpet to fly away on. On reaching your destination, friends would invite you to play ball on the sand, or perhaps build sand castles. Fairground music would tempt you to spin round on a wooden horse, never stopping until a faithful Skegness donkey arrived who you could ride for hours. Strolling towards the clock tower, there was chance to join the crowd watching a Punch and Judy show.

Local Radford men's outing
Fred (Bobo-Booth) far right of photograph

With the sun now high in the sky, the time arrived to walk across the golden sand clutching an enormous pink ice cream. This was the moment you finally achieved your ultimate dream of paddling in the sea at Skeggy.

As the memorable day on the beach began drawing to an end, you returned to the boarding house, where a welcoming waitress smiled as she served you a generous helping of delicious Lincolnshire chips and crisp freshly cooked fish.

Oh, what joys that a holiday at Skegness could provide, for those fortunate to have their dreams came true.

Having announced her exiting news, Rita perched herself on the edge of the sturdy fender surrounding the old large black fireplace. Lost in thought and both mesmerized we stared at the flame licking around the battered old kettle, steaming away on the old hob.

We were free to dream. Mavis was at Grandmother's reading her book, undisturbed by her young sister. If Granddad were there, she would eagerly listen to him reminiscing – as he was a great teller of tales, especially after visiting the local public house.

Sea side holiday
Rita and Pat with Rita's mother

Outing to Trent Bridge, 1946 – Bernice, Rita and her Aunty Ivy

Grandma disapproved of Granddad's outings to the pub, but in our company refrained from expressing her opinion (unless he began relating street gossip or repeated a raucous tale he had heard). Then, bristling with indignation, Grandmother would protest, especially when mockingly he mentioned "The Lady", who he referred to as "Mrs Farquarson of Todd Hill."

Grandmother, realizing a pint of local brew had loosened his tongue, would then become agitated. Especially when he ignored her warning to stop relating derogatory stories, and continued talking about toffee-nosed dwellers, who – he suggested – lived a stones throw away on Todd Hill. This was a place he vividly described, and sounded remarkably like a dwelling I knew on the Grove.

Grandma, now in a panic, usually cried out, "Do stop that talk Charlie, both the girls go to Sunday school."

Granddad would look at both of us; then dramatically he would wink at us as he tapped his finger on his nose and solemnly stated, "Always remember the Ides of March".

I would nod in agreement, but had no idea what he meant. Mavis would smile, as if she understood the hidden message. Being older perhaps she did, while I was left wondering.

My sister's interests and hobbies were different from mine; she found no pleasure in boisterous games and frequently hinted that my actions and activities were both foolish and immature. Now she often reminded me that in just a few short weeks I would be attending a secondary school. She was desperate to make her younger sister act with some dignity, but being barely ten and half years of age, dignity and commonsense was an asset I sadly was lacking.

I was not overly concerned about her disapproval, for my friend Maureen was my role model. Although she was only six months older than I, she appeared full of confidence, so I attempted to emulate her. Maureen – perhaps because she had older brothers to guide her – seemed confident and self-assured, and by walking in Maureen's shadow I felt more confident.

Chapter 15

*D*espite being summer, it was necessary to keep the fire alight. Raking out dying ash from the grate, I began to place small lumps of coal on to the remaining hot embers. For I suddenly realised Dad would soon be home. Knowing he enjoyed hot tea, I began to fill the kettle. For unlike Grandfather who frequently called at the local pubic house, Dad always came straight home from work.

Entering the kitchen, he would remove his coat and then gratefully sink down in his old wooden armchair. Titus, anxiously seeking his attention, would approach Dad, who bent down and assisted the old cat onto his knee. Dad reached over and picked up his library book; then, happily, he would pour out his freshly brewed tea and drink the saccharin sweet liquid from his old tin mug.

Rita, who was keeping me company, knew my Father was expected home and was not concerned – for she knew Dad would make her welcome, as he always welcomed my friends. They felt relaxed in his company, unlike the unruly lads who visited the Forest Park grounds where Dad was employed as a special constable. He was kept busy there on his beat, for Nottingham Forest Park could be a hectic place, being situated close to the heavily populated and busy Hyson Green. Dad had the hard task there of sorting out any local vagabonds who created mischief.

As we waited for Dad to arrive I offered Rita a drink of Dandelion and Burdock. I poured the dark frothy liquid into a chipped cup, then curiously asked her, "When will you be going to Skeggy?"

Clutching her cup Rita replied, "As soon as we start school holidays."

I pondered as I recalled how, a few months ago, I had told Rita of my own holiday plans, when Grandmother had announced that Mavis and I were going on an out of season trip to the east coast. There we would be staying at a boarding house situated at a resort called Mablethorpe. Smaller than Skegness, its main attraction was its spectacular golden beach, which stretched for miles.

When Grandmother, Mavis and I arrived there, it was a complete contrast to what I imagined Skegness would be. Especially out of season, for Mablethorpe lacked the bustle and excitement its neighbour situated twenty miles further along the coast had.

Grandmother arranged this out of season holiday thinking it would benefit my sister's health. Suggestions had been made the sea air would do her good. Excited at the thought of this unexpected journey to the coast, I had waited eagerly to leave behind the smoking chimneys and grime of Nottingham.

From the window of the steam train I noticed the green flat open land of Lincolnshire unfolding, a memorable sight for a young city dweller. Grandmother had booked us a room at a small boarding house situated in a back street situated close to the shops and within walking distance of the sea front. Shown into a sparsely furnished room I noted a dressing table; on it stood a large washbowl and jug. Near the window, a double and single bed and large wardrobe completed the scene. Still excited following the train journey down to the coast, I hurriedly helped unpack a few items from the old leather suitcase. Then with Grandmother urging us to mind our manners, we made our way towards the sitting room. There the landlady explained we had to vacate our room promptly each day at ten o'clock and not return until after four when high tea would be provided. Each day we ate breakfast in a small drab dining room. The menu never varied: a small serving of grey uninteresting porridge, toast and runny homemade blackberry jam, all washed down with a lukewarm cup of weak tea.

On the first morning of the holiday, at ten sharp we left the premises. Wearing our hats and coats, briskly we set off down the road, glancing into the windows of any shops we noticed as we continued on our way towards the small promenade. It was there I caught my first sight of the beach. Stretched before me was a sight that filled me with awe and amazement. A brisk wind was now blowing the golden sand into the air. Without hesitation I pulled off my hat. Clutching it firmly in my hand and not stopping to remove my best pair of shoes, I ran across the wide stretch of sand heading towards the sea. Soon my grandmother and sister were left trailing far behind and when I reached the edge of the shore I stood enthralled and listened.

The waves were roaring in and I was fascinated. I had never imagined the sea to look or sound as it did. The unique echo as the waves hit the shore were something I had never expected, despite studying watercolour paintings of seaside views that talented Uncle Laurence had painted. I had no idea the sea was able to speak, for clearly it seemed to speak to me. In a unique language, it softly whispering a greeting at first as each wave rolled in; eventually gathering momentum a strong rhythmic sound developed and it

Bernice and Grandmother 1948

began to roar. I plainly heard it cry: "I hold the power come closer child and listen to me. I'm God's mighty creation, his majestic and glorious sea". The power and the message fascinated me.

As each new day of the holiday dawned, Grandmother walked us down to the sea front. With her coat wrapped firmly around her, she braved out the cold sea breeze. I kept warm by running up and down the deserted beach and gathering seashells. I used them to decorate a growing sand castle and then watched in fascination as the waves rolled in and reclaimed them.

At four o'clock we made our way back to the boarding house, Grandmother satisfied we had received an adequate supply of the healthy bracing sea air. We retraced our steps, Grandmother realizing that thankfully at last, we officially could return to the lodging house.

We opened the door, headed straight towards the sitting room, where at last Grandmother was able to sit in comfort and get warm. She slowly removed her coat, placed it on the heavy wooden coat stand, then with great dignity adjusted her hat and sat down on the velvet covered high backed armchair. Tired she might have been, but she acted as dignified as anyone who lived on the Grove.

Later we entered the dining room and under Grandmother's watchful eye we ate an acceptable but modest high tea. Both granddaughters strived to do their best to create the impression of well-behaved young ladies, an image that Grandma so wanted us to portray.

On my return to Radford, I was eager to explain to my friends how surprised I had been at the sight of the sea. Childlike I failed to fully understand the reason or principle of the sea appearing to move ever upwards until it reached the sky. I silently pondered on the idea that if the sea and sky joined, did it mean one day – as ancient people had believed – we would make our way to heaven on a boat? I intended to ask the question at Sunday school, but the first person I discussed the theory with was Maureen, who listened then forcefully said: "Bernice that's really stupid; I have read a book from the library about the sea and there are mermaids, what you think would happen if mermaids tried to get on a boat and sail to heaven?"

Before I had chance to reply she continued, "Mermaids don't wear vests and I bet God won't let anyone showing their titties get on board a boat that travels to heaven".

So having that thought planted in my mind, I decided Grandmother wouldn't approve of me asking anyone at Sunday school about boats or bare-breasted mermaids. So my question remained unanswered for a long time.

Chapter 16

When I visited the local park, my close friend Rita Bell addressed as Ding Dong by her close friends often accompanied me .

However when Maureen appeared and things began to get hectic, Rita would disappear. For she was not as robust as some members of the Radford group and did not relish being bold.

I valued my friendship with Rita and never could remember a time when she had not been part of my life. Rita came to live at 15 Bloomsgrove Street as a toddler , and being close in age had been my playmate since we were very young . She was the only child of mature parents, both previously married. Lottie and Jack Bell both had adult children, who were surprised at the arrival of a dainty dark haired half sister. For they imagined their parents too old for new parenthood. The age gap between the half brothers and sisters made them unlikely playmates for Rita. Seeking the company of other children she became a frequent and welcomed visitor to my home. Our relationship developed over the years and we became as close as sisters.

Unsupervised, we occupied our time playing games or sitting and talking in the small back kitchen. Hitching up our skirts we perched on the rim of a heavy metal fireguard, watching a coal fire blazing inches from our thighs as we chatted away.

Rita was fortunate as a small child to be indulged by Ivy, a dark haired unmarried lodger who had lived with Rita's family for years. She assumed the honorary role of "Aunty", and being childless happily accepted the title.

Radford REC, 1949 – Maureen, Rita and Bernice

Taking the role of Rita's favourite loving Aunty, she played an important part in Rita's life. Over the years she purchased fancy outfits and new toys for Rita, enabling her to be well clad and owning more toys than the average Bloomo child. However, these unsolicited gifts did little to provide Rita with young playmates, so Aunty Ivy encouraged other children to enjoy the fringe benefit of having an adopted Aunty by also providing little Rita's playmates with small gifts. Being a constant friend, I benefited by having Ivy as my honorary Aunty, as she often invited me on joint outings. Rita and I shared our most intimate secrets and although we differed sometimes in our points of view, we rarely argued.

Some days we wandered away from Bloomsgrove Street and visited a small backyard situated on Denman Street. There we helped feed a horse kept stabled there by its owner, Rita's dad.

Another favourite haunt we frequently visited was the local park, where we occupied ourselves playing ball games on the grassed area or on the swings, during the long summer holidays it was a very popular place to visit .

My last day at Douglas Road Junior School had finally arrived and I began to wonder if Maureen Sylvia would stay in contact during the summer. With no big ceremony arranged, we marched as usual into the hall to attend morning assembly and sang a favourite hymn. At the end of the day, instructed to take our belongings from the cloakroom, the schoolchildren were wished a happy and safe holiday. Then with final goodbye wishes extended to those moving on to Radford Boulevard School, we collected our personal items. In an orderly fashion, we filed out of the classroom.

Gathering in the schoolyard to say farewell to everyone, I spoke to Maureen Sylvia. She informed me that she had acquired a new pencil case to use at the secondary school. It had a red "M" clearly painted on it. Maureen Sylvia indicated the letter and informed me that, as she was changing schools, she wished now to be addressed by just one name, that name was Maureen.

Having stated her intention, she pointed to her new pencil case and strolled out of the school gate. I watched her departing and pondered if going to a senior school would bring other changes and perhaps using a simpler name indicated that our relationship would also alter. Feeling uneasy, I watched as she raced down the road to join Barbara, who lived in her direction.

I glanced around, wondering if anyone had waited to walk to home with me, but everyone had disappeared. I slowly began to walk down the hill alone; knowing as I did there would be no one at home to greet me. Dad as usual would be at work. I wondered if I should call at Grandma's house and speak to her. Suddenly I realized someone, at great speed, was running down the hill; the figure was getting closer, heading towards me. It was Maureen. She stopped some distance away, then cupping her hands close to her mouth she began to yell: "Bernice I'll see you tomorrow, we can go on the Rec."

My spirit now uplifted, I waved back as I replied, "I'll wait for you on Bloomo".

She waved and, as swiftly as spring winds can change directions, turned and quickly disappeared out of sight. I smiled with relief: tomorrow would not as I had feared be lonely or boring. I felt certain it was going to be an interesting summer. For with Maureen around it usually was.

Chapter 17

The summer holiday was ending. Soon the days of freedom and fun would disappear. Another chapter of my life was about to begin and I began to wonder what changes I would encounter once my secondary education commenced. For having been pre-warned that being a pupil at the Radford Boulevard Secondary School was going to be rather a different experience, I had started to become rather apprehensive.

For seeds of doubt planted by an exhausted teacher at Douglas Road Primary School now sprung into my mind. The teacher in question, after spending a stressful day teaching a class of fidgety children, had exclaimed: "All the pupils who shortly are leaving to become pupils at Radford Boulevard Secondary school better make the most of these last few carefree days at Douglas Road. For I have no doubt some of you will soon be experiencing how teachers at your new school demonstrate their particular method of sorting the wheat out from the chaff."

Rather puzzled by this odd statement, I decided later that day to ask my father for an explanation.

"Dad, what does the teacher mean, sorting wheat from chaff?"

Dad smiled as he replied, "Your teacher is describing weeding out children who get up to mischief. Chaff describes the sort of bad lads I escorted to the police station last week."

His answer left me even more puzzled, for what did weeds and wheat have to do with the lads Dad caught last weekend damaging equipment on the Nottingham Forest? Perhaps the teacher was right;

I had better make good use of these last precious moments of my summer holidays.

Maureen had of course found many interesting ways of filling the hours, enjoying every moment she spent energetically swimming at the local swimming pool. Having made arrangements to join her there I hurriedly began rolling up my bathers in an old towel, then proceeded to set off to walk up Denman Street, heading towards the directions of Boden Street baths.

The swimming pool, housed in one section of a public complex, was a busy place and local people made good use of every facility available there. The swimming pool, being a decent size, was popular with the local community, as were the bath cubicles. For few homes in the area had bathrooms and a weekly soak in a hot bathtub was one of the few luxuries available. The public laundry house, also located in the complex, proved a lifeline for Little Mabel and many other Radford women, for without the facility life would be more difficult. Each department at Radford complex was staffed by enthusiastic Little Generals. Men and woman who delighted in putting up posters demanding that, without question, you obey their strict rules. Few people it seemed dared challenge or even question their orders. For on the rare occasion an individual did raise their voice the outburst attracted unjust attention. Maureen did begin to speak out when young and shocked the authorities with her outbursts; hell bent at seeking fair play at every opportunity, she forged ahead to achieve it. Self-promoted Generals soon discovered what a determined character she could be. Although winning verbal battles against powerful opponents in her younger days was rare, gradually Maureen gained experience and became self-educated and an expert at overturning petty unjust rules. Speaking out became her forte and her reputation as an outspoken character continued to grow.

Arriving at the baths I was surprised to discover there were no lengthy queue, for during holidays usually this area teamed with activity. Today it seemed, however, that everyone had decided to go paddling in the River Leen.

Maureen and I paid the admission and entered the changing room. It seemed strange the pool looked so empty. Pulling our bathers on

Radford Swimming/Bath House

quickly we proceeded. Rolling up our outdoor clothes, we firmly placed them in a towel and left the bundle on the wooden bench. Entering the inner area where the pool was located, a familiar eerie sound greeted us. A noise we had previously been informed was echoes resonated off the high unusually shaped roof. Listening to the sound that was intensified by shouting from inside the building had become part of the fun. For swimmers attempting to communicate with each other found it difficult distinguishing the location the owner of the voice – and that could be useful when playing a game of water tag.

Maureen hurried towards the pool. Being a good swimmer she didn't hesitate and immediately jumped in the deep end. I joined her and we began to swim up and down; there seemed plenty of space as the pool was almost empty. We practiced underwater swimming and handstands. Before long Maureen instigated a game of chase and touch dobby; several local children had now arrived and they also jumped into the pool, recognizing us and needing no urging to join us in the game. The more swimmers joined in the merrier the game became. Maureen was in her element; she loved competitive games and she bustled around organizing everyone. Another game of water dobbing was soon underway, Maureen having now elected herself as the team leader. With newly recruited players, we now numbered eight. As the pool was still half-empty, there was ample room to spread out and safely swim around.

Loudly issuing orders our team leader bellowed: "Ready, Steady, Go!"

I was just about to jump in the pool, when I noticed the pool attendant waving his arm in Maureen's direction. He blew a loud blast on his whistle. Maureen, unable to hear, proceeded to jump into the deep end of the pool. Swimming like a fish she ploughed through the water, chasing another swimmer. The attendant blew his whistle again; still unable to hear she paid no attention. The furious attendant, his face red with anger began shouting, "Hey – you in the blue bathers."

Maureen, now hearing his angry cry, looked up in surprise.

"Who, me?"

The attendant replied, "Yes you, stop bumping into people."

Maureen gave him a defiant look.

"I'm not bumping, it's a game. I'm playing dobbing."

He replied, "No dobbing in this pool."

Maureen, bobbing up and down in the water, replied by pointing to a large notice fixed on the tiled wall.

"It doesn't say we can't play dobbing on those rules"

The attendant ignored her protest and furiously said, "No bumping or dobbing, get out."

Maureen, still bobbing up and down replied, "Why should I? I haven't broken any rules and my time's not up yet."

Then turning around she began swimming away towards the deep end of the pool. By now the swimmers in the water were straining to hear the attendant's reply. Furious to have his instructions ignored, the attendant roared, "I make the rules here – now get out".

"I'm not, my times not up," replied Maureen. Then she proceeded slowly to swim towards the centre of the pool.

Other swimmers, aware of the shouting, began to wonder what was about to happen next: mutiny at the Radford pool?

Had Maureen been reading tales of Captain Blythe, I thought, as I climbed out of the pool. The other nervous swimmers reluctantly now stopped playing dobby. I sat on the edge of the pool. Maureen was happily swimming up and down, obviously not intending to climb out.

The attendant with an expression of blind fury on his face continued to stare at her. Suddenly he moved away from the pool. Reappearing like a flash of lightning carrying a long pole he proceeded now to move towards the edge of the pool.

Maureen, swimming up and down, did not notice him or see that he was now holding a long wooden object with a heavy metal hook attached firmly to the end.

The attendant noted Maureen's actions, and carefully moved into position. Expertly he struck out, harpooning the strap of her bathers, and with one foul swoop he pulled her towards the side of the pool. Taken by surprise, before she could gather enough power to escape, he leaned over, grabbed her upper arm, and dragged her out of the pool. Still attached to the hook her vigorously struggle resulted in a tearing sound of material being heard, as she was hoisted upwards.

Maureen spluttering lay on the side of the pool. The attendant threw down the wooden pole and began yanking her up on her feet and angrily shouting, "Time's up you little bugger."

Maureen started headed towards the change room and I followed, both of us realizing we now had little choice – for our allotted time officially had ended. It was not until she was getting dressed that she noticed the rip in the strap of her bathing costume. Closely examining the damage, she let out an almighty roar.

"My Mam only got me these bathers last week from the jumble sale," she said.

Then, furiously yelling like a banshee, she charged out of the change room and headed back towards the pool.

The attendant was still standing close by the side of the deep end. Maureen suddenly noticed the long pole and hook he had used to cause the damage. Racing forwards, she firmly grabbed it, attempting to lift it up. Struggling she raised the lengthy object; the heavy metal hook scraped across the tiled floor, causing a sound of grinding metal to be heard. The attendant looked up and noticed her coming towards him.

"Put that down you cheeky little sod," he bellowed.

Maureen shouted back, "Fetch it, Hitler. You ripped my bathers, I'm going to tell me Mam."

Then with out another word, she managed to hoist the pole high above her head – and, standing there framed like an Olympic javelin thrower, with all her strength she launched the pole into the air. With a mighty splash, it landed in the middle of the pool. The attendant looked on in disbelief as the pole, weighed down by the heavy metal hook, proceeded to sink to the bottom of the pool. Maureen without a backward glance then strode towards the exit, while I, clutching tightly to both wrapped sets of wet bathers, hastily followed her out of the door.

Silently we both walked away. I was convinced she would permanently be banned from entering the pool and strongly suspected that I would be blacklisted too. A sobering thought but I couldn't help admiring Maureen's nerve: she had made a stand, the attendant was behaving like a dictator, as there was nothing in the rule forbidding us from playing dobby. We were only having harmless fun.

Bugger him, I thought. Then, as my bravado began slipping away, rising panic overtook me – for I started wondering, what will happen if Grandmother gets to hear about Maureen's latest escapade?

Chapter 18

The house felt cold. I looked inside the cubby hole under the stairs to see if Dad had left any wood and was relieved to find a supply of chopped dry kindling. I was puzzled for it seemed unusual to come home and find an empty fireplace; perhaps Dad had failed to realize that despite it being summer the forecast said it would be cold today. Mavis was absent and was probably drinking hot tea over the road at Grandmother's house, for she seemed to spend most of her time over at No. 19 these days.

Gathering up an old newspaper I crumpled it into a ball and placed it in the bottom of the iron grate; this was followed by dry kindle. Now picking up a box of matches I struck the match and bending down lit the paper; the dry wood crackled and spat. In haste, I threw small lumps of coal on top of the sparking wood. Then I watched as gradually the sparks appeared to settle and a steady flame appeared. So far so good. From experience I knew this was only the beginning of the task, for it was not always easy to get the coals to glow; the flames could still simply fade away and die.

I was impatient for I wanted to sit and read my new library book and now I began urging the fire to burn quicker, using a method I had seen my Dad use many times. Dad was an expert at drawing up a slow reluctant fire, so knowing his technique I reached out and grabbed a sheet of newspaper and placed it firmly in position over the grate opening. Blocking the gaping hole in the fireplace created a swift up draw of air and stimulated the fire. As if by magic, the flames roared into life. Continuing to hold the newspaper over the grate, the

Woodville Yard 1950/51. Seated – local child with Rita.
Standing – Bernice and Maureen

sound of the front door opening caused me to briefly glance up. Rita rushed into the kitchen; distracted I turned to speak to her, failing to notice the newspaper I was holding had drifted closer to the flame. With a whoosh, the newspaper caught fire; attempting to escape the inferno I tossed it aside and burning paper floated down, landing on the pegged rug placed by the hearth. In a panic, I pushed Rita roughly aside and rushed to the sink. Noting a saucepan full of dirty water there, I picked it up and threw its contents onto the burning rug. An odious cloud of steam rose from the singed rug, the emergency was over.

The fire, confined now to the grate, was burning brightly.

Rita glanced at me, and simply asked, "Is that the rug you pegged?"

"Yes," I answered.

"Good job you only singed it," she said.

I glanced at the roughly made, multi-coloured rug.

"Yes – but it smells as if I will have to wash the bloody thing, for it's soaked in stinking water. Dad must have boiled fish heads in that water."

Rita leaned over without saying a word and stroked my old cat Titus, who had jumped down from Dad's wooden armchair. Titus stretched out a paw and began investigating the source of the enticing smell.

I bent down and clutching hold of the ragged end of the rug dragged it towards the back door. Titus was still examining it as I threw the rug out from the house, tempted by the fishy smell. Eager to investigate, he ran out the door in hot pursuit.

Rita now started to explain she had called with an invitation, extended to both of us by her Aunty Ivy, who had offered to take us to a variety concert on Saturday. This was to be held at the bandstand, situated on Trent Embankment.

I hesitated. It was a mixed blessing going on an outing with Rita's Aunty Ivy, for although she was generous and treated us to ice cream and comics, without any warning she would sometimes get annoyed, berating and accusing us of unwarranted sins. The last few outings had been unsettling experiences, for what usually started as enjoyable outings seemed to quickly deteriorate into disturbing unhappy events. For Aunty Ivy was increasingly demonstrating unreasonable behaviour, and this erratic situation caused Rita to frequently blink, a habit she did when anxious. I also felt stressed and uneasy now in Aunty Ivy's company; when I was with her I remained silent and would stare straight ahead, not sure of what I had done wrong.

Aunty Ivy was not Rita's blood relation but for many years she cared for Rita, buying her gifts of shoes and other items; she was most generous but her moods and actions were unpredictable.

Rita was puzzled and embarrassed at how she would complain about our behaviour, as we had both tried to obey Aunty Ivy's every wish. . So gradually, despite the lure of Rita's company and ice cream, I became most reluctant to go on outings that ended with Rita and I trailing home upset and worried.

Grandmother and Rita's Aunty recently had to everyone's surprise become friends and, afraid Grandmother might think I had caused offence, I was reluctant to disclose the reason I had avoided these outings. Despite the constant fear of being reprimanded it was a groundless worry, for Grandmother never asked me to account for any supposed misdemeanour.

Years later I was informed that Grandmother and Dad had been aware of the strange situation. Feeling sorry for little Rita, they thought she needed a friend, and felt I would with confidence cope with the problem. In truth I was as nervous and out of my depth as Rita was.

As time went by it became clear to others that the unpredictable behaviour demonstrated by Rita's aunty was out of control. Eventually it resulted in her having to stay at Mapperley Psychiatric Hospital, for she was in need of long-term medical treatment.

Now looking back, Little Rita did not have such an easy time despite her ribbons, fancy buckled shoes and lacy dresses. For at times her life must have been difficult. Yet Rita never complained, proving to be just another Bloomsgrove survivor, battling on despite everything and believing there were many other children with more problems to face than we had.

It may have appeared to affluent outsiders our life and horizons seemed bleak, yet in some ways we may have been the lucky ones, for day-by-day we were receiving a most precious gift – for true friendship and a feeling of belonging to a community, however humble it seems, is a treasure worth having.

For from an early age we played with neighbourhood children that we trusted and shared adventures and childhood secrets. Sometimes we heard things we did not fully understand, snatches of discussed adult conversation that Mavis, who was older, perhaps understood, but refused to explain. When snatches of local scandal were heard, I felt frustrated as Mavis smirked and insisted I was far too young to understand such grown up matters. Therefore, I never attempted to question my sister about the reason for our mother's absence. As a younger child I also overheard rumours regards my questionable origins and wanted to ask but never did, and so the subject was never raised at home. It appeared the mystery would never be unearthed. Puzzled, I accepted that our family was obviously not free from hidden skeletons, but gossip and speculation also seemed to touch many residents of the street. Family battles developed, and were sometimes overheard because of the close proximity of the houses. These arguments created something for the gossips to discuss, as preserving privacy was difficult. Some Bloomsgrove Street residents, being rather fond of the local public house, would claim the right to sit in the same seat every night. There were two local public houses, The Peacock Inn and The Dog and Pheasant, conveniently placed at the top and the bottom of Bloomsgrove Street, both popular destinations for Rita and Pat's parents.

Herbert, a small, strongly built and hard-working coalminer, was Sandra's dad, who well deserved his regular nightly tipple. Exhausted after a long hard shift at the pit and covered in coal dust, he made his way home. There he would find, placed in the small kitchen, a large tin bath, half-filled with warm water. He was not a shy man and once submerged in the water (that soon became murky) he never objected to the audience of children who trooped past him to play with his daughters. His modesty preserved by the opaque water, he continued to lay back and soak his tired muscles. In time, revived by his bath, he would get dressed and be served his evening meal. Later he would make his way to a local public house; there he relaxed as he enjoyed his well-earned evening pint. Lily, a tall woman with dark hair, was his wife, and it seemed they were an odd matched couple. She had a deep voice, and often startled people when they first heard her booming tone. A talented musician, she regularly entertained customers at the Peacock Inn by skilfully playing the piano. Lilly encouraged Pat, her oldest child, to watch over Sandra her younger sister – not an easy task if her young sibling was playing with her friend Donalda. The locals all addressed Donalda by her nickname Bubbles, a term of endearment given to her as a baby by her own family.

Bubbles and Sandra were a well-matched pair. They both attended Douglas Junior School and shared many interests. Both were quick thinking children, live wires and the youngest members of their families. Bubbles, who was dark haired, delicate and attractive, was Pearl's sister, while Sandra her constant companion (who was also small) had blonde wispy hair and a pale complexion. Both girls were born during the war and looked small and young for their age. In character and wit, however, they were wise beyond their years – bright individuals who were reared under tough wartime conditions

During those unsettled years, mothers would despair at the prospect of safely raising their wartime babies. The post-war years provided different worries and new experiences.

Sandra and Bubbles were noted for having a sense of great self-worth; they were full of humour, constantly giggling at everything. Neither of them robust children, yet they appeared tough little characters. Sandra suffered a medical condition rarely discussed in the 1940s. Lack of understanding had created a blanket of silence around suffers of epilepsy and Sandra's parents declined to discuss their daughter's medical problems with others. And without the benefits of modern drugs, Sandra sometimes suffered grand mal seizures.

As I watched the girls skipping I noticed two young brothers arrive. I knew both Trevor and Donald, close neighbours – who recently had informed me that plans were underway for them to go and live in Canada. Their father was a member of the Canadian forces, and was rarely seen on Bloomsgrove Street for he was stationed and living at a military base outside of Nottingham. Soon he was returning to Canada and Donald and Trevor, who, having grown up in Radford, expressed concern about moving away from their maternal grandparents, who lived close by. Both boys had been promised that when they reached Canada, they would be able to ride horses and become cowboys.

Growing enthusiastic at the prospect of living overseas, I listened in awe as they related their exiting news – for ever since I had spent an exhilarating holiday leading donkeys up and down a beach I believed myself a specialist on the equine world. Donald began promising he would invite all his friends to visit him in Canada and provide every visitor with a horse to ride. Hearing such fantastic news, in great excitement I had rushed to find my dad and ask if he would let me go to Canada.

He smiled as he answered, "Well, I hope if you get a firm invitation, you turn out to be a good traveller, it's a very long boat ride."

Radford Boulevard Sports Day
Maureen leads the way

I was puzzled. I had never been sick on the boat travelling a mile down the Trent River as it headed on smooth water towards the local pleasure park. I wondered what caused Dad to think I would get sick travelling to Canada.

However, I never had chance to discover if I would survive such an exciting long journey, or be seasick. For when Donald and Trevor eventually left the street and sailed to Canada, I never heard from them again.

For some local children their first experience of the sea was when their parents managed to obtain free tickets that would enable their off-spring to visit the east coast – and there catch their first sight of the sea. Some accompanying adults also managed to spend the day there, and were most happy to view the sea as they sat at the windows of a beachfront inn. There were popular places to visit and landlords welcomed the ever-growing number of Nottingham customers, who all helped boost their daily takings.

Maureen and her younger brother Kenny had once obtained a treasured ticket to travel on the bus and had joined the throng on a days outing. Maureen dreamed of staying at the coast for longer; it was not possible but eventually her chance came. When the extended family holiday arrived, Little Mabel had carefully folded her clean clothes with delight, and placed them in a large sturdy bag. This proved a new experience for her. For previously when she placed a collection of clothes in a bag, she always included a large bar of coarse washing soap, a dolly blue bag, and then had proceeded to place all the articles in a pram. For any clothes she carelessly had tossed in a bag had been destined to be taken to be scrubbed clean at the local Radford washhouse.

Chapter 19

The lucky day-trippers, who managed to secure seats for the annual pub outing, would, once the appointed day arrive, gatherer outside the public house. They waited for the bus to arrive, clutching their tickets anxiously. A cheer erupted as the bus came into sight. Then people wasted no time in boarding the vehicle and securing a seat, impatient now for everyone to be seated. With everyone aboard the bus began to move, and good spirit was restored. Before long someone would begin to sing a popular song; soon everyone on board was joining in the chorus. With great enthusiasm, they belted out familiar words. Eventually voices grew hoarse from singing; eagerly they began to open up the bottles of lemonade and free crisps provided. The exciting day at the coast passed by quickly. Almost before they realized it, their day at the seaside was almost over – and, with the bus driver now urging them to climb back on board his bus, they set off for the return journey.

Triumphant but tired, many of the passengers, still wearing the souvenir hats they had purchased, fell asleep. At the end of their journey, the children who had been unable to obtain a ticket for the trip were sometimes waiting to greet the lucky ones who had. Pitying them, some kind returnees would hand out sticks of Skegness rock to the disappointed children who had missed the chance of experiencing such a wonderful day.

Fortunately, Mavis and I continued to visit the coast with Grandmother. One memorable summer, arrangements were made for us to stay at a church army holiday home. This was a new experience for all of us. We travelled by train to Western-Super-Mare and by the end of the week we were well-versed in church army hymns; unlike the Skegness day-trippers, however, we failed to gain insight into seaside hostelries. For with Grandmother as our escort, however quaint a seaside inn might look, we were to remain ignorant of such places.

Still – despite that ban, I had the most glorious time, and was thrilled to be given the chance to meet and help a local boy! He had a job working on the seafront caring for a team of seaside donkeys. Eager to be involved, I boldly asked the owner of the donkeys if I could assist him. Having obtained his agreement, soon I was holding and checking the donkey's reins and saddle straps, then assisting excited children as they clambered on to the back of the bored and passive donkeys. Grandmother rested nearby on a deck chair, and she watched as proudly I held the worn out leather reins and slowly led the donkeys up and down the beach. I walked for hours and became something of an expert at handling the placid donkeys. I eventually returned home at the end of the holiday sporting a wonderful suntan.

On my return from the Western-Super-Mare trip, I wondered how Maureen had been spending her time, so decided to pay her a visit. I was startled when first I noticed her standing in the doorway of the local shop. I knew it must be Maureen, but she acted sounded and looked unlike the Maureen I knew. She was leaning against the door of the shop and talking to a small crowd of children I didn't recognize. She noticed me approaching and then slowly waved. As I drew closer, I noted the children: two girls and three boys. Two of the boys were older, dark-haired and handsome; they seemed to be the ones capturing everyone's attention. Articulate and full of confidence, I was surprised to hear they spoke with unusually pleasant accents. They looked up as I approached and gave me a beaming smile. I was amazed now to see they were identical; Maureen introduced them as the Irish twins.

Maureen seemed bewitched by them, as were most girls who met them. I was surprised at her sudden interest in these boys. For until these teenage Adonis' made their appearance, boys had been a species Maureen had ignored or often deliberately avoided. However, this matching pair seemed to have changed everything. Full of Irish charm and obviously blessed, it seemed they must have kissed the blarney stone. Life it seemed from that moment was to change for Maureen and myself, for until then we had failed to recognise our developing hormones. Grandmother it seemed would have more problems controlling me now. She would never approve of a granddaughter standing on street corner, talking and laughing with handsome twins who oozed Irish charm. They were boys who, I feel, would not have met with approval by a certain lady who attended the local church. Grandmother's mission of keeping me on a straight and narrow path, seemed to be growing more difficult day-by-day. Yet, she still seemed to be determined as ever to turn me into a *little lady*.

Weston Super-Mare 1949 – Bernice and holiday friends

Chapter 20

Maureen and I spent the latter part of the school holiday playing on the Radford recreation ground. It was within easy walking distance of Bloomsgrove Street and a popular playground and local park.

Another area we enjoyed visiting, during the school holidays, was the local park. There surrounded by bushes lay a green patch of land: it had swings, roundabout, seesaws and a slide that stood on solid ground. A larger section of the park housed a bowling green; this was the spot Lenton and Radford adults gathered to play lawn bowls. It was a restricted spot, immaculately kept and off limits to children.

Maureen was familiar with every inch of the park, or "The Rec" as locals usually called it. The backstreet youngsters in their droves descended there, especially in good weather. For there was a chance there to let off steam and act out fantasies. Unsupervised by their parents, and with only one regular overworked keeper to keep order, many long sunny days were spent there having fun. One of my favourite pastimes was climbing the rails surrounding the top rung of the seesaw. Foolish risk-takers like me scrambled to the top and, swinging from the high bars, would attempt to imitate a jungle ape. Dangling dangerously suspended, my unprotected head pointing downwards towards solid concrete ground, foolhardily I would hang. Then I would foolishly begin to swing back and forth, whooping and hollering to catch attention, giving what I believed to be a great performance. The idea for this game came after a visit to the local picture house, where Johnny Weissmuller was starring in his latest

Tarzan film. I had been greatly impressed watching Johnny bravely fly through the air on a rope, making it look so easy. Before long immature young risk-takers like me attempted to recreate these jungle episodes using the bars of the seesaw at Radford Rec. Tarzan had one a big advantage over me and others – for he had never had to face the wrath of the Radford Park keeper, who, having recognized the dangers, tried to deter all foolish children from attempting this silly practice.

Rita was not a risk-taker, unlike Maureen or me who frequently played dangerous tricks. So it was a shock to everyone when little Rita became injured on the park. The accident she was involved in, caused by a swing, was undeserved. For through no fault of hers, she received a severe blow to her chin. Bleeding profusely, Rita was quickly taken home by her friends. Arriving in a dazed state, her mother in great haste and panic rushed her to the local hospital, where a doctor examined the gaping wound, promptly cleaned and sutured it. The local hospital, recently having become part of the new National Health Service, was already used to dealing with Radford children. We certainly kept the casualty department busy.

For weeks following her accident Rita was the centre of attention. The gang clamoured around to inspect her vivid wound. Gradually the novelty faded. Interest was lost as Little Rita's sutures became boring; the gang all returned to the park, leaving behind Rita – banned from going near the swings – left alone at home. With just the scar on her chin to remind her of her brief hour of glory Rita began to mope. Eventually, to her relief, her mother lifted the ban and the little heroine was able once again to join the gang on the park.

It was shortly after Rita recovered from the episode with the swing that Nottingham Education Department announced changes in the allocation of school places. Rita discovered, as did other Radford children, that she was to attend the Lenton-based Cottesmore Secondary School. She was unsettled and apprehensive, because the modern school situated on Derby road she thought a "Snooty Place".

Pupils attending the modern designed school usually lived on The Groves. The school had a grassed play area and seemed elite. Bloomo kids, hearing they were to attend Cottesmore, were stunned and protested they did not want to. However, to everyone's surprise the protesting future pupils soon settled in and became proud of being at Cottesmore. Folk did wonder how the children from Bloomo attending the new school would cope, especially as long-established relationships between local children would be disrupted. However, it was soon clear that the bonds existing between The Bloomo kids were not easily broken, regardless of attending different schools, as their close friendships continued to thrive.

Rita continued to join me in out of school activities and the only time School rivalry reared its head, was on the interschool sports day. For all the local schools were keen to become sports champions and practiced diligently. Girls at Radford Boulevard School however remained confident that, having Maureen on their team, they would remain victorious – for any opponents that a rival school selected would have little chance of out running, jumping or leaping that final hurdle before Maureen.

Doctors continued being amazed at her stamina, finding it difficult to understand how she continued to perform so well. Her flamboyant character also raised eyebrows as she constantly refused to conform. Her mother chose to dismiss any complaints. For Little Mabel long

Radford Boulevard Sport's Trophy Day

ago had noted how doctors shook their heads and planted doubts that Maureen would ever survive, or even enter secondary school. They had portrayed a frightening future for her daughter, and it seemed they were wrong. The prognosis had caused great anxiety; now Little Mabel felt justified in ignoring other pessimistic views expressed by those in authority who searched for answers and hidden reasons that made her daughter act in such high-spirited ways.

For Little Mabel firmly believed that Maureen's erratic outbursts and the zest she displayed were the reason her daughter had survived. Maureen on the threshold of puberty, however, was now having to deal with awakening hormones; as they stirred her outbursts increased and she sometimes behaved irresponsibly. Her mother shrugged her shoulders, accepted her daughter's unorthodox ways, and exclaimed, "Maureen was born with the ability to walk where angels fear to tread and emerge unharmed."

In short, she was a miraculous survivor.

The testing time for Maureen however lay ahead, for years of secondary school education were waiting. Radford Boulevard School's reputation of sorting the wheat from the chaff indicated that Maureen would need to tread with greater care. And it has to be said that the Archangel Gabriel himself would have found some of the problems Maureen was about to become involved in difficult to handle.

Chapter 21

I came downstairs. It was still early, Dad was awake and a good fire burning in the grate. The morning cuppa was mashing in the metal teapot. I took out the loaf and started to cut a thick slice of grey looking bread. Crumbs dropping everywhere, I reached towards the fireplace. Grabbing hold of a long metal fork, I speared the uneven slice and held it close to the glowing coals.

The appetizing smell soon began to fill the small kitchen. Dad did most of the cooking, although Mavis occasionally would try out a recipe she had seen demonstrated at school. Food rationing being strict, many ingredients were hard to obtain; one day, planning to make bread and butter pudding and having no dry fruit to use, I suggested she use rhubarb from Grandma's garden. Looking at me in disgust, she exclaimed, "That will be a soggy mess."

I continued trying to persuade her, but gave up after she said mocking tone, "You would eat any old rubbish."

Oh well, perhaps she was right. I knew little about cooking. Perhaps it would have been a soggy mess, but interesting – and anyway children in those days were so easy to please. The highlight of any children's celebrations was when jelly and custard were on offer.

Dad on one occasion surprised me by obtaining a ticket inviting me to a children's Christmas party organized by the Nottingham Parks Committee. I hoped for jelly and custard and was in seventh heaven when I realised musical chairs and pass-the-parcel games were also planned. The big day arrived, the games commenced and the expected desert was served. Just one incident clouded the day's event; it happened towards the end of the party. Santa arrived and handed labelled gifts taken from the tall Christmas tree one by one to all the other eager children. Finally, the tree stood bare and with every child's name but mine was called. After a few moments I anxiously watched a hastily wrapped parcel tied up and handed to Santa. He shouted out my name and handed me the crumpled package; it contained a soiled secondhand comic. Why had I been the one forgotten? I never discovered the reason. Perhaps Dad had been too busy to organise getting one. As Mavis and I became older, it appeared life became easier for him. For Dad began taking us to the Odeon cinema on regular outings. Rita or Pearl often would join us, and Dad never worried how many children trailed behind him on our Wednesday picture session. When I started big school, I had been pre-warned that my life would start becoming hectic. "No time at secondary school for you to muck about," people had been telling me. So I hoped the picture sessions would continue. Would everything be so very different at Radford Boulevard School?

Dad tuned in the wireless. He always checked the correct time by listening to the chimes of Big Ben. Looking at me, he warned, "It is getting late I will be off to work in a minute. Don't get late on your first day at the new school."

I nodded.

"I won't. Maureen and Barbara are going to call for me."

Fiddling with his watch, he instructed, "Barbara is a nice girl; try and stay close to her today."

I nodded. He was right, Barbara was a nice girl; though she was rather shy and stuttered badly, she was a good friend who I played with at school but rarely met during the holidays. Not encouraged to roam the streets, her mother preferring her to stay close to home, and Barbara never seemed to object to being restricted. Our close friendship seemed odd in some ways, for we appeared to have little in common. There were differences in our backgrounds and temperaments, yet despite everything, we remained good friends.

Barbara lived in a terrace house just a street away from Maureen's home. I expected they would join forces and walk down Denman Street together along with the other children about to begin secondary school; we had all had decided to group up today and walk towards the Radford Boulevard intersection. At that point, a clear view of the large imposing school building was possible. Then you only needed to cross this busy corner and the entrance door to your future life was waiting for you.

The Four Corners, as it was known, had given its name by the local population because of the four buildings standing on the spot. Each building served a very different purpose. On one corner the parish Church of All Souls stood. Across the road, there was a smaller building housing a well-used pawn shop. Situated opposite was a popular public house. Finally the tallest building to dominate the scene, clear from a distance, was the well-occupied Radford Boulevard Secondary School.

Local folk laughingly referred to this intersection as:

"The Four Corners.
As good a representation of life in Radford as you will ever see:
Salvation, Ruination, Damnation and Education."

Chapter 22

I hurried to finish my breakfast, then washed my hands and face at the kitchen sink. We didn't have a bathroom and although a tin bath permanently hung on a nail outside the back door, it was rarely used these days because I was able to join Rita sometimes and share her bath, or wander to Grandma's house where a modest bathroom had been installed that Mavis and I were allowed to use. Many folk still relied on the public bathhouse.

Leaping up the stairs, I entered my room and began pulling on my new school clothes: navy blue gymslip, jumper, black lace-up shoes. I now looked the part, a secondary school pupil. I was at the *awkward stage* – barely eleven, feeling grown up and brave one day and vulnerable and worried the next. It was my first day at a secondary school and I was glad my friends were planning to accompany me.

I heard the front door open. A voice rang out, "Are you ready Bernice, I will race you to school. Bet I get to The Four Corners first."

I responded quickly to Maureen's challenge.

Collecting my dinner money from the mantle piece, I raced out of the door.

Standing waiting on the pavement was Barbara; before she had chance to realize what was happening, Maureen and I took off, running down the street and round the corner at great speed. On and on we ran and Barbara was left far behind as we belted down the hill. Barbara never given to running, and she was especially reluctant today being dressed in her brand new school outfit. She attempted a hurried walk but by now was lagging far behind us. Maureen, well ahead of me, was on top form. The Radford Runner kept up her impressive speed, while I did my utmost to catch her up. Faster and faster I went, but Maureen was faster. My gymslip now seemed to have a life of its own, flying up in the air and exposing my new navy blue elastic leg school knickers, on view now for everyone to see.

Almost at the school, Maureen had already sighted the tall stone building; as she reached the front entrance door children and parents were milling all around. Elbowing her way through the crowd, she was determined to be first inside the building. Close on her heels I did the same, impatiently pushing my way in. We were both now standing on school premises and Barbara was still nowhere in sight.

Maureen laughed triumphantly, and then shouted, "I won you by a mile."

I was just about to answer, when I felt a hand tap me on my shoulder.

"What's your name young lady?"

A voice full of authority asked me. Before I could reply, she asked the same question of Maureen. We muttered our names.

"Well you two, this is not a race track, we expect you to behave in an orderly fashion if you expect to keep on attending this school."

Then in a softer tone, she said, "This school encourages all athletic sports, but in future save your energy for the sports field."

She strode away, and later that day surprised us at a school assembly, where she introduced herself as the school headmistress. Later she proved a fair-minded but strict principal.

Regards athletics, she was keen to encourage all sporting activities and anyone showing promise was given chance to shine. Living a healthy life was the upper aim in setting the school curriculum. The theory being that pupils with a healthy body had healthy minds. Rumours abounded that the school principal had been a top class athlete and represented England in the pre-war Olympic Games. One school sports day, she appeared to confirm the rumour by wearing a well-cut blazer that clearly on its pocket displayed an impressive badge.

The pupils at the school took great pride in interschool competitions and Maureen on sporting occasions always did the school proud.

She continued however to be forthright in stating her opinion on other occasions and before the first week at the new school was over she had already earned a reputation for being outspoken. Firmly believing she had the right to speak and heard, when others disagreed, often a battle of wills would begin.

After the school assembly, given instructions to march towards the classroom, a desk would be allocated to each pupil. Maureen, Barbara and I were directed towards class One A. Several children from the Douglas Road School joined us; we also met children from different junior schools who were destined to become our new classmates. We made our way through the corridors and up a flight of old wide stone steps. The classrooms had big windows and around the lower walls ran large metal pipes. It looked rather shabby, unlike the hall we had just left, for the assembly hall was part of a newer addition to the building and housed an impressive gymnasium and large stage.

We sat down at the individual desks as instructed. All the children were asked to call out their name and if they had a sister attending the school. Then the teacher began reading out a list of rules. The first rule emphasized was that no fraternization was allowed on the premises with members of the adjoining boy's school, even if it was your brother. The boys playground was strictly an off limits area. The teacher continued reading some other rules. Having clearly conveyed the most important messages, she proceeded to explain that every child at the school became a house member and she named the four separate houses – the aim being to be part of a selected team. By representing your own team and winning points, you gained honours for your house.

The class teacher then announced, "The names of the four houses are, St Andrew, St David, St George, St Patrick."

We all were anxious to know which house we would be placed. The teacher produced a list and began to read out names. One by one, the girls received a paper bearing the name and colour. Write your name on the paper, we were instructed. The girls glanced at the colour written on the paper, given blue for Saint Andrew Patron Saint of Scotland. I wrote my name on the line. The girl next to me had the colour green Saint Patrick, Patron Saint of Ireland. One by one, obediently we wrote down our name. Then Maureen received her paper. It was yellow for Saint David, Patron Saint of Wales.

She reacted realising instantly. Loudly she announced, "I am not going to be a member of that house."

Everyone stopped writing and turned to listen.

The teacher looked at her in surprise; she had never before met Maureen, or knew of her forthright ways and how other teachers had become accustomed to dealing with her outbursts.

"What do you mean?" she asked.

Maureen pointed to the paper and waving her hand in Barbara's direction said, "I don't want to be in that team. I am not supporting anyone else but St George. He is an English Saint, I am not Welsh, cannot even speak Welsh. Give it her, she is called Jones, She has a Welsh name."

The teacher had never before encountered a pupil who challenged the decision of the house allocated to them – or, indeed, challenged anything else on the first day at a new school.

The children in the class who had never met Maureen before were astonished. Not so the ones who knew her from Douglas Road School, for they had often encountered her rebellion, and feared once more this was going to lead to trouble.

The teacher quietly beckoned Maureen to follow her. Maureen stood up; with a look of determination showing on her face, she followed the teacher out of the classroom. Before she left the room, the teacher instructed the rest of the class to write in our books all we knew about patron saints. It seemed most of us seemed to know very little.

We were still attempting to write when the door opened – and back into the room came the teacher, followed by Maureen. I noticed my friend was now wearing a small badge pinned to her jumper. On it was a picture of a daffodil. She stood at the front of the classroom as the teacher asked Maureen to explain to the class what the head mistress had said. To my astonishment, Maureen began to say she was proud to wear the flower, for Saint David was not just for people named Jones. Saint David was also for the Kings Welsh Guards and tough rugby players who admired him, so it must be a good house team. She added that the two princesses had Welsh dogs. As she sat down, I gasped in surprise, for her change of heart was so unexpected. Maureen climbing down was something unheard of. The head mistress was not only a champion athlete; she must be able to cast spells. When eventually I grew up and chanced to think back on my school days, I realized Maureen had been lucky to be educated at a school where the head teacher used a great deal of common sense. For she had recognized early on that someone with Maureen's personality could debate a subject and, given enough information, might not always oppose rules and regulations. But without being given a valid reason, she would simply dig her heels in and rebel.

Maureen would go on to become a loyal member of St David's House and won points galore, especially on sport days. Eventually she was the holder of a coveted title and cup. And how proud she was the day she became a champion! She was the unbeatable Radford Runner.

Chapter 23

The first term at secondary school went by quickly; life had settled into a regular routine. On any given school morning Maureen and Barbara now would meet near Boden Street baths and walk together down Denman Street as they made their way towards my home.

Barbara made efforts to hurry Maureen along; her pleas, however, were in vain – for despite her anxiety Maureen continued at a slow pace, stopping at every shop window along the way. Barbara, who never wanted to be part of Maureen's early morning plan, became more agitated as the clock ticked by. Eventually, arriving at my unpainted front door, Barbara, worried she would be late for school, would open the door and shout, "Bernice come on, are you ready?"

I had been ready for ages, but understood why there had been a delay in their arrival. Maureen had once again delayed getting here until the last possible minute, for she relished a challenge at the start of each day – and defeating the school bell and me was a stimulating experience she thoroughly enjoyed.

Each school morning she set out to prove she was the unbeatable Radford School champion runner, and as well as trying to arrive at the school before me she also wanted to enter the schoolyard just before the school bell ceased ringing. She increased the thrill of the race by allowing as little time as possible to cover the distance between my home and the schoolyard.

The ritual never varied and, although we had performed this feat so often, Maureen still considered me her worthy opponent.

Having competed against each other in both friendly and formally organized races, the recent results had consistently been a close finish: *Maureen Sylvia first; Bernice (a close) second.* All other competitors were left trailing far behind.

However, this daily race to school was an event she planned for just the two of us. Maureen, poised and ready, would be waiting for me as soon as I stepped out of my door: "Come on Bernice, we've only got five minutes before the school bell rings," Barbara shouted. Not being an athlete, she worried about her ability to arrive at school on time – but Maureen, who loved an audience, always managed to persuade Barbara to witness our daily races. I continued to accept the challenge, and lived in hope that one morning soon I would win.

Situated right next door to my home was the Harts bottling factory. On school mornings, workmen always seemed to be busy out on the street. I was accustomed to seeing these men, loading or heavy beer crates on to the wagons. Recently the workers had become interested spectators, and would turn to watch as Maureen shouted, "Beat you getting to school, Bernice." The workmen, hearing the taunt, would laugh, and gathering closer begin to clap and shout encouragement. This it seemed was the signal for the race to begin.

Maureen streaked away, and running like the wind was soon leading the way. I raced to catch her. In desperate pursuit I followed, hoping that this time I would run faster and win. Reaching the first corner and passing by the Peacock Inn, we headed on to Ilkeston Road. By now almost flying, we ignored the busy morning traffic and dangerously crossed the road.

Now we began dodging the queues of people anxiously waiting for the No. 39 trolley bus to arrive. We ran on and on, speeding past the cob shop; panting and puffing, I was just managing to keep up with my challenger. We arrived at the park gates and, with the final hurdle in sight, we approached the intersection and raced across the road. Now we could hear the school bell beginning to ring. As we both entered the schoolyard, heavily panting, Maureen led the way, wearing her ever-victorious smile. Triumphantly and loudly, she began to exclaim, "Beat you again." As usual, I was too breathless to reply.

The bell ceased to ring as Barbara scurried nervously across the schoolyard, scrambling to join her classmates who were already standing in line.

The school assembly was held as usual in the large school hall, where the head mistress gave her pep talks and awarded prizes and accolades to worthy pupils. Each week winning points were counted and great applause rippled through the hall as the results were announced. For winning points for your house was an honour. Saint David's House, due mainly to Maureen's sporting success, seemed to be forging ahead.

The head teacher began the day's meeting with an announcement: "The school choir has been accepted to take part in an interschool competition, more singers are required. Any interested pupils may now apply to join the choir."

Maureen leaned over nudged me and whispered, "Did you hear that?"

I glanced at her, puzzled she was showing such interest.

The pianist began to play and the children stood up to sing the final hymn, one of Maureen's favourites. With her shoulders held well back, proudly she began singing in a good strong voice, "I vow to thee my country all earthly things above." Several of the teachers' standing near by listened and watched Maureen with interest. Aware they could hear and see her, singing at her musical best, she proudly continued.

The assembly almost over, the headmistress addressed members of the choir, reminding them extra rehearsals would soon be necessary, especially if they hoped secure the winning trophy.

Maureen gave me another nudge.

"I want to join the choir."

I was surprised, for although I knew Maureen loved music, her wanting to join the goodie-two-shoes choir just shocked me. Members of the choir were often considered teacher's pets by the less disciplined members of the school. For being a member of the choir appeared to indicate that you never got into trouble. Always seen as obedient, neat and tidy, it was no surprise that they were so often the pupils at assembly who others applauded when the good conduct credits were awarded.

Maureen's decision now of wanting to join the group who achieved these lofty heights stunned me. Had the tide turned? Was this a reformed Maureen? Just what was she up to?

Her true motives would eventually emerge, I thought.

That weekend Maureen decided against our usual visit to the local recreation park. The weather being clear and crisp I asked, "Do you want to go down to Wollaton Park instead?"

She looked up in surprise.

"Are you allowed to walk around the pond now?" she asked.

"Yes," I replied, hastening to add, "But Dad told me to keep away from the barbed wire fence surrounding the old huts."

Maureen listened with interest.

"What – the huts near the Hall where the soldiers were billeted?"

I vigorously nodded, knowing Maureen would be impressed that I was supplying new information of events happening at the park.

Having decided that we'd go, we set off. Being young fit and brimming over with enthusiasm, we made it to the park in record

Wollaton Hall, Nottingham

time. It was nice to walk in the park again and I gazed in awe at the historical hall. There was the added interest of looking at the rows of army huts, for troops a few short years before had occupied these hastily erected buildings. Allied servicemen who seemed unlike any soldiers we had seen before – for they looked, dressed, talked and acted very different. Maureen and I sometimes discussed our first experiences of seeing these troops! Especially our surprise the first time we encountered a group of smartly dressed, friendly, white-toothed men, who greeted both of us with a smile. For until that moment, we had never encountered a black person. The only experience we had previously known was of an image viewed on a silver screen. The soldiers we met, having been in training, now were able to leave the camp, on recreational leave. At last able to enjoy all the attractions Nottingham had to offer, they visited the local public houses and became acquainted with the residents. They also taught the Nottingham girls to jive at the local dancehalls. The girls proved themselves good company as well as quick learners and the troops found visiting local dancehalls a popular past time. Maureen and I were far too young to be interested in entering dancehalls but nonetheless we were fascinated, watching the troops in action. To young ears, their accents sounded like characters depicted in the Hollywood films. Handsome heroes acting in make-believe stories had been shown on the big screen at local picture houses; now we were enthralled with the real thing – though never bold enough to actually approach the soldiers, as many local boys did to ask them the usual question ("Got any gum chum?"). These generous soldiers usually obliged and handed out handfuls of gum and candy to the eager children.

At that time, we were all too young to realize these men would soon go away in their thousands to fight, many never to return to Nottingham or to their loved ones who grieved for them in lands far across the sea. Maureen and I as we grew older began to understand more of their sacrifice, and the tragic reality that so many of these smiling young soldiers paid the ultimate price to secured the freedom of others. It was so brave – yet what a futile loss it must have seemed for their loved ones, who were left to mourn. We also realized that being young during the war years had an advantage. For our youth helped shield us from the harsh truth and anguish the adults endured.

The ancient hall at Wollaton Park came into sight and as expected, the camp huts there situated in the place Dad had explained. He accurately described row after row of temporary buildings. Surrounded as they were by tall wire fences, we did not venture too close. Instead we began climbing the hill, moving ever upwards as we approached the ancient impressive hall. From this vantage point, you could imagine the history of the past and begin to wonder what interesting stories the trees in the surrounding woods would relate if only they could only talk. We were some way up the slope before we turned to face the camp. It was a chilly but bright day; the large driveway of majestic trees standing in the distance made a wonderful backdrop. For children born and raised in the overcrowded backstreets it truly was an awesome sight. Stretched out below us was another view that made us gasp, and was unlike anything we had experienced before. For behind a barrier of wire that resembled a large cage, rows of huts stood, and wispy smoke could be seen rising from the oddly constructed chimneys.

Standing at a vantage point on the slope of the hill, we observed a group of men; they were standing and talking to each other. Others seemed to be exercising while one man appeared to be hanging garments on a line. Another seemed to be reading, and on a bench situated close to the wire fence a group of men sat together.

One young blonde man appeared to be looking in our direction; suddenly he stood up and stared. He was not an American soldier. None of the men were, and they looked very sombre. They did not smile at us with white gleaming teeth, and the wire fence that reminded me of a cage began to trouble me. The atmosphere was heavy and grey. I felt like an intruder, standing on the hilltop watching this scene. I suggest to Maureen perhaps we should move away.

Suddenly one of the men seated on the bench started to wave in our direction. Startled Maureen stared towards them; then several of the men began shouting and laughing. They were speaking together in a language we failed to understand. Maureen was stunned at first at this turn of events and for a brief moment remained silent; then loudly she exclaimed, "They are bloody prisoners, cheeky sods they are waving at us."

Then walking down the hill towards them until she was within hearing distance, she suddenly stopped; pulling back her shoulders she stood tall as loudly she began to sing, "Land of hope and glory, Mother of the free…"

The men looked and listened, then these sombre clad prisoners, far from their own homes, who barely could understand the English language or the significance of Maureen's song, came closer towards the wire smiled at us and politely began to applaud.

Chapter 24

The weather had been severe; the roofs of the old terrace houses were now heavily covered in snow and ice. Mavis and I huddled close to the old kitchen range; the kettle had been on the hob all day, kept constantly boiling. I was waiting and hoping my sister would mash a cuppa! Mavis was very fond of tea and would often make both of us a drink – and if I was lucky, and rations permitted, she would make a toasted cheese sandwich.

I heard the front door open, followed by footsteps, for no one felt it necessary to knock: they just walked in through a door that rarely needed locking. My father was an easygoing man who imposed few rules, and No. 16 Bloomsgrove Street was a place of refuge for my friends. Friends in need of company could call without worry of being hassled or rejected; they simply entered the house and were welcome. Invited into the untidy warm kitchen everyone there shuffled up to make room for the visitor to join us around the fire. Pearl, who lived next door, was a regular caller. Just three calendar years older than me, in terms of lessons learnt the hard way she was years older, having had to develop survival skills from a young age. For she had problems and burdens that many grown ups would have found difficult to cope with. Sometimes they overwhelmed her, as the difficulties she experienced deprived her of enjoying an innocent carefree youth. Pearl was the oldest girl in the family; she had a younger sister Donalda, known to everyone by her nickname Bubbles. She also had two older brothers, Raymond and Terence. Pearl's mother and father had for several years led estranged lives, and Pearl shouldered responsibilities that no child should have to endure.

Living with Pearl's family was her maternal grandfather, an old sick man who suffered from severe Parkinson disease. As time progressed he gradually became worse and it became difficult for him to talk or walk. In the summer months he would sit for hours outside on an old wooden chair, watching the children play in the street. His chair placed on the pavement outside the front door of No. 18, he passed the time watching people walking by. Residents on Bloomsgrove Street knew him well, and were familiar with the sight of the old man constantly shaking. Visitors passing by did not always seem as tolerant and if strangers stared at her granddad, Pearl – a sentimental girl – became distressed. For in her troubled life, her maternal grandfather had attempted to protect and show her a little kindness.

Pearl was shivering as she entered the kitchen, dressed in a thin dress and old cardigan, her hair wet and bedraggled. She said, "Are your water pipes frozen?"

Mavis answered, "Don't think so."

Pearl sat down on the rail of the fireguard, and for a few minutes there was silence. Then Mavis spoke again. "Grandma had a pipe frozen upstairs last week."

I listened with interest. Mavis spent a lot of time across the street at Grandma's, and being older, heard far more news about grown up problems than I was made aware of.

Mavis continued, "Dad says if it gets any colder it will kill the wild birds."

Dad was still working daily on Nottingham Forest Park, and despite the cold weather people were still visiting the park. Dad had been busy at work recently, as there had been a flurry of accidents. Children arrived at the park with home made old sledges, and delighted in dragging them to the highest point of the hill. Launching off at rapid speed, attempting to steer a wobbling sled past the sturdy trunks of numerous trees was a recipe for disaster. Although these children were used to playing rough and tumble games, these tough little individuals were no match for a direct confrontation with a mighty tree. The injured children, nursing bruised and broken bones limbs, were taken to hospital where the staff had grown used to dealing with resilient street children. What made these children's visits different was not the courageous reaction of tough little locals to their own injuries, but the concern they expressed regarding damage inflicted on their precious homemade sledges.

Pearl's brother Terrance was one of the lads who enjoyed a bit of rough and tumble; her oldest brother Raymond was more interested now in adult entertainment. Having left school in his early teens, Raymond had adopted grown up ideas, and he now considered himself above childish games.

As Pearl sat in our kitchen, discussing frozen pipes and commenting on the long icicles hanging down from the house roof, she exclaimed, "We have icicles on the inside of our bedroom windows."

I listened as Mavis asked if Pearl was still sleeping in the upper front bedroom.

Pearl nodded, and said, "Yes and the windows are still broken."

I knew the big room well, for just a few short years ago I had spent nights sleeping at Pearl's home. I had been very young then, but I still remember the crush of four children sharing a bed and huddled up trying to keep warm. As I got older I pondered how odd it was I could clearly recall the nights spent at Pearl's house and yet had little recollection of my own mother.

Mavis put more coal on the fire. Now the bucket stood empty, so, without stopping to put on a coat, I opened the kitchen door. Outside it was bitterly cold as I crunched my way up the icy path; glancing up I noted the long icicles hanging from all the roofs. Holding the coal bucket in one hand and a small shovel in the other I opened the door of the coal store and, reaching inside, quickly scooped up a few small pieces of coal. Then, struggling to pick up a larger black shiny lump, I placed it in the bucket. Deciding to pay a visit to the lavatory, which was situated right next to the coal store, I opened the lavatory door. Stepping inside the small brick building I gingerly sat down; then with a gasp I immediately leapt up as icy cold water doused my head and shoulders. The lavatory's rickety roof had sprung a leak; a jar containing a lighted candle (purposely left inside the small building) had created enough warmth to melt the previously formed icicles. I realized then why Pearl's hair had looked damp and she was shivering as she entered the kitchen. She too must have visited the little brick building.

When Dad came home from work Pearl was still there, and Pearl politely spoke to him.

"Did you see Terence on the park?" she said.

"No not today. If he has any sense he will stay indoors in this weather," Dad replied.

Then, taking off his heavy coat, he sat down in his big wooden armchair. The tea in the big pot was still hot; he asked me to pass the mugs out and proceeded to pour out a cup for everyone; then, nodding to Pearl, he pushed a mug in her direction. She looked at him and gratefully sipped the warm saccharin sweetened tea. In the years to come, Pearl often reminded me of the kindness Dad had always shown to her and would simply say, "When I was little, I loved coming round to your house." Dad would have been happy to know that his simple act of welcoming a young troubled girl was later recalled with fond gratitude by an older woman.

Although, for all Dads gentle ways, he did have a couple of rules he preferred I keep. Normally I kept them, too – but on one memorable occasion a strict rule was broken. As usual, my friend Maureen was by my side when I did it.

Joining the school choir had given her the idea. For now I had joined Maureen as a member of the choir, we practiced singing in unison. As usual with Maureen, anything she undertook was competitive. Striving to prove she could sing longer and louder we practiced together. At first, I was puzzled why she seemed desperate to join the choir. Then I realised she had mistaken the venue of the forthcoming singing contest. Believing it was being held in Wales and desperate to visit there, she clambered to be accepted. And although soon after she realised the truth – that the venue was in fact close to Nottingham – she enjoyed singing in the choir too much by then, and decided to sing on.

The winter holidays had started and Maureen and I had been practicing singing Christmas carols. We had heard the Salvation Army singing in Market Square and witnessed them passing among the

114

crowd with a collection box. It prompted Maureen to say we should try our luck at carol singing. I readily agreed, keen to sing a few hymns and collect a few coins. We decided that the best place to try was where the rich folk lived – that is, on the Groves! We believed these folk had spare money and would be certain to attend church and enjoy supporting poor carol singers. Yes, the Groves were definitely the place to go. Being December and with shorter days upon us, it was already dark as we crossed over Ilkeston Road.

As carols were God's business, we decided it appropriate to knock on the resident's front door. Nudging each other, we began to sing, "Away in a manger". After a few minutes of singing and loudly banging on the door, we sang another chorus and banged on the door again. No reply. Puzzled, we stood for a while, then walked away and repeated the performance at the next door. This time after singing a few words, the sound of a bolt drawn back on a door was heard; it suddenly opened and a man's voice boomed out, "Good, good – where is your tin?" What tin?, we thought. Maureen stuck out her hand instead and he handed her two pennies. Then he shut the door before we could sing another verse or even say thank you.

Fired by enthusiasm we knocked at two more doors; one asked us to sing a hymn we had never heard of and then told us to come back when we know how. The next one who opened the door looked down at us and asked what street we lived on. I was afraid to answer, for in the shadows she looked a lot like Mrs Farquarson. I felt certain by the sternness of the woman's voice that Grandma would not approve, so I ran off, telling Maureen as I left I was not going to sing outside any more houses on the Grove. Maureen raised no objection, for as she pointed out we had only collected two pennies for our troubles.

As we walked across Ilkeston Road and made our way back to Bloomsgrove Street we passed the public house. Hearing a piano played, Maureen had an idea. Grabbing my hand, she shouted, "Come on."

I followed her as she ran up the street and she never stopped until we reached the door of the Dog and Pheasant Pub. To my surprise, Maureen pulled the large door open.

"Come on," she said, and then added, "My Dad always gives

money to the Salvation Army when they sing in the pub, we can sing here."

Before I could stop her she pulled me inside – and I found myself standing inside *forbidden territory*. For not only had my Dad warned me to keep away from public houses, he had also explained it was against the law for young people to be on these premises. Maureen just shrugged at my hesitance and reassured me.

"Don't be silly," she said. "No one takes notice of laws at Christmas."

I had no idea what happened inside a public house. It may have been unusual because it was the season of good cheer – or perhaps it was the over indulgence of bottled spirit – but the reception we received on entering the building seemed welcoming so we started to sing. The patrons of the pub, many of them neighbours who knew me, began shouting encouragement. They urged us to carry on singing and before long the audience began to join in, clapping with vigour and shouting suggestions for other Christmas songs. We were getting a tremendous reception when a man suddenly appeared from behind the back of the bar.

"Hey you two you're not allowed in here – out you go."

Maureen and I went towards the door. As we reached it a paying customer stood up and shouted, "Come on you lot, give the kids a copper it's nearly Christmas."

The landlord did not say a word, just watched as we stood in the doorway. We waited open mouthed in astonishment, noting the gathered crowd adding coin after coin to a pile of coppers they placed in the big sturdy ashtray. The final coin added to the pile was large and silver and placed there by the proprietor himself – who, as he gave it, said, "Don't come in here again. I will lose my bloody licence, even if it is Christmas."

We promised him we wouldn't as the man who organized the collection ripped up a large sheet of newspaper and, wrapping up the money, handed it to me. Then, bending down, getting so close to my face I could smell his fume-filled breath, he whispered, "Don't let your Dad know you have been in here. The landlord will be in trouble and knowing your Dad so will you."

Later Maureen and I counted the money in amazement, for we had never seen such a pile of coins before. Maureen and I made a pact never to tell anyone about going into the pub, especially to my Dad, and so we never did.

Chapter 25

The snow was thawing. Long spiked icicles that had dramatically hung down from every rooftop now started to melt. The heavily packed ice that had covered the roofs now reluctantly submitted to the increased rise in temperature.

All around were strange echoing sounds, as inevitably the progressive movement of thawing snow produced a chorus of moans and creaks. Long weeks had passed by since the snow had tumbled from the sky, totally disrupting daily life as it settled on rooftops and there quickly froze. Thick layers of dangerous, solid ice restricted people from walking. The roads and pavements were dangerously coated, as were ice-blocked windows; now at last it was melting. The strange noises intensified, groaning and crackling as the dripping mass made its final descent to earth.

I watched in fascination as in an undisciplined and destructive way slabs of ice slid forwards. Edging ever nearer to the edge of the high roof, eventually it lurched forwards – and loud thuds began resounded all around as the dislodged ice landed on the ground with a final defiant roar.

I stood watching the scene for ages, my nose pressed close to Grandmother's kitchen window. In the distance, I noticed water beginning to cascade from under the door of the outside lavatory. Clearly visible from my vantage point were a row of brick buildings that housed the lavatories. These were the primitive draughty outdoor facilities, standing near the bottom of the yard and used by the residents of Woodville Yard.

Grandmother's lavatory, securely locked and the key conveniently placed on a hook in the kitchen, had become frozen weeks ago.

I watched in amazement as water now cascaded out of the building. Woodville Yard began slowly disappearing, the cobbled yard transformed before my eyes into a small lake. I came away from the window, then, without putting on a coat, I opened the back door and ran outside.

Looking over the yard, I could see Rita standing at her bedroom window. In great excitement, I waved and called, "Rita, come on, get your wellies, water's everywhere out here."

Rita seemed always to be the first child on the street to acquire new clothing; recently she had been sporting shiny Wellington boots. The past weeks of harsh weather she had worn them often, wading through thick snow and ice.

Rita heard me shout and so did her mother, who shouted to me, "Get your coat on you silly sod – you will freeze to death."

I nodded in reply but ignored her instruction. For happily I noted Rita appearing at her back door; warmly wrapped, she quickly joined me outside.

We stood together on the last water-free patch of ground in the yard and watched in astonishment. Contaminated water continued to pour from under the doors of several of the small buildings. As folk had predicted the lavatory pipes had burst, for despite their efforts of placing lighted candles inside these small buildings, the protective tradition had been unable to prevent a calamity this time. For weeks of freezing bitter conditions had been too severe to prevent this havoc occurring. As the rapid thaw continued the disastrous result of lavatory pipes being blocked by ice for weeks were now being revealed.

Rita looked on in horror as human sewage, old soggy soiled newspaper and other items floated on the newly formed lake. I watched with interest; it took more than an unpleasant sight to make me feel queasy, for I was made of sterner stuff. Unfortunately, Rita had a delicate stomach and unpleasant sights and smells caused her to wretch. Local children, knowing of her weakness, would sometimes relate gory stories that swiftly made her run away. As to be expected, after Rita briefly surveyed the sight she began heaving, for she noticed an undesirable object floating on the newly formed lake. Turning pale, she hurriedly informed me she was going home.

Now left standing alone to witness the dramatic scene of what was happening in Woodville Yard, I decided to go indoors and talk to Grandma. For despite her strict rules and fussy ways she always found time to listen to me. Grandmother I thought would be interested to hear of the flooding, for long ago she had given me the responsibility of looking after her little outdoor building. At Woodville Yard every Saturday I had earned my pocket money by doing a task that now prepared me to handle the sights and smells of faulty overflowing drains.

For ever since I was old enough to carry a heavy pail, I had staggered down the pathway leading to the little outbuilding. Gripping the handle of a bucket of soapy water, I staggered on until I reached Grandmother's outside lavatory.

Woodville Place, Bloomsgrove Street

120

My first task was removing rubbish; then came the job of cleaning the lavatory. Using soapy water carried in an iron bucket I scrubbed the pan and seat, the task not complete until all the soapy water was sloshed onto the lavatory floor and swept away. The final touch was hanging cut squares of newspaper on a nail. Then, locking the lavatory door, my work was complete. I had earned my weekly pocket money.

Over the past few weeks it had been impossible to walk on the icy path and Grandma did not expect me to try. Instead different tasks had been selected. Granddad Charlie, who always paid my weekly shilling, never asked if I had performed my set task; he just reached into his pocket each week and handed me the money. Granddad was a generous man as local children discovered, for they often benefited from his generosity. For he had the habit of sharing out loose change from his pocket, something he performed often, especially when staggering unsteadily home from the pub.

When he arrived home in a merry state, Grandmother, a strict teetotaller, pursed her lips and sighed as she gave him a long sidelong look.

Granddad Charlie dismissed the look and being deaf due to injuries received in the First World War paid no attention to the sighs. Grandmother found his drinking bouts difficult, but had once suggested he drank to block out disturbing memories of a long ago war that still affected him. For it seemed as a young man he had witnessed many dreadful scenes that made him totally opposed to all wars.

He rarely discussed the subject with me; however, being a natural storyteller, he enjoyed relating other memories of the past. For Granddad had lived on Bloomsgrove Street since the year 1910 and had many amusing antidotes to recall and memories of old Radford. Well known in the area as a local printer, his services were in great demand after the Second World War. He printed a popular local football gaming ticket. The public house landlords did a roaring trade distributing and selling these tickets of chance, with money prizes awarded to the holders of winning tickets. Granddad was fortunate the tickets proved popular, for due to the regular orders given by local landlords he always had a valid reason to visit so many pubs.

He had seen many changes occur on Bloomsgrove Street, especially at Woodville Place – a spot holding memories for older Radford folk. For years ago the terrace houses that stood there had been back-to-back dwellings; these houses had been where hardworking women had laboured to produce Nottingham's finest lace. They were poorly paid workers, who made the lace merchants grow rich. These woman and their families lived and worked in unsanitary buildings. The workrooms were situated on the upper floors of the dwellings, with rickety staircases placed on the outer wall that allowed access for wagons to be able to collect bales of the finest lacework made. This lace was destined to decorate the tables of gentry, fortunate people who occupied the finest homes in the land. As time passed, large factories began to appear and smaller home-workers' accommodation and workshops were demolished. The remaining houses were converted and were to become homes for the local factory workers or coalminers. The front room of Grandmother's home had been converted into a shop, and in her younger days, she ran a small general business there.

I was amazed when I first discovered Little Mabel had been born in one of the now demolished back-to-back houses at Woodville Place. She had no recollection of living there, but spoke of her own mother's memories of the old place. It thrilled me having this common bond with her, as Bloomsgrove Street was my birthplace also. How strange fate seems to be, meeting Little Mabel – a true Born Bloomo Girl and now a loving Mother Hen, who always seemed willing to cluck around any poor little chick who needed her. And how fortunate that this particular chick – who was so keen to be mothered – benefited from her attention.

Chapter 26

Woodville Place continued to provide vivid memories for so many people. For with the outbreak of the Second World War a large underground communal air raid shelter had been developed there. An entrance door led down a flight of steps into a large underground building. It had been in use as a shelter until late 1945. Converted later on, it became a useful storage area for a busy local factory.

People who had taken refuge there during the war had memories of the nights spent deep underground and always referred to the building, as "The Woodville air raid shelter". In common with so many local children, I had my own private memories of being in the large underground shelter during air raids, taken there when warning sirens alerted the locals.

During the middle 1940s my sister and I would pull on our siren suits and hurriedly leave our beds, heading for the communal shelter. The first task was making our way down a steep flight of steps. Once inside the shelter it was always a scramble, for the dimly lit building was a warren of narrow corridors. We hurried towards the area that led to rooms furnished with rows of primitive canvass covered bunk beds.

Some adventurous youngsters from Bloomgrove Street would try to get as far away from adult supervision as possible. For going into the underground shelter seemed a great opportunity to explore this strange underground world. Deep inside the shelter, however, you soon became aware of strange noises; although, being young, we were unaware that these noises indicated that danger was lurking outside the thick walls. We treated the whole experience as great fun at first. Huddled together in the gloom, young friends entertained themselves playing guessing games; then, as time passed by, we would climb up on to the upper bunks and, resting on the lumpy mattresses, begin telling spine-chilling stories of strange creatures who lurked and lived in the dark spooky corners of the shelter. The children with good imaginations were the most ingenious storytellers and would spin such eerie tales that in the gloom of the poorly lit setting, they almost came to believe the scary tales themselves. After a prolonged spell in the underground rooms – and by now to feeling uncomfortable on the primitive beds – they became overtired and cold. Listening to strange clip-clopping echoes created by the air raid warden's boots as he marched around the corridors, young imaginations ran wild, and became convinced that ghosts were lurking around every corner. A catalyst created by fear had every child hurrying down the corridors to locate the safe arms of their parents. The air raid warden, busy making his way around the labyrinth of corridors – on a mission to record the number of residents inside the shelter – would become confused at this sudden exodus of children. The grown ups, meanwhile, would put on a brave face as inwardly they prayed they would survive the night, and the diversion of children arriving to rejoin them was very welcome. Some parents did, however, wonder why the children with the most vivid imagination were now sitting so silent and still. For unknown to their parents, they were recollecting the scary story of the ghostly floating figure (who unexpectedly creeps up on you and, with one blast of cold clammy breath, imprisons you forever by sealing you in a solid block of ice). These tired young children were by now feeling the effects of being in a raw, cold, underground room. It became so easy to imagine that a ghostly figure had already begun its evil work. The horrid thought of being captured and sealed inside a solid ice block terrified them.

For young children were, it seems, able to dismiss the fear of Hitler's night-time bombing raids. Ghosts who lurked in the dark corners of underground shelters were a very different matter.

Bloomsgrove Street provided us with a second communal shelter during the war; this one was a plain and simple building placed half way down the street. Alongside the building large pipes were installed, running close to the kern way. The emergency buildings and pipes were a constant reminder to the locals that Great Britain was at war. The shelter was never as popular during the blitz as the Woodville underground refuge had been, but seemed to attract more interest later in the forties. For by then certain individuals began to realize what a useful spot it was to hide. For inside its solid windowless walls you could hide safely from prying eyes. For the poor light and dark shadows inside effectively concealed any occupants.

Maureen, alert and worldly, mentioned she had seen couples sneaking into the shelter. Curious and bold, it occurred to her that on this occasion perhaps it would be unwise personally to investigate these suspicious privacy seekers who were inside the shelter. For she had a notion there may be a possibility they were secret agents, who, hidden from view, might be exchanging secret information. We discussed the situation and contemplated the possibility of communication equipment being hidden inside the building and even secret messages being transmitted. The thought intrigued me; however, it did puzzle me that the suspected agents were young local girls I recognized, while their partners were usually unknown young men dressed in strange military uniforms. Eventually I decided to mention my concerns to Dad.

He listened carefully to my story, as I assured him Maureen and I had not divulged this information to anyone else. Then I explained in detail how we for some time had noted the unusual activity going on at the local shelter and suspected something suspicious was happening. I added that we thought they must be spies.

Dad smiled as he said, " I don't think you need to worry about any secret activity being exchanged in that shelter, for their activities would be of no interest to the government. Just in case though, it would be wiser you don't repeat what you have seen to anyone else, or tell other folk what you suspect is happening in that shelter."

Years later, by now enlightened, Maureen and I giggled wildly as we recalled our naïve suspicions. I laughed even louder as Maureen declared, "Bet the only secret ever revealed in that shelter was the easiest way to undo the hook of a girl's bra."

As the early post-war years passed by, life began to alter and the large pipes laid down the road disappeared. With great excitement the children watched them being removed. As the workmen struggled to dig up the heavy pipes, lost treasures began to be uncovered. Items accidentally dropped years before were at last revealed. Generous workmen sometimes tossed the minor coins retrieved to waiting children, who patiently stood watching. Around this time, we were also experiencing the joy of discovering the taste of bananas and juicy oranges and a variety of different sweets now on display in large jars, which temptingly sat on the shelves at the local shop. Rationing was still in place but things were gradually improving.

Chapter 27

As we became older, we became interested in youth clubs and group gatherings, and Saturday afternoon children's picture shows continued being a great attraction. It was around this time Mavis passed a selective exam to go to The Nottingham Technical Textile College. How odd to see my sister dress up like a toff in blazer tie and shiny shoes. We had never shared the same interests or hobbies, but we sometimes discussed our views on the teachers we liked or disliked. With Mavis now attending a formal college we seemed to have even less in common and slipped further apart. Mavis was becoming a serious-minded academic young lady and developing into everything Grandmother hoped she would be. I continued, however, causing her more anxiety and worry. Especially the antics I got up to when I was out with Maureen.

Grandmother was surprised and relieved when I informed her Maureen had decided to join a local church youth club. I decided to go along as well and Grandmother had no objections; in fact, she began to believe a miracle was underway and God in his wisdom was guiding Maureen down the right path. However, the journey Maureen chose started out to be an unusual choice for her and ended up becoming slightly bizarre for both of us.

Unwittingly Grandmother encouraged my involvement in these activities. She strongly would have disapproved of some unusual adventures we became involved in, as some exploits made me shudder and goodness knows what the Lady from the Grove would have thought.

It was a Sunday. I arranged to meet Maureen on Denman Street as she had asked to join me at classes held in the church hall. She had declined invitations before and showed little interest in undertaking religious study, but recently Maureen's curiosity on the mysteries of the afterlife had grown and she was keen to learn more about the subject. I introduced her to my friends at Sunday school but soon she became bored. It was shortly afterwards she asked me to accompany her on a different quest – and, like naïve pilgrims, we set off together to pursue and discover the truth!

It turned out to be one heck of a journey, for it enlightened and educated us both. During the search for answers, we met some interesting people; however, the journey of discovery was destined to end in an abrupt strange way.

My Grandmother, if aware of the bizarre things we were becoming involved in, would definitely have tried prevented me from going.

Maureen and I were to meet many jolly people who ushered us in with a smile. Among the first was a group we met at the local Salvation Army hall. Warmly welcomed in and seated near a group of other youngsters, soon we were joining in the noisy activities, singing with gusto and loudly banging on tambourines. We had been impressed to discover the founder of the Salvation Army was a man called General Booth – Maureen's paternal and my maternal ancestors had the same surname. This link with the past helped us at first to feel part of the Salvation Army movement and we boasted about it at school. At the beginning it seemed jolly going to evening meetings, and the Army Captain soon asked us to become involved further. At that time, the Salvation Army demonstrated their faith by holding public meetings at a prominent spot in the centre of town. Old Slab Square was a popular place for the Army to gather. I began to feel rather nervous when I realized that Grandmother might discover I had been absconded from my former Sunday school. Although she respected the charity work the Salvation Army provided, abandoning the lessons conducted by her chosen church certainly would not meet with her approval. So reluctantly, I decided banging a tambourine on Slab Square was not for me. Maureen did not appear downhearted at my decision, for she had decided to search for salvation at a different location. She had discovered that a local vicar was organising a youth club at a church hall close to Hyson Green. Maureen arranged to meet me at the hall.

The evening program was scheduled to begin with a short prayer meeting, followed by a missionary speaker. Afterwards free refreshments and light entertainment would commence.

Regardless of faith, indications were given that everyone was welcome.

Maureen was full of enthusiasm, for it seemed it was exactly what she was looking for. We enquired about becoming members and looked forward to being welcomed into the fold. Our names were recorded as soon as we arrived, then we were invited to take a seat at the front of the hall.

The room soon began to fill up. Maureen waved on as she recognized a number of people. The door closed and the prayer meeting began. After the opening prayer, the Vicar introduced the speaker. The man began by informing us he was on a mission. Smiling, he acknowledged the applause and began relating stories of how he travelled the world spreading the gospel. He captured our interest at first but after repeating the same tale several times with only the geographical locations changing, it all began to be rather boring. Maureen, anxious to sample the refreshments, grew restless and began to shuffle her feet on the floor. In doing so, her heels scraped repeatedly across the floor. The speaker sternly stared in Maureen's direction; other people stared at her and began to tut-tut. A pompous looking boy Maureen had earlier recognized turned to face her and gestured her to be quiet by putting his finger to his lips; he made a dramatic loud hushing sound. Everyone's attention was now directed on Maureen, who was furious. In a mock whisper, she stated abruptly, "Bloody stuck up choir boy, bet the vicar doesn't know he pinched a pencil sharpener from Woollies on the Green."

The man giving the talk heard the comment and for a moment hesitated, distracted at what he had heard; then, looking annoyed, he continued his long drawn out lecture. Eventually the man left the podium and the priest, to Maureen's relief, announced we could now partake in light refreshments.

Maureen and I made our way towards the table where pop water and homemade biscuits were available. We finally could start enjoying our evening out.

I was the first to notice the pompous choirboy was ahead of us in the queue. He was talking to a lady assistant; she was busy pouring cordial out of a large jug. As we edged closer to the table, the boy attempted to block our path. Maureen leaned towards him and, putting up her finger, waggled it close to his face; as she did so she uttered a loud hushing sound. He jumped away, startled, then loudly he began shouting to the lady serving the cordial.

"Look Mam that's the girl who tells lies and is trying to get me in trouble, I didn't do it," he concluded.

Maureen immediately replied, "Yes you did, every one knows you pinch from Woolworth's."

The boy went white and continued protested loudly to his Mother.

By now, the vicar noticing the delay in serving the refreshments came over to investigate. The boy's mother seeing the vicar approaching was blushing with anxiety, her voice rising in panic as she shouted at Maureen.

"You wicked, evil girl coming here telling lies."

Maureen did not hesitate and shouted back.

"I'm not the bloody liar, he is and he is a bloody thief."

At this point, the vicar standing close enough now to hear the confrontation, attempted to sort the trouble out. Addressing Maureen, he said, "Young lady that sort of language is not allowed, apologize at once for your remark or leave."

Maureen, now in full fettle and oblivious to the type of collar he was wearing, refused to back down or apologize. I stood by in silence, unable to confirm the accusation Maureen had made but knowing she was most unlikely to retract a single word. For Maureen in her own unorthodox way had a code of honour; if she made a statement believing it to be true she would not retract a single word, for her rule book stated that was not fair play. Adamant she was right, she would not be giving an apology – even if a vicar had asked. So the outcome became inevitable: both of us being evicted with little ceremony from the meeting.

As we stood outside the hall eating our biscuit we realized we had missed out the free cordial. Maureen was livid and stated, "That priest shouldn't expect an apology from me. I am right and God does not expect me to say sorry to a thief or his stuck up mother."

The unfair eviction did not upset Maureen for long. Head on, confrontation had become something she was very familiar dealing with.

Chapter 28

The last year had sped by, so much seemed to have happened. Maureen and I had been rushing about in a constant frenzy pursuing numerous activities. There was one activity we both enjoyed: singing as members of the school choir. We had an opportunity to perform at the Nottingham Albert Hall and it was a memorable and magnificent occasion. Enthusiastically we also joined many organized sporting activities. Maureen continued to hold the coveted Victor Ludorum trophy and her title "Winner of the Games" was an honour well-deserved, for she was a good all round athlete and a spectacular runner.

Maureen wanted to keep her title forever and remained keen to compete against anyone willing to challenge her running abilities.

On one occasion her brother Ronnie, a fit, able and determined young man, threw down the gauntlet and his younger sister eagerly accepted, for she had been waiting for the opportunity to race against him for ages. Full of confidence she could win, Maureen stepped forward.

The venue for the race was the Forest recreation park. Brimming with excitement Maureen was on top form; the signal to begin the race given, away they sped, each runner determined to pass that winning post first.

This brother and sister, who both inherited a strong desire to win, lined up. Olympic competitors could not have tried harder. Putting every ounce of effort into the race Ronnie ran like the wind, but his sister ran even faster. Maureen was triumphant, and satisfied that once again she had proved she was truly *Radford's Victum Ludurom*.

Ronnie, the family joker, laughingly threatened a rerun, but secretly felt proud of his sister's sporting victories and graciously accepted his defeat. For he reflected on her health problems and her past struggle to survive and felt reassured. For so many tense difficult moments had occurred in the past, with the family needing to make sacrifices in order to secure the extras needed to help Maureen's recovery. Her parents and brothers had already experienced the heartbreak of losing two sons and siblings and there remained the fear of losing Maureen. Each milestone she had reached was an amazing triumph and survival against such adversity a miracle. The Booth family and the doctors who previously had given her a poor prognosis were astonished at her progress.

Ronnie accepted, as I eventually did, that despite our best efforts we would never beat Maureen on a racetrack. Instead, wholeheartedly I threw myself in to other activities, hoping to succeed by doing other things. The journey down the road of life carried on and was becoming a real breeze. Everything we did together produced a laugh. Giggling was how we spent a large part of the day, but things were about to change and my adventures at Radford Boulevard Secondary School were unknowingly about to end.

For I discovered that big changes and plans unknown to me had been under discussion. Hidden agendas involving my education had been set in motion. The coming year revealed a manoeuvre destined to push me towards a crossroads in my life, prompted by Grandmother who was determined to map out my future. Her aim was to stop me aimlessly wandering through life and prevent more adventures with Maureen. For my unruly conduct was not part of Grandmother's plan of rearing a respectable little lady!

A recent outing with Maureen that had reached the attention of my Grandmother caused her great concern, and despite my continuing to attend local parish meetings, she felt I was in need of a firm hand and guidance.

Grandmother in the past had made an effort to assist my father rear his two young daughters. No easy task for an aging grandparent, especially one determined to transform a wild tomboy into someone that the Lady on The Grove would approve of. With that thought in mind, Grandmother would not admit defeat and ignored the fact.

The best laid plans of mice and men do not always…

She therefore carried on dreaming her dreams.

Her anxiety increased when I began straying further from home and getting into bolder ventures. One particular weekend she was informed that, dressed in my Sunday outfit, I had been seen near the local river, loitering in the company of unruly boys. It became more serious when Grandmother also discovered I had been dangling from the bridge that spanned the River Leen. For not only was the activity dangerous, it was illegal. Not a wise thing to do I was reminded, being the daughter of a special constable. My actions would cause him great distress, knowing I had flouted the law. To intensify the serious misdeed, the act had taken place when Grandmother believed I was attending Sunday school. A heinous crime in her opinion and she was very upset. I was sorry to have caused such bother but felt relief she had not discovered another secret – that for weeks I had been sneaking away in the evenings to go on outings with Maureen, visiting a destination that was strictly off limits. Maureen and I began going to a secret spot after hearing older children discuss a venue where groups of teenagers gathered each evening. It was a dark corner situated near Canning Circus and it intrigued us. Being curious, we decided to investigate and discover what happened there. When we first arrived the gang ignored us, judging us far too young to be involved, so we hung around on the edge of the crowd until their initial coolness faded and eventually we were tolerated. The reason they perhaps eventually allowed us to join the group was that they discovered Ronnie – a well-known young Radford fellow – was Maureen's brother, and the fact obviously impressed them.

The teenage group, ignoring cold weather, would sit on the pavement, talking, laughing and joking together. The hideaway situated close to a local factory was a popular place to meet at night because the area was deserted. It was located on a dark deserted backstreet and hidden from the prying eyes of adult's. Parent seeking wandering offspring had little chance of locating them there. No serious mischief happened, although teenage boys sometimes to impress would produce a woodbine and clumsily light it. Alternatively, the boys told wild scary tales to frighten silly teenage girls. When the girls responded by loudly screaming, pimpled youths would verbally battle to assume manly roles. Adults would have been baffled at the attraction that drew us on the coldest of nights to sit on dirty hard pavement, while half a mile away a youth club welcomed all young callers to enter warm comfortable premises. However, this group of children preferred sitting in the gloom, as they rejected grown up supervision.

The children had discovered the best stretch of pavement to sit on, for directly under one area of the pavement pipes carried a constant flow of hot liquid. This was discharge being released from a large factory. The constant flow of heated fluid, running through waste pipes under the pavement, acted like under-floor heating. The teenage gang aptly named the spot *"THE HOT PIPES"*.

For a long time it was an innocent danger-free area, until one evening an unpleasant happening there changed it into a place of fear and apprehension. The incident caused the bravest of children to stop gathering at such isolated dark areas; soon afterwards all meetings there ceased.

Local children vividly related the story when I returned from a school camp. I was shocked to hear of an unknown man who had visited the area. At first he engaged the children in simple conversation; they assumed him to be a parent attempting to locate his wayward child. However, this stranger began making regular visits and some of the children became uneasy. They tried ignoring him, hoping he would go away. He persisted hanging around until the older boys, offended now by his strange comments, began to drift away finding a new place to gather. Eventually just a handful of younger stragglers continued to meet at The Hot Pipes. The man still appeared; the few naïve youngsters who remained, unaware of his reputation, were surprised one evening when he grabbed hold of a child's arm and attempted to coax her away. Her companions, startled and then frightened, did not react or respond until she began screaming in terror. The abductor by now had travelled some distance away and was dragging the captured child into a deserted old building. Fortunately, the older teenage boys had gathered that evening on a street close by and hearing the screams ran in the directions of The Hot Pipes to investigate.

As they approached, realizing the situation, they began loudly shouting for help, attracting the attention of patrons from a local public house. The men inside responded immediately to their cries. Soon the sound of heavy footsteps and men's voices echoing around the street attracted attention. The villainous man, hearing the sound of commotion, bolted out of the deserted old building and ran away. The terrified child was located and carried out of the building, shaken by the ordeal but thankfully physically unharmed.

The story travelled quickly. I felt certain my father heard of the incident. Although he never mentioned it or issued warnings of the dangers involved in frequenting dark deserted places, he appeared rather relieved when Maureen and I, after hearing of the event, decided to join the adult supervised local youth club.

Chapter 29

I now began spending more evenings at the YWCA. The order and supervised activities there I found enjoyable. For ever since I spent time at Pipewood School Holiday Camp, I realized a disciplined, well-arranged routine could be fun. Although I missed my gentle father when I was away at camp, there youngsters had the opportunity of learning new skills and coping with everyday tasks. Staying there now made me aware I had missed so much growing up without a mother. There seemed comfort in having feminine supervision. At camp, each child was checked daily, ensuring they had all bathed and cleaned their teeth.

I was reaching the age of development, a special time when young girls needed reassurance and guidance. Something an on-the-spot mother would provide a growing daughter.

The order and routine I experienced being away from home felt an attractive way to live.

There was something comforting having routine and order in your life; everything around looked clean and tidy, and we were encouraged to respect our simple wooden billet huts. Set in the heart of the lovely countryside of Staffordshire, it was a peaceful place. Basic as the accommodation was, in many respects it was an improvement on the homes of some children.

Looking back on the experience, it assisted me to put down firm foundations. Something in far off days that was not an easy task of living in a one-parent family My sister and I were fortunate having a

Pipewood School Holiday Camp

kind sober father, although he worked long hours and often this led to both of us being unsupervised. At those times, I was tempted to stray.

Being away from home, I had a chance to push open the door and view a scene of a more organized world. Day-by-day from then I left my early childhood years behind. As I approached teenage years everything around me now was about to change.

Grandmother opened the door shouting, "Hurry up, its time you were going to school."

I pulled on my coat and started to walk towards Ilkeston road. A new term was about to start at Radford Boulevard School. I was unaware plans to push me towards a respectable career were being plotted. However unwilling I may be, Grandmother had selected a route not intended for Maureen to share. However, destiny rules. Maureen and I continued to walk together down a shaky pathway. The activities we pursued caused more anxiety as the long summer holidays began drawing to an close. Maureen and I made secret plans, unaware a completely new chapter in my life was about to begin. Grandmother's mission became more difficult as, day-by-day, she attempted to keep watch over my teenage encounters.

As I walked down Ilkeston road, I waved to Rita and Pat making their way up the Groves, heading towards Cottesmore School. Maureen, having become bored with the early morning races, arranged to meet me in the school playground.

She was already waiting when I arrived, and as I approached I noticed her talking to Margaret and Thelma, who had been practicing netball. Joined by Maria and her friend Mavis, they earnestly began discussing just whom their teacher had selected for the class netball team.

The school whistle blew, and I had no time to enquire if I was one of the elite to join the team.

As we made our way into school, I glanced across at the noticeboard that displayed the morning schedule. It was then I became aware that a teacher was beckoning me.

"Bernice, make your way to the head mistresses office, she wants to speak to you."

I was bewildered. I wondered if I was in trouble; I could not recall breaking any school rules recently. In fact, everything for a long time seemed to have been running smoothly.

I slowly left the schoolyard, aware everyone was staring at me – and I returned a few minute's later totally stunned, having been

Radford Boulevard Sports Gym 1949

informed that with a couple of other selected pupils, I had been nominated to sit a special entrance exam. The information came as a total surprise, I had no idea why I had been chosen. The other prospective candidates had known about it for weeks; I had only just discovered the news. It was many years later that this mystery was solved. For eventually I discovered that my determined Grandmother had played a major role in my being among the few chosen to sit that exam. She could be very determined and had insisted I sit the entrance exam, hoping that if I passed the exam and interview (as previously my sister had) I would gain a coveted place at the Nottingham Textile College. Then all the other problems will solve themselves – especially those concerning her wayward youngest granddaughter.

I was dismayed at the prospect, for I had no interest in pursuing a career in the textile industry and no ambition to attend the college; in fact the very idea of leaving my friends at Radford Boulevard filled me with horror. And hidden from me for as long as possible had been these secret plans for my future. They had only disclosed at the last possible moment! And it really was the last possible moment, for just a few short days passed by before I found myself with lots of other Nottinghamshire children sitting at a desk in an overcrowded large hall. Presented with a set of exam papers, I faced instructions to begin answering the questions set before me. I wasn't at all worried about filling the paper in, as I as I was not the slightest bit interested in gaining a pass. It also seemed highly unlikely to me I would be among the thirty bright pupils who secured a place at the textile college. My older studious sister had gained entrance three years before, but she was a keen student who never got into mischief. She settled into life at the old Shakespeare Street college with great enthusiasm and enjoyed all that college life had to offer.

After the exam was over, I discussed it with Maureen. We laughed together as I attempted to describe the exam papers handed out and the procedures performed before we were able to begin answering the numerous questions. She especially laughed as I describe silly drawings and odd questions about shapes dots and odd pictures we had been asked to sort out. The exam was unlike anything I had experienced before; strangely it was apparently a new method of measuring a pupil's abilities.

A few weeks later, to Grandmother satisfaction – and my own and I am sure my teachers amazement – I found I was among the selected pupils asked to attend a formal interview. More surprising was the news that followed the interview, when to my total amazement I received a letter congratulating me on gaining a place at the college.

Given little chance to protest, Grandmother hastily proceeded to deck me out in the required outfit. She was so pleased at seeing me at last looking the image she desired, dressed in a smart regulation blazer. Soon afterwards, continuing to complain sulkily at my fate, I discovered a brand new world I never experienced before.

Chapter 30

Finding myself transported into a world where people failed to appreciate my Radford slang or sense of humour, I began to wonder how I would cope in this strange environment. I missed the familiar routine of being in my old classroom and yearned to be back at Radford Boulevard School and there be able to listen to Mr Gallagher talk with enthusiasm of famous poets and his love of the English language. I recollected with delight the day I discovered I was among a handful of pupils selected to visit a local theatre to watch a dramatic performance of a Shakespeare play. Memories of that day revived as I walked by the Theatre Royal on my way towards the impressive front entrance of the technical college; it occurred to me the street I now travelled on had been named in honour of the famous Bard.

I continued making my way along Shakespeare Street until I reached the impressive wide steps at the front of the college. Climbing up the stone flight, I entered the building. The lessons had not yet commenced and the students as the technical college, having a break in lessons, gathered together at their meeting place downstairs. I joined them in the refectory.

At first it had seemed strange having freedom to wander around. I began following the pattern that had been set by the crowd, and before long began to feel one of them. Mixing with other students, especially young teenagers who displayed prominent badges on their blazers, I discovered my fellow classmates came from all areas of Nottinghamshire. Securing a place to study textiles, I realized they commenced the same time as me. In the refectory there was also the opportunity of meeting mature-age students attending various courses – and despite the difference in our age group, we all were encouraged by the tutors to be progressive thinkers.

To my own and other folks astonishment I appeared to settle quickly into the routine and soon was enjoying studying in the old building situated in the heart of Nottingham. Soon afterwards to my dismay changes were made and limited time was now spent in the impressive old building, as the younger students now moved to premises situated on Bath Street. This involved travelling further each day on over-crowded, smoke-filled trolley buses. So many things occupied my mind, as daily information and extra academic knowledge was discussed about subjects previously I knew little about. I was also received invitations to visit fellow classmates at their homes. There I became aware that others lived a more affluent and orderly life than I did. I recognized also how neglected and shabby my home on Bloomsgrove Street appeared to be. This insight prompted me to attempt changes, and with little skill but lots of enthusiasm I decided to start decorating the untidy terrace place I called home. It was no easy task. On reflection my impulsive to alter my surroundings perhaps was stimulated by the strong feelings of needing my puzzling questions answered. For continuing to wonder about my mother and the reason for her absence greatly contributed to having unsettled feelings of where I really belonged.

Dad seemed unaware of my deepening worries or my concerns about the mess and clutter we lived in. Being an easygoing character, when I approached him concerning decorating the house, he readily agreed to purchase paint and brushes. Mavis, who joined me in the plan of brightening up our home, also approached Dad with a request. She boldly suggested purchasing a leather suite, and once more Dad amiably agreed. Concerned that Grandmother might hear of our plans and veto any changes, with Mavis helping we removed from the house the soiled antique chaise-lounge and shabby velvet armchairs and gave them to the local children who were keen to add the items to their growing mountain of rubbish they had collected for a forthcoming bonfire.

Getting to work, Mavis and I mixed up a quantity of white distemper, then set about painting the front room, splashing the stuff everywhere. With a surplus of energy but little skill the task was soon finished. I decided then to paint my bedroom.

I began by removing from my bedroom wall a picture of my favourite horse and planned to replace it with a photograph of a Hollywood film star. When the task was complete, I could now study the object of my desire each day. Happily I gazed around, oblivious to the fact my recently painted walls had an abundance of streaky patches, or that I had failed to remove the large splashes of distemper I accidentally dropped on the cold grey stone floor. The room was far from perfect but I was satisfied, for now it smelt of fresh distemper. As I laid down the made peg rug I hurriedly had made, everything to me seemed a big improvement.

Other changes were happening, what with Grandmother reaching advanced years. Thankfully being tall for my age proved a useful asset, for I was now having to take on extra duties – and a task willingly shouldered was that of family washerwoman. In order to carry out this task efficiently, I needed to gain access to the local council washhouse. This meant encountering Bossy Boots, the official who worked there.

I had no problem convincing the officials that I was a young adult and my regular trips carrying piles of soiled clothes up Denman Street soon began. Heading towards the busy council washhouse I often met Pearl, also struggling with a heavy bundle of clothes. We chattered happily together as we staggered on our way. On arrival at the Boden Street building, we joined queues of older women waiting to pay the entry fee. I soon became an expert at picking a suitable washing stall – an important task, for with a lack of labour saving equipment all the dirty clothes needed to be hand-washed. An arduous task and sufficient knowledge was necessary to choose a well-maintained washtub, a skill well worth acquiring. By the age of 13 years, I could wash and iron as expertly as any well-trained housewife. This enabled me to arrive each day at the textile college looking reasonable clean and tidy. I never discussed my washhouse outings with my new friends and found myself becoming a *Jekyll and Hyde*

1951 Nottingham textile students outing.
Bernice first left, bottom row

character. For listening and observing laundry methods used by the older woman, I confidently found myself able to discuss in class the benefits to be gained of textile manufacturers solving problems of fading dyes or material shrinkage. The scientific discovery of the new synthetic materials intrigued me. My tutors, having no idea I was leading two very different lives, must have wondered why I asked so many questions on the laundering properties of these newly discovered fibres.

My friend Pearl also in time benefited by discovering easier ways of coping with a family wash, but was too busy to worry about how the scientific development of new materials had been achieved. For Pearl, having coped from an early age with a family wash and other grown up duties, simply performed these duties without complaining. Thinking of people's lifestyles, I realised now how they could vary. For mixing in a wider circle was proving an education. Probably this was what Grandmother planned and hoped would happen.

I agree it broadened my outlook and stimulated my mind, and yet my closest companions continued to be my Bloomo friends!

Grandmother still attempted to rein me in and curb any signs of rebellious activities, and within a few months she had a valid reason to do so. For with the departure of Donald and his family to live in Canada, new residents arrived to live in No. 17 and their presence caused great speculation on the Street. Eventually the new neighbours who settled on Bloomsgrove Street became a catalyst that due in part to our youthful indiscretion created a catastrophic chain reaction. Our behaviour enraged Grandmother, causing her to ban Maureen from visiting the street.

Chapter 31

It was almost three o'clock and Maureen had not arrived. I decided to walk towards Mitchell Street to meet her, for previously we had discussed plans to shop together at Hyson Green. Yesterday Maureen seemed keen on the idea, although shopping was not something we often did together. With no signs of her and time slipping by, I decided to walk towards Alfred Street in hope of meeting her along the way.

As I approached Maureen's home, I spotted Little Mabel walking along the street; she was carrying a large bag. Hurrying to acknowledge me, she eagerly began to explain that she had been to a jumble sale and had managed to purchase many bargains. In great excitement, she began pulling garments out of her large bag and thrusting them towards me, urging me to inspect them. With words tumbling out of her mouth, she began painting a vivid picture of her morning activity. Little Mabel, when necessary, could be very descriptive with words, especially when she became agitated.

"Look at this bargain," she said, and then before I could reply she continued to explain that she had arrived early at the jumble sale and was the first to join the queue. After patiently waiting, she was upset when an arrogant latecomer rudely pushed her way to the front. As the doors opened, the waiting crowd surged forwards to enter the church hall and the cheeky queue jumper gained entrance before Little Mabel.

Furiously watching as the woman marched towards a stacked table, Little Mabel ran and reached the table first. Grabbing hold of a bargain, she began examining the coat. It was then that the queue-jumper who towered over Little Mabel had reached over, trying to wrestle the coat from her hand. A battle royal commenced. Little Mabel fiercely held on to the coat and despite being half the size of her opponent she managed to cling on. For Little Mabel, if fighting a just cause, was a fierce opponent, and the situation called for drastic action.

Continuing breathlessly to explain how her opponent had lost the first round, Little Mabel told me how she outwitted the queue jumper again. Having raced to reach the entire number of well-stacked tables, and securing many more bargains. Finally, her treasured buys placed firmly in her bag, Little Mabel sought to attract the gatecrasher's attention. In great triumphant, she had mockingly pointed towards her bulging bag.

Having related her victory, she proceeded to grab my arm. Her eyes glinting behind the thick lenses she wore, she thrust the bulging bag towards me.

"Look at the bargains I managed to get," she urged and thrust the bag forward for me to inspect the spoils. As I did, she concluded her tale. "That will teach the snooty bugger a lesson, trying to jump the queue."

I smiled, picturing the described battle – for taking on little Mabel I imagined would have been an awesome experience.

As we entered the communal yard I noticed Ronnie standing with two of his friends. He grinned at his Mother, and in a teasing manner pointed to the bag she was carrying.

"See you have bought our Maureen a new coat from Griffins."

Little Mabel looked at him and replied, "Cheeky sod."

Then looking towards me, Ronnie said loudly, "Bet your Dad's got loads of money and buys you and Mavis fur coats from Griffins?"

I was still trying to think of a witty reply when Little Mabel advised me, "Take no notice of him, he always shows off when he is with his mates."

Then, opening the back door of the house, she ushered me in.

I was not upset. I had become used to Ronnie's remarks and manner and enjoyed his light-hearted banter. For like his sister they

1950 Maureen the cup holder

Maureen and Bernice 1953

both enjoyed light-heartedly teasing friends, and it was well meant.

Maureen's oldest brother Arthur I barely knew; he was more studious than Ron, and being the oldest surviving brother Maureen had explained that he took life seriously. He was a busy young man who was hardly ever at home. Maureen explained he was soon to commence national service, but for now was busy studying.

Inside the small house, young Kenny was sitting alone at the table, surrounded by pieces of paper he was scribbling on as he listened to the wireless. It became obvious a football match was underway, and that Kenny was scribbling down what the football commentator was saying.

There was no sign of Maureen.

"Where's our Maureen gone," his mother said.

Without looking up Kenny replied.

"She has gone with a crowd of lads to see the football match."

Little Mabel turned to me.

"Did she tell you she was going?"

"No," I replied and added, "she asked me to go shopping with her to Hyson Green. "

Little Mabel shook her fist in the air.

"Wait till she gets back, I gave her the money to buy a tin of spam for tea, she was supposed to call at Marsdens and buy it. I bet she has spent the money."

I did not answer, for I never could guess what Maureen was capable of doing – and, it seemed, neither could her Mother. Maureen made her own rules, unaware her actions might be unacceptable to others. On impulse, she grabbed any opportunity that presented itself and forged ahead regardless of the consequences.

I had been waiting in Little Mabel's kitchen for ages and had been about to return home when the back door suddenly opened. Standing in the doorway was a tall heavily built man; he wore a cloth cap and dark jacket. He stared at me directly, then without speaking leaned towards me and smiled and stretched out his large workers hand. Then, to my astonishment, he began uttering a most peculiar sound that resembled a frog croaking.

I stared at this stranger, puzzled at his unusual behaviour; however,

I was the only person who seemed surprised. For young Kenny, after glancing at the figure in the doorway, loudly began laughing. Then he startled me by making the same peculiar croaking sound. His mother seemed perfectly at ease and smiled as Kenny returned to writing down the football results.

Little Mabel, her attention now focused on the man, spoke to him. "Our Maureen's gone out to a football match. Bet she has spent the money I gave her. She was supposed to go to Marsdens to buy some snap."

Maureen's Dad made no effort to reply. Then, waving in my direction, she continued, "This poor sod is her pal Bernice; she has been waiting here for ages. They were supposed to go shopping down the Green together."

Hearing this lament, I expected the head of the household to feel dismayed. However, Maureen's Dad, *Bobo*, gave a response that further stunned me, although his wife and son seemed at ease with his reply. For he began now uttering unusual alien sounds. I was becoming increasingly bewildered, as Mr Booth pointed his index finger first at Kenny then at Little Mabel and finally at me and in a loud voice boomed out, "Juped, Juped, Juped."

Kenny, having sprung from his chair, began jumping up and down on the spot. Pointing his index finger towards his mother, he chorused, "Juped, Juped, Juped."

Then both he and his Father began jeering and laughing. Little Mabel remained unaffected, not a bit puzzled. Unlike me who was completely flabbergasted.

Eventually down the track of time, I grew to understand this strange ritual was a family tradition. It was a sign of family bonding, and as the years passed I witnessed their tribal gesture on many occasions. I would often hear the cry of "Juped, Juped, Juped." It was a verbal expression I happily accepted, along with some strange dexterous gestures.

Around this period I had discovered my maternal ancestors bore the same surname as Maureen's family; it seemed they had also lived in the same area of Nottingham where my Mother originated.

I began to wonder if possibly there was a connection. For having little information about my maternal family background, surrounded by Maureen's family I reflected on their close family bonds and how comfortable I felt in their company.

It had been a shock to discover there might be maternal relatives living a few streets away. With no photographs of my mother, I could not imagine what she looked like. It had taken ages to find any clues; incredibly due now to hearing news of Maureen's family history, the mystery surrounding my mother would be revealed. For I had listened to gossips in the past discussing the possible reasons why my mother left home. I understandably was anxious for more information. Especially as the gossips indicated that she was a selfish cuckoo who flew away from her nest and abandoned her youngest chick, leaving us behind for kind but unrelated carers to rear.

Maureen's dad Bobo by a strange coincidence worked at the Royal Armaments gun factory; he met my Mother there, as she also worked there. This information intrigued me, at last here was someone could describe what she looked like. I was anxious now to ask questions and hear firsthand information about her.

Bobo hesitated to discuss the subject. Perhaps this was because I was young; but as time passed, he informed me that she had worked in the office canteen. I ask him to describe her. He stated she was small in stature but had a fierce reputation that put the fear of the Lord in the tallest of men. He ended the conversation by saying, "Your dad is probably better off living on his own."

I didn't reply. For having no memories of my mother, as a child I had only dreamt how it could have been if my mother and father chanced to meet again. As I became older and a little wiser, I realized it was a most unlikely scene. For unlike the romantic images viewed at the local picture house, the reality was that a loving meeting between my parents was never destined to occur. So just as discarded sweet wrappers are thrown away at the end of a film session, I began to toss aside my dreams – for they were only fantasies created by a disturbed and troubled child.

Chapter 32

Over the years, many post-war changes happened on the street; we watched the large water pipes, which had been put down at the start of the war, finally dug up and removed. A public air raid shelter that stood in the middle of the street was also removed, and with these wartime necessities gone it became obvious the long war really was over. Other changes crept in, altering life in dramatic ways. New ideas were prompting people to move forward and enter a different type of world.

The inquisitive were taking the chance to explore new opportunities. By viewing other lifestyles, their expectations were changing. New hobbies sprang up and different ways of passing time emerged. Experiencing other lifestyles somehow became easier and the timid slowly gained confidence, while the brave ones jumped in and forged ahead. The most adventurous among us cast off the invisible chains that had previously held them back, eagerly seeking fresh ideas and soaking up academic knowledge. Some pulled up their roots and departed to live in far away places, no longer content to remain in a life of hard tedious grind that their parents had accepted. Watching the changes was both incredibly exciting and sometimes tinged with sadness – for as the exodus continued the old lifestyle we knew was slipping away.

I also was changing. Discarding my childhood pursuits, I threw away my collection of racehorse drawings and in its place gathered a mountain of newspaper cuttings of my idol: Mario Lanza.

This hero besotted me! His voice, his looks and charm captivated me, I thought of no one else. Maureen alternated between collecting cuttings of stage artists and became unable to decide who her favourite was. However, her main loyalty and enthusiasm was Nottingham Forest Football Team. Everything about the team had captured her heart she was a dedicated supporter.

I accompanied Maureen a couple of times to watch the local team play, dutifully standing in the cold biting wind, but I never understand the rules of the game or Maureen's fanatical dedication. Eventually one freezing cold day, to Maureen's surprise I declined accompanying her to the football match. For now, I realized, once the warmer weather arrived, playing tennis would be far more appealing. I was an amateur player and did not even own a racquet. Eventually Dad acquired one; it was secondhand and I asked my sister if she knew where it came from. She refused to answer, so I then asked Granddad the same question. He laughed and replied, "Well seems it's a toffs game, they enjoy playing tennis. Even the blokes get rigged out in white knickers, so I wouldn't be surprised if your Grandma got it from Mrs Farquarson."

I smiled at the fact I was now playing a game that would meet with Mrs Farquarson's approval.

Maureen and I still enjoyed seeing the latest movies at the local picture house. One place we visited often was The Savoy on Derby Road; it was there we watched our film idol Mario Lanza. Sitting in anticipation on the front row, we waited for the curtain to rise. From the first moment Mario appeared on the screen, we were besotted. As he sang to his leading lady we imagined he was singing to us. With great enthusiasm, we tracked down any announcements of his forthcoming films, then rushed to be first in the queue where other dedicated fans impatiently also waited. Sometimes fans jostled each other to secure a seat but we usually managed to be on the front row. I spent ages collecting cuttings of Mario from the paper and at home sat in raptures whenever they played his songs on the wireless. On one memorable occasion, when Maureen and I were sat on the front row watching the film The Great Caruso, when Mario appeared on the screen we sighed so loudly and burst into such exclamations of joy that the usherette threatened to evict us. That evening as we

Bernice and Cousin Pat 1952

waked home, we deliberately choose the longest route, for we wanted the magical evening to last forever. Singing snatches of the songs we had heard and discussing scenes from the film, slowly we made our way up Ilkeston road.

"Oh what a magical night," we proclaimed in joy.

Mavis, observing us arriving home in this enraptured mood, shook her head, muttering "You two are so immature."

She had no time to hear my explanation. However, what with my being so elated, her scathing opinion did not bother me. For Mavis I realised had her own hero – although unlike mine, he was not seen on the screen of the local picture house. For Mavis was involved in a secret romance. Her boyfriend, an unknown to me, was someone she refused to discuss or mention. Mavis had no intention of discussing the subject with her young immature sister.

As a sophisticated research assistant employed by a prominent Nottingham textile laboratory, Mavis was taking further studies. Her mind focused on a higher level, she considered I was unable to comprehend anything of importance.

Regards my own studies, however, Dad and Grandmother had little to worry about, for I was enjoying life at college, and after hearing about the famous Nottingham-made Battle of Britain Lace to be displayed in a hall at the Shakespeare Street Building I felt proud. For the work of art demonstrated the skill and glory of Nottingham's famous lace industry. This fine work was a great achievement and although textiles was not a career I choose to pursue, I applauded the skill involved in its manufacture and design.

My mind however was set on doing something very different. Life was gliding along it seemed in a smooth and orderly fashion and Grandmother must have felt that at last she could relax, as there were no major problems to worry her.

Chapter 33

Perhaps life would have continued to run smoothly, if only Donald and Trevor still occupied No. 17 Bloomsgrove Street. However, the newcomers living there unwittingly became a major talking point among the other neighbours. Maureen and I had discussions on their comings and goings, for they were fascinating new occupants, who spoke in unusual accents and gathered outside to sing and play musical instruments. Their behaviour intrigued us and spellbound we watched as the men vigorously danced in the backyard of No. 17. The new owners provided board and lodgings to these men and Maureen and I were full of curiosity as to where these people could possibly be from.

Maureen commented that one of the younger men seemed rather handsome and our interest in the newcomers slowly grew. Being young naïve girls, soon we tossed common sense aside and tried to discover everything we could about these fascinating strangers.

We did not realise our actions were causing folk to talk. However, other Bloomsgrove Street events also began attracting the attention of local gossip-makers. It began as a mere whisper, then rapidly hit the Street headlines at the speed of light, for one young occupant of the Street was about to embark on a life-changing journey.

The young person who caused the stir was Pearl, who made an unexpected and dramatic decision. To everyone's astonishment, she announced, "I'm getting married on Saturday."

Her friends were shocked, having no idea she had a boyfriend. Pearl, not yet seventeen, was romantically involved with an unknown man. It prompted long discussions and wild guesses about the identity of her future husband.

Filled with curiosity, everyone began asking questions.

Who had swept her off her feet? Did anyone know him? What did he look like?

Pearl became the prime target for all local gossips and managed to keep everyone guessing. Eventually she disclosed his identity to someone she trusted, a person in the past who had listened to her problems without being judgmental. The person she spoke to was my father.

Explaining to him the courting couple had a dilemma, Pearl told him her boyfriend came from Italy; his name was Fulvio and they had met at the ice cream factory where they both worked. Although they had known each other for just a few short weeks, the young Italian man had captured Pearls heart. She described him as a reliable young man who had proposed marriage.

Having listened carefully my father asked, "Why are you in such a hurry to settle down? You are so young."

Pearl explained that Fulvio had entered England on a limited permit. He would have to return to Italy soon and it would be difficult for him to return here. They wanted to be together and getting married was the only solution.

They needed her parent's permission to wed and had other difficulties to solve. Realizing the situation but never having met Fulvio, my father was reluctant to give advice on such an important matter; instead he chose to simply extend his good wishes for their future happiness. To a casual observer, a proposed marriage between them appeared a huge gamble and the possibility of hardship and difficulties lay ahead. However, when my father extended his good wishes, he realised that although by calendar years Pearl might appear naïve and young, she had coped with difficult life experiences – for as a child she often performed the duties of an adult. Perhaps Lady Luck now had opened up a door of opportunity to a better life, and all would be well.

Within a few days of discussing the situation, the young lovers were man and wife and Pearl became the first of the Blossoms to be married.

The couples first years together were not so easy; they lived in a crowded downstairs room situated in Pearls modest childhood home. However, they managed to survive their first difficult hurdles. The unexpected marriage eventually ceased to be a topic of conversation, as other events captured people's attention.

Maureen and I would discuss the possibility of fate playing an important role in our lives and wondered if we would encounter such a magical experience. Who knew what was waiting around the corner for both of us? Having these deep discussions led to Maureen and I sharing the secrets of our family background. She already knew how curious I was to discover the truth of why my mother left home. I had found it impossible to knock down the wall of silence surrounding the subject. For it never seemed to be the right moment to broach the delicate subject with Dad. Maybe I was afraid to do so, scared that I would strike a verbal sledgehammer that would open a Pandora's Box.

Bernice, Rita and Maureen
Woodville Place 1954

Maureen revealed her own family mystery concerning her maternal grandparents. She was curious and hoping to unravel the truth of past events that concerned her elderly relations. I knew her grandparents, a friendly old couple who did not seem to have anything to hide. Their small Radford home was a place where, sitting behind unlocked doors happily, they welcomed folk in.

Maureen seemed determined that there was a hidden secret be revealed, and her keenness intrigued me. On visits to her grandparents, usually they would be sitting by the fire. On some occasions her grandmother was alone; it seemed her husband had wandered off to the local bookies to place a small bet. On a good day Grandfather returned as a winner, arriving home carrying a jug of beer and a bag of sweets. Generously he would hand a handful of boiled sweet to both Maureen and me. Then joining them by the fire, noisily we chomped away enjoying our barley sugar or humbugs.

Maureen was fond of her grandmother. Despite her being an old lady, deaf and almost blind, in spirit she remained young and strong. She had a wonderful personality despite her disabilities and retaining a sharp mind and cheerful youthful outlook.

A wonderful teasing atmosphere existed between her grandparents. I was amazed hearing them tease and laugh with each other. I was not accustomed to hearing light-hearted banter between elderly couples. Their closeness reflected how much they enjoyed each other's company. I realized as I matured what wonderful gift laughter brings to any relationship.

Maureen explained her grandmother was many years older than her grandfather was. At the beginning folk had judged them to be an ill-matched couple. For not only were they mismatched in age, but they had also been raised in very different circumstances. Many people had frowned upon their marriage – yet time proved the doubters wrong, for the bond between them was rock solid many decades later.

Maureen questioned her grandmother, Ruby Rebecca, for information.

"Why did you leave London and your family to live in Nottingham?"

Her grandmother looked at Maureen and remained silent.

Maureen in time discovered that Ruby Rebecca had settled in Nottingham around 1886, there she met and married John George, a young man with no riches to offer. History revealed he was from a harsh background, an illegitimate child born in a workhouse. The couple had very different backgrounds and religion, yet despite the obstacles they decided to marry. Their union would cause far-reaching and lasting waves of disapproval.

Maureen gradually discovered part of their intriguing story some years later when, able to investigate, she filled in some of the mysterious gaps from the past. It was by travelling to a London graveyard that Maureen eventually traced the resting place of her distant ancestors and there placed a traditional pebble on a grave. Visiting that spot, she felt her Grandmother would have approved her action. For the strong forthright personality Maureen possessed always reminded Ruby Rebecca of how she also displayed the same traits when young. For being determined, despite everything she followed her heart, although doing so had caused her to lose contact with her family roots.

Maureen, proud her diligent search had born fruit, eventually paid a visit to the Shakespeare Street Synagogue; there she was welcomed by the Jewish community. Her journey of discovery had come full circle, the lost piece of the family jigsaw slotted into place.

Other members of the Booth family were also fitting together their own jigsaws, for Maureen's oldest brother Arthur, his National Service pending, decided to marry his sweetheart Joan. They met at a local youth club; Joan was a gentle kind-hearted girl who also possessed a great sense of humour, an asset if you intended to join the Booth family. The wedding, to be conducted at St Stephens Church, would be a great family occasion; Maureen was delighted at the thought of being a bridesmaid. She was also worried the wedding date seemed likely to clash with a Saturday football match, but was determined however to attend both events. Thank goodness, it all went well and as planned. Maureen behaved with decorum and enjoyed her role as bridesmaid.

However, soon Maureen and I would discover that not all romantic interludes end so happily. For by stepping over parental boundaries, placed there to control our youthful enthusiasm, we ended up in a difficult situation.

Chapter 34

The summer holiday was drawing to a close; it had passed slowly since Grandmother banned Maureen from visiting Bloomsgrove Street and I had strict orders to stop bothering the new neighbours.

Not being certain Dad knew about the warning, I hesitated to bring the subject up and was left wondering if he agreed with Grandmother's harsh decision. I pondered on whether I should approach him as I walked across the street to Rita's house. When I knocked on the front door, Rita's Dad opened it; he glanced at me and turned away as he called out, "Rita your pals here, it's that Gledal gel."

He spoke my name as usual, pronouncing it in his own peculiar way. He was a small built elderly man, who could often be heard talking mildly to himself and muttering under his breath about the weather. Nobody in the house appeared to take his comments seriously, and he never expected anyone to reply.

Rita came to the door and beckoned me in; we sat together on the settee discussing the final plans for us to visit Lincoln. I became aware a small bed had been placed in the corner of the sitting room. I realized it had been placed there for Rita's mother, who was finding it difficult to climb the steep stairs to her bedroom. Poor health prevented her now from travelling, so she had arranged for Rita to travel to Lincoln on holiday with me. My father had agreed I could go, and Rita and I were all set to board a train to Lincoln without an adult. This would be a brand new experience for both of us.

We were to stay at the home of Rita's elderly distinguished Uncle Ernest. He lived in a cosy house situated near the stone bow, close by the historic cathedral. His unmarried daughter Joyce shared his home, a young woman who had little to say but made us both feel welcome. Her happy go lucky fiancé Doug owned a smallholding and appeared to enjoy the job of rearing pigs. Occasionally Rita and I visited him there and helped by feeding the young pigs. Grabbing an old iron bucket, we scooped up scraps of food and tipped them into the feeding troughs. Doug, a good-hearted man, praised our work and generously rewarded us by sharing his sweet ration.

Uncle Ernest's oldest daughter Dolly was married to a local butcher, who conducted his business from a thriving little shop in the centre of the town. Sadly, I could easily imagine that the little piglets we fed ended up being sold there.

Dolly, an outspoken jolly woman, was a buxom landlady. Her public house, situated in the heart of the market place, was a popular place.

Rita and I, being young, were never allowed on the licensed premises during opening hours. Instead as, adult members of Rita's family gathered in the bar, we spent time wandering around Lincoln market, where we entertained ourselves for hours until time passed and we could return and join the family gathering.

Due to the wide age gap between Rita and her cousins, she addressed her female cousins as "Aunty". Childless Aunty Dolly was a great favourite, for she spoiled her young cousin – as did Rita's married half brothers and sisters. Her mother smiled as she explained the big surprise her older children received when Rita was born.

Her Lincolnshire relations rallied round when they realized that Lottie needed to recuperate from her illness, and willingly agreed that Rita and I could spend our Lincolnshire holiday unaccompanied.

As we climbed aboard the large steam train and secured a window seat I sighed with relief, we were actually on our way.

With mounting excitement as the train puffed along, I watched the green fields coming into view. Arriving at Newark we both recognized the station and realized we would soon be reaching our destination. The train arrived at Lincoln on time and although I had travelled this journey before the magnificent cathedral still impressed me. I loved everything about this small town. All the stories and history fascinate me, for truly it is a magnificent place.

Each time I visited the area, I gazed in awe at the famous cathedral that dominated the Lincolnshire skyline and noted the intricate details carved on the ancient figures on the outer walls. Whenever Rita and I entered the building, we first made our way to view the little imp. Often as we stood admiring this famous little figure, we spotted visitors searching for him in vain. Then proudly we approached them and pointed out his location, relating to the bystanders the legend of the little mischievous imp who turned to stone. Small children present seemed enthralled by the story, as I had been when first I heard it. Another story repeated often was of the Lincoln landmark that played an important role during the grim times of the 1940s. A recent history story worth retelling – for it tells how Lincoln's unique outline helped visually to guide home its brave battle weary pilots, returning to their Lincolnshire base. For on sighting the famous landmark they must have rejoiced, knowing they were so close to their home base.

Leaving the cathedral, we would happily skip over the cobbled pathways, descending the steep hill until eventually we reached the bottom.

We encountered a few small shops on the way, but rarely stopped to buy anything until we reached the cake shop. Eagerly we opened up the door, entered the old shop and purchased two hot doughnuts. With the jam dripping down our fingers we munched happily as we journeyed on our way.

Reaching the spot in town where the water flows under an old bridge, we would linger awhile. Moving on, we then investigated the interesting side streets until eventually we made our way back, travelling up the steep hill with the energy of youth to arrive at the stone bow in time for the main meal of the day. We were grateful to eat whatever was on our plate and proud our parents trusted us to conduct ourselves correctly.

This was all very unlike the behaviour Maureen and I had recently displayed – which culminated in us both getting into trouble and

Maureen being banned from visiting "The Street".

It all started when Maureen decided to persuade Rita to let us into her backyard for a specific purpose. For sited there was a wall that separated the gardens between No. 15 and 17. Anyone sitting on that wall had a bird's eye view of the comings and goings of the interesting new neighbours.

We were not the only ones on the street curious about the strangers who frequently called at this house – but none were as persistently interested in the visitors who called at No. 17 as we were. We had become silly giggling teenagers, obsessed with the intriguing male lodgers, and we planned to be nearby when once more they came to visit Bloomsgrove Street.

When I realized that my house had a clear view of No. 17 from the front room, I told Maureen; before long we were experts at being net curtain twitching. One glimpse through the window at these young male strangers caused us to dissolve into uncontrollable giggles, and the interest only heightened when Maureen decided that one of the newcomers resembled her latest film star idol.

Watching these new neighbours became our favourite pastime and eventually our constant vigil attracted attention, as attempting to hide behind thin curtains was not very successful. Inevitably the young male lodgers noticed us and laughed, pointed in our direction and waved. Their response heightened our interest – and soon they were not the only ones to notice twitching curtains, for by now Grandmother became aware of our bizarre behaviour. Marching across the street, she confronted us and ordered us to move away from the window. Had we not been so blatant with our window watching, perhaps we could have continued observing from this safe vantage point and Grandmother have remained unaware of our foolish activity... For banned now from window watching, Maureen and I devised a far more dangerous plan and decided we would try to talk to these exciting strangers.

After Rita informed us that her mother had met and spoken to the new neighbours over the back wall, it all seemed so a simple. All we needed to do was gain access to Rita's backyard and there casually meet the strangers face to face. Being a frequent visitor to Rita's home, our entering her backyard did not arouse suspicion – and dainty Rita, as yet untroubled by surging hormones, had not shown the same interest in these young men; she'd even failed to notice that one of them resembled a film idol. The weather was pleasantly warm as we all sat together on the back wall. Maureen commented on the small garments hanging on next door's clothesline and Rita informed us that the young couple who owned the house had a young son. She added that the couple and their lodgers seemed friendly, but that understanding them was rather difficult as they spoke limited English. Maureen and I were captivated by the information; we yearned to know more, and wondered where these strangers came from.

Grandmother, unaware we were now visiting Rita's backyard, was reassured that any problems had been solved.

However, she only had to glance out of her kitchen window to have her allusion totally dispelled. For perched on the garden wall mere inches from the back door of No. 17 sat three giggling girls, two of them with ulterior motives.

A thin, tired looking young woman suddenly emerged from the house, looking startled to see someone sitting there. As we began swinging our legs, she looked up and shyly smiled. Hurrying to the clothesline, she began removing small garments. Quick as a flash, Maureen seized the opportunity and jumped down from the wall. She ran towards the line and proceeded to unpeel the small items from the line; as she did so Maureen gave the started mother a beaming smile and handed her the dry clothes. Seeing Maureen had attracted the woman's attention, Rita and I jumped down to place small garments into the woman's basket. The woman smiled politely and took the clothes indoors.

"Time you went home, Bernice."

It was Rita's mother. I looked up, feeling puzzled for I visited Rita's house frequently and often stayed late. Never before had I been told to go home.

Maureen arrived early the next day. As we sat on my front door step together, I became aware of Grandmother watching us from across the street. I felt uneasy, for I had never been so closely supervised before.

All my childhood I had wandered at will, visiting any of the neighbour's homes; no one had ever raised objections, and now every action was being monitored. Naively, I failed to understand why these restrictions were necessary. Some time later while sitting on the dividing wall at Rita's, Maureen and I – despite being closely supervised – seized the opportunity to talk to the young men. We soon realized that Rita had been correct about the communication difficulty. These men spoke little English; however, speaking a language fluently when handsome male lodgers are involved seemed no hardship, as other means of communication it seemed were possible. The group of men smiled and waved to us and we waved back. A couple of the older men seemed very friendly and moved closer. Eventually they were sitting on the wall beside us. They produced cake and sweets and smilingly offered them to us. One began admiring and stroking Maureen's auburn hair. Another produced a large comb and, leaning forward, attempted to comb my thick tangled curls. Mesmerized by

Maureen at Alford Street

their attention and charm, we made no effort to move away.

It was at this stage that Grandmother became aware we were sitting outside communicating with these strangers. She had watched in dismay as her youngest granddaughter simpered, giggled and obviously enjoyed male attention. Her reaction was swift and furious. She lost no time making her presence known. We were left shocked, as we had not been aware she had been watching us from her kitchen window.

Flinging open her back kitchen door, she stood on the outside steps and shouted, "Bernice come in at once and that pal of yours can go home right now, she has put you up to this behaviour."

Maureen looked surprised.

"What have I done?" she said.

Grandmother answered, "Get back home and don't come down this street again."

Maureen clenched her fists and flushed bright red; she was on the defensive. Ordered to go home when you do not feel the slightest bit guilty – as well as being embarrassed in front of these good-looking strangers – was not going to be acceptable to Maureen, and she was livid.

By now, I had already crept slowly up to Grandmother's door.

Realizing it would be a waste of time to offer any explanation, I went inside – and seeing Maureen approaching, Grandma angrily slammed the door closed. Maureen, without a moment's hesitation, marched up to the door and without knocking flung it open. Grandmother was startled.

"You're a spiteful old bugger," Maureen exclaimed and continued, "You can't stop me coming on the street; I don't care about your rules. Or that stuck up bloody church committee."

Grandmother did not answer. She just took her arm led her outside and locked the back door.

I stood silently waiting. What was Grandmother going to do now? She had forbidden me from looking out the window at the young men, now she had caught me talking to them!

To my surprise, she simply sat down and began to read her book; she did not speak or discuss the dispute. I waited, expecting some reaction; after a lengthy spell of silence I began to feel uneasy, so quietly I walked out of Grandmother's house, crossed over the street and headed home. I knew the house would be empty for Dad was working as usual on the Forest Park. He said he worked longer in the summer holiday as the long days bought out the worst in unruly villains. Now I began to wonder what he would say when he found out that Maureen and I had flouted Grandmother's orders. Feeling totally deflated and with just a few steps to tread, I soon entered the front door of my home. Going towards the untidy, lonely kitchen and with no one else at home, I had nothing to do but think over the results of what my actions had caused. Thank goodness, the summer holidays were almost over. Perhaps when Dad is not as busy at work, he would have time to sit and talk to me about this difficult problem and I could try explaining how it had happened.

Chapter 35

The nights were drawing in and the weather-getting cooler; carelessly I threw some small lumps of coal on the fire, then gathering up my study books I pushed them to one side and reached for my interesting Agatha Christie. Before I had chance to read a single sentence the door opened and into the kitchen came Rita. She perched herself down on the sturdy rim of the fireguard and began to chat.

"Have you seen Maureen since she was rude to your Grandma?" she said.

I quickly started to defend Maureen.

"She didn't intend to be rude," I said.

Rita simply gave me a strange look and failed to reply.

Deep down I realized swearing at Grandmother was over the top, for even Maureen must regret doing it. So sadly, I added, "Maureen is still not allowed to come down Bloomsgrove Street."

I carefully omitted the fact I had recently been in contact with Maureen and had met her just yesterday at place far away from the street.

I was only half listening as Rita began explaining how she had visited the foreign property owner at No. 17. I paid more attention when she began mentioning the babies. For a few weeks earlier when I heard news of the streets' latest arrivals I had felt peeved to discover I had missed the chance of meeting two brand new tiny infants. It seemed so unfair; I missed the chance of visiting the newborn baby twins and it was just because I sat on a wall and let someone comb my hair. I did not intend to defy Grandmother; she had ordered me to stop looking out of the window, but she never mentioned sitting on old walls.

Rita, unaware I was feeling upset, continued speaking.

"I went to see the twins yesterday, they are really small. They are going to be christened, their mam let me hold them and I helped push them in a big pram."

I listened with interest, though I felt cheated it was Rita and not me who first held these new arrivals. Being twins they seemed really special and I hadn't yet had chance to seen these tiny new residents because I was still barred from approaching their home.

Usually when a new baby in the area was born I would be first to knock on the door and ask to see the new arrival, for I loved being around small babies. I often paid visits to Pearl and Fulvio's young daughter Lucia who lived close by, and my interest in caring for her and other babies had prompted me to enquire about professionally caring for infants. I hoped soon to visit Nottingham General Hospital to enquire about becoming a children's nurse and was instructed to return and speak to them when I was older. Once my final year of textile studies was complete I intended to do so. I enjoyed being a student but unlike my sister I had no desire to pursue a career in the textile industry.

I chatted to Rita as I mashed a pot of tea and as we sipped the brew we discussed our weekend plans. Rita had promised to visit her honouree aunty who lived on the Aspley council estate. Aunty Ada was sister to Ivy the lodger; she always made Rita welcome when she paid a visit. The bond of warmth and friendship that existed during the war was still found among our close neighbours and other unrelated folk.

I was finding it difficult that Maureen was unable to drop in and keep me company. It was difficult sneaking off to talk to her and recently even on the local playground I had felt uneasy.

I hadn't yet found the right words or courage to talk to Dad about this problem and as no one at home was mentioning the window-watching event or garden walls, I couldn't gauge how Dad would react if he discovered I was still in regular contact with Maureen.

Hearing a strange noise I glanced towards the back door, then became aware of a movement at the kitchen window. Glancing up I saw a strange terrifying apparition: a distorted face was pressed close up to the glass pane, a pair of eyes was staring straight at me. It let out a blood-curdling scream. I felt the blood draining from my head, my knees sagged and I collapsed with fright in a heap on the kitchen floor. Rita, taken by surprise, was spared by my sudden reaction of actually seeing the horror at the window.

While I – still reeling with shock at seeing such a ghostly vision – looked up in horror as the back door slowly open, I heard a familiar sound: a peal of uncontrollable laughter. It was my friend Maureen, her face partly concealed by a dark hood. She stood in the doorway. She had decided to ignore the ban imposed on her and had sneaked over the back yard fence to pay me a secret visit. To add to the excitement she decided to distort her features by pressing her face to the window.

"You frightened me to death! What are you doing here? Did anyone see you come down the street?" I yelled out.

Maureen being Maureen just laughed but didn't answer my questions; instead she began giving me the reason for her making this urgent visit.

She was intending to join a new club situated close to Ilkeston road and before they filled the membership book, she wanted me to join as well. Bubbling with excitement at the prospect of my accompanying her, Maureen talked enthusiastically about all the new activities we would be able to enjoy. Rita listened but showed little interest in becoming involved in a girls club. I had not noticed how quickly the time had ticked by. Suddenly I realized the neglected fire needed stoking. Before I had chance to move I heard the sound of the front door opening; startled, I looked up as my Father walked into the kitchen.

"Fire's almost out, and its really cold out there," he said.

Then without stopping to remove his coat, he reached into the store cupboard, picked up a few sticks, and threw them on the dying fire, followed by a handful of coal. Grabbing the poker, he started prodding the dying embers.

I looked at Maureen anxiously as I wondered what to do or say. Father spoke again.

"Let's have the kettle on. I called in at Skillies chip shop and I've bought a big bag of chips."

I did not answer.

Then, as he looked at Maureen, he said, "Thought it was you I noticed racing down Bloomo – it seems a long time since you galloped down here. "

Maureen opened her mouth to reply, but before she had chance to speak Dad spoke to her again.

"I know you can always eat a few chips, better get the brown sauce out the cupboard and let's get the kettle on – its hungry work climbing over our back garden fence."

I placed four plates on the table, got Dad's big mug and three chipped cups out and put them on the newspaper-covered table. Dad mashed the tea. Later, the unexpected chip supper now eaten, we all sat and watched as Titus climbed up on to Dad's knee. As Dad stroked the old cat Titus happily purred. Then Dad began again to speak.

"It seems a silly sort of past time you girls sitting outside on cold walls, especially now the weather is getting frosty, you will all end up getting piles. Best for everybody if all three of you do your chatting in here where it's nice and warm; "

He winked and smiled as he continued, "At least, it is if you remember to stoke the fire!"

Maureen, Rita and I nodded in agreement. Dad was probably hoping that by the time the warmer weather returned all thoughts of window-watching or wall-sitting would have faded away. And Dad was right, for front room window-watching was soon replaced by hobbies.

Chapter 36

ow Maureen was visiting Bloomsgrove Street life seemed good again and we both decided to show everyone just how responsible we could be. So proudly we explained we had decided to join the local YWCA. Grandmother, deeming it a respectable place, gave it her full approval.

As we made our way down Ilkeston road we headed for the hall; there we met several classmates from my previous school who also had become members of the club. It was a good to see them and it became obvious that time had not stood still for any of us. For we had one by one begun to develop our own interests and style. Despite Mavis objecting I still insisted in wearing my favourite old navy jacket, but I had exchanged my gymslip for a pair of denim trousers and a flimsy scarf casually tied around my neck.

The girls who didn't worry about a sharp-eyed Grandmother continuing to supervise them were already experimenting using lipstick and combing their hair in unusual styles. I had attempted to change my own hairstyle but curly unruly hair had a mind of its own and quickly reverted back to the shape nature intended. As we entered the club that night Maureen excitedly pointed towards a notice placed on the information board. It read:

MIXED NIGHT.
MUSIC, DANCE AND DRAMA.
LIGHT REFRESHMENTS PROVIDED.
MEMBERS FREE.
GUESTS BY INVITATION TICKETS ONLY.

There was a buzz of excitement. For the club officially was for girls only. It was only on rare occasions that these mixed groups entertainments were permitted. We began discussing the coming event and immediately decided it sounded too good to miss.

Maureen suggested I invited my friends from the textile college. When I hesitated she appeared disappointed; this surprised me as it was the first time she had shown interest in them.

I had even hesitated telling her when months ago I was selected by my fellow students to be their elected captain, although I had considered it an honour.

Mavis on hearing my news had raised her eyebrows in surprise, then dryly commented, "Well you should be thanking Grandma for getting you that honour; it was due to her efforts you got chance to study there. If you had your own way, you would still be getting into trouble at your old school."

The statement made me feel uncomfortable; for I could not deny I had protested at leaving my old school. Now I realized that by doing so, it had lost me nothing. For it seemed I now had the best of two worlds: my valued old friends and my new classmates, who although they had seemed different at first I now appreciated. For mixing with a different group of people had enriched my life. My childhood friends continued to provide me with warm security and a comfortable glow. The new friends I studied with were both stimulating and loyal company. The groups were different in some ways and destined to remain apart, but life has a funny way of joining pieces together – and at the end of the day I suspect that this produces a better picture.

It was difficult for outsiders perhaps to understand how "Backstreet Dwellers" have bonds that hold them together – for although close ties in Radford did exist, it was something difficult to define. Often expressions and words used by the locals, outsiders found as difficult to understand as a foreign language. We also acted in ways that puzzled strangers, making us seem a higgle-de-piggley, rag-tag and bobtail set of people. Yet although having a childhood others might describe as deprived, we felt an unexplainable surge of pride as members of Radford's Survivors Club. We might have appeared to lack ambition and social skills, yet our hidden strength proved us

Trent Bridge outing 1953, Bernice and Mavis

masters of adversity. For Radford dwellers in the past have shown they can produce memorable sons and daughters. Who, despite being raised in an area devoid of recognized formal beauty, have left their mark on a wider world. From the starkness of their small, rundown terrace houses, where their ancestors toiled in dirty noisy factories, the descendants of these battlers have gone forth. Producing engineers, writers, poets and scientists. Their forebears helped make the factory-owners rich and their master's names were the ones displayed on goods recognized around the world. Yet the old local salt of the earth battlers who produced these goods, whose names were never spoken, were proud of the fruit of their labour, despite the meagre pittance they received. Other Radford dwellers risked their health by working underground; it was their efforts that provided the fuel to keep the factory engines turning. Time and a war slowly changed the situation and their sons and daughters were able to push away barriers, changing their world by using their newfound knowledge. They were still proud, however, to recall stories of how their parents had been born and lived worked and died in the overcrowded back streets.

Many memories are best appreciated by the Radford folk themselves. A mixed entertainment night at the local YWCA turned out to be one of those occasions. For at one particular gathering, flamboyant Maureen provided an evening to remember as she dominated the show.

Having decided to dress up for the evening's entertainment, Maureen made a real effort choosing her new outfit. Heading into town, we headed towards C&A Stores. There I selected a floral dress while Maureen chose a black flared skirt and white shimmering blouse adorned with a large red flower.

Wearing the outfit, Maureen became transformed an elegant fashionable young lady. As soon as we entered the club Maureen spotted a record player placed in the corner of the room. Making a beeline towards it, quickly she took control. Examining the records provided she stated they were unsuitable, loudly grumbling that they sounded like funeral songs. The person elected to organize the music was not in sight, so uninvited Maureen began to eagerly search through the pile of old records. Suddenly Maureen exclaimed with joy.

"I'm putting this one on at least you can sing to it."

Maureen had discovered a record that met her approval; this she demanded was played first, and she made her way to the centre of the room. There she waited for the music to begin; when it did, Maureen began her performance. Maureen had sung this song many times before and performed like an expert, having a captive audience thrilled her. I knew Maureen could hold the tune well. After hearing her rendition of "The Rose of Tralee" the audience politely clapped; flushed by her success and the round of applause she received, Maureen began to repeat the song once more. All would have been well if she had stopped then, but a fresh group of people arrived, among them a tall handsome young man who Maureen noticed and recognized. He waved to her. I was surprised for I did not recognize him. Maureen later informed me he was a football player. Maureen dashed across the room to talk to him. Already a crowd of admirers had gathered around him. One particular girl dressed in an unusual fur trimmed cardigan was possessively clinging to his arm. Maureen pushed her aside and grabbing him by the other arm stated, "I have just been singing, you missed it, I will get them to put the music on and sing it again."

By then a different piece of music was playing and some dancers were already on the dance floor attempting to jive to the tune. Maureen strode across the room, heading towards the record player; reaching over, abruptly she turned it off. The floor, occupied now by a bunch of lively energetic teenagers, loudly protested and insisted she turn their music back on. Among the confusion, the girl who seemed smitten by the handsome football player pointed to Maureen and loudly exclaimed, "Who does she think she is – Dianna Durban dressed up to visit the Ritz?"

Maureen, furious at being thwarted and annoyed that the girl appeared to be claiming the attention of the football player, turned around to face her opponent.

"Well at least they would let me in the Bloody Ritz," she said and added, "Dressed in that bloody fur cardigan you look more like King Kong climbing the walls of that American sky scraper."

Then Maureen began her vivid and well-practiced impression of a ferocious chest-banging ape, ending the act by making realistic grunting ape sounds. People at the club who knew her well laughed, clapped, whistled and applauded.

However, the strangers among us seemed shocked at her display and had no idea what to think of this eccentric character called Maureen. For despite her elegant black skirt, shimmering white blouse and demur look, in fact she was a fully loaded powder keg. On the one hand, she seemed to be growing up and changing into a woman; on the other, her strong personality and bewildering actions indicated that she remained as unpredictable as ever.

With her school days soon ending, Maureen would be stepping into the wider world. How would she cope with that experience? Would she alter her ways? There was no way of predicting the answer, but in time I was certain the answer would be revealed.

Chapter 37

hristmas was almost here and Grandmother had managed to get a few meagre branches of holly. I noticed the box containing a few old decorations was already out of the cupboard. Grandmother unpacked the fragile baubles.

Dad never bothered with decorating a tree for usually he worked at Christmas time and never seemed to have time to celebrate. Last year had been a particularly gloomy Christmas dinner, for I had spent most of the day alone. Mavis had been invited to celebrate with a new friend and had returned home bubbling with excitement and relating stories of the wonderful time she had spent and how impressed she had been with everything she had seen and done.

This, year however, Christmas was turning out to be a very different state of affairs, for Mavis surprised me by asking if I would accompany her to an evening function. An event organized by a group of people I had never met, it was to be a formal affair with her work colleagues. The function to be held at The George Hotel situated in the centre of town; it sounded rather grand. Mavis usually chose to spend her leisure time with her friends, who she indicated are far more mature than my pals. Mavis also stated that I was a troublesome younger sister who acted in a childish way. Therefore, after her comments I was surprised that she now wanted my company, and I worried about accepting the invitation. One dilemma was my lack of knowledge on what was suitable to wear on such an occasion. I pondered awhile before accepting the invitation, then agreed to go and decided to leave clothing arrangements to Mavis.

Dinner at the George Hotel, 1952.
Mavis and Bernice far right

The big event arrived and Mavis began urging me to hurry. I already had expressed doubts about even attending this particular outing and now I began threatening to stay away, but with the tickets already purchased, I decided I was being unfair.

Looking at the outfit I was expected to wear, I sighed. Feeling overdressed, I pulled on the ill-fitting evening gown and reluctantly joined my elegantly dressed, sophisticated sister. Who appeared to be oozing confidence.

The George Hotel was impressive. I had never been into such a large hotel before and had no idea of the protocol. So I was surprised when a cloakroom attendant offered to relieve me of my coat and hat. Closely watching Mavis, I did my best to imitate everything she did, nodding and smiling at folk as we walked into the lounge.

The waiter announced, "Dinner is being served in the inner room."

Mavis proceeded to enter the dining room and slowly I followed her. She seemed at ease as we took our places at the large table. Several people were already seated and talking happily to each other. Leaning forward, Mavis now paid close attention to one particular young man, listening intently to everything he had to say, as did

181

several others young ladies. The young man, a colleague of my sister, was obviously used to admiration and was enjoying the attention. Sitting smugly back in his seat, he reminded me of a Sheik surrounded by his Harem. As the evening passed, the young ladies – all intent on securing his attention – were competing with each other with flamboyant gestures and witty stories. Mavis left the table briefly to visit the cloakroom. During her brief absence, assuming I was to contribute towards the conversation, I began to speak. At first the group showed little interest in what I was saying, and looked rather bored at my chatter. I hesitated a moment before nervously talking again, this time I began relating an experience that happened to me the previous week. As I unfolded the story of a scary incident I recently had encountered, their bored expressions changed to one of shock. For it was of an event that happened one dark evening, when a sinister character decided to stalk Maureen and I. We realized someone was padding softly behind us. An odd looking character was getting closer and closer, eventually he was walking right along side us. Fearless Maureen, never one to avoid a confrontation, swung to face him and loudly asked what he wanted. His non-verbal response gave us a shock, for to our horror with one swift movement, he opened his coat, fully revealing his naked lower region. Maureen's reaction was sharp and rapid, as loudly she shouted, "Put it away you dirty sod. The cats got better tackle than you."

As I concluded my tale, everyone around the table fell silent. They were no longer looking bored by my after dinner conversation – instead they were obviously disgusted and haughtily they turned away, adjusting their chairs and pushing their long stemmed wine glasses nervously around the table. I heard someone asking where Mavis was and realized that unwittingly I had made a huge mistake. Sophisticated gatherings were obviously not the place for relating informative stories of a delicate nature, even if it was tale I would have no hesitation of laughing about with my friends. I sighed, realising that the art of small talk and polite social conversation were far more complicated than I had expected and something I yet had to learn. Then, feeling sheepish, I slumped back in my chair and for the rest of the evening remained silent.

Mavis returned to the table, unaware of the bombshell I had dropped. I decided not to tell her of my faux pas. I knew she would be embarrassed and angry at my outburst – unlike Maureen, who on hearing of the incident the following day laughed wildly as she said "Well at least those posh girls will know what to say, if ever they meet the creepy sod one night."

During the next few months Maureen and I avoided going to secluded areas in the evening. We also outgrew and avoided standing in a group on dirty pavements or huddling in local doorways. It now seemed more comfortable to visit her married brothers and enjoy the warm drinks and biscuits on offer. Her older brother Arthur and wife Joan lived near Sherwood Rise they had settled comfortably into married life.

Ronnie also lived close by; he was having health problems but battled on earning a living and supporting his family. Little Mabel constantly worried about Ronnie's diet, expressing the opinion that fatty food was aggravating his medical problems. Her criticism it seemed was justified, for Ronnie developed a stomach ulcer and the doctor told him to avoid fried food.

Maureen and I sometimes visited another home where the standard of cuisine was always good. For Jean, Maureen's friend, was a good cook. In the past, she had commenced nursing training, but gave it up in order to become a wife and mother. Now she was spending her time and skills rearing a family. She lived in an immaculately kept little home close to Denman Street, where everything was kept in apple pie order. This place Maureen stated was her favourite place to go.

Another favourite spot we used to visit often was the local picture house, although our past obsession of sitting on the front row screaming in delight at our favourite film stars had waned. It had become rather frustrating constantly told by the patrons and usherettes to "Keep quiet you two."

Eventually sitting in total silence admiring our favourite stars was no longer appealing. So instead we began visiting local church halls and clubs or just sitting and chatting together. On occasions we joined other teenagers at the local hop, where the organizers seemed surprised, for we were beginning to act more respectably. Perhaps this sign indicated that gradually we were approaching the gateway to unknown territory, and would soon be stepping into the world of grown ups? Our life journey hopefully would stay on track and head us straight towards the sign marked "maturity".

Chapter 38

Maureen had been busy over the last few months gathering information she hoped would make her future dreams come true. Her sights set high, she was keen to secure a job working in a high-class music shop; with this in mind she applied for an interview at Farmer's music shop. Maureen was eventually given a date to attend an interview. She appeared confident about the situation. Knowledgeable on so many aspects of music, I felt she could handle that part of the interview well. She was more than capable of answering complicated questions on so many subjects. However, lurking in my mind was a concern that Maureen would find it difficult accepting the golden rule that "a customer is always right!" Maureen would find that policy a bitter pill to swallow.

To everyone's delight, the interview went well and Maureen succeeded securing a job at Nottingham's leading music agents, Farmer's Music Store, the shop part of the impressive Pearson of Long Row Store.

I was pleased knowing it had all gone well, for Maureen had been keen to work at this particular shop. It was place recognized as being an establishment of excellence. Working there was going to be a big step up the ladder towards achieving her goal – that was, to be a leading authority on all branches of the music industry.

The shop attracted customers I always imaged were rich and influential – the type of folk who I believed occupied the houses found on the Grove. I had little personal knowledge of the store, although once I had entered the premises with Grandmother as my chaperone. Confidently she had walked through the front entrance, while I, being immature, had been awe struck at the grandeur of its façade. Grandmother's attitude also impressed me; she was undaunted by the fancy fittings and wide impressive staircase. It was obvious Pearson's of Long Row was no little corner shop. I had been reluctant to accompany her but had no choice, for I needed to collect an information booklet. For Grandmother, wanting to keep me fully occupied, had arranged for me to have piano lessons. Despite my protests, the first lesson was to commence soon and the piano teacher had given instructions that a music book was to be collected at the store. Reluctantly I trailed behind Grandmother, who marched in to the shop. The uneasiness that I felt reminded me of another occasion when I accompanied Grandmother into a large city bank. Inside that stone building all was strangely quiet, and I imagined people watching me enter as I whispered to Grandmother, "Everything feels odd and creepy in here."

Concentrating now on depositing her meagre savings, she ignored my whispers. She frowned and made no attempt to reply. I watched her approach the polished wooden counter. The ornate brass fittings that decorated the solid counters reminded me of the heavy wooden pews found at Grandmother's favourite church.

The courteous diligent staff at the bank spoke in soft low voices, and they handled each customer with great respect. Hearing them address my Grandmother as "Madam" sounded rather grand to an unsophisticated Bloomsgrove Street girl. Many years passed by before my childish awe of such buildings disappeared and I felt confident about entering premises where they employed forelocks-touching banking officials.

Maureen, about to present for her first interview, appeared confident. Knowledgeable on many aspects of the music industry, I felt she could handle the interview well. She was capable of answering the most complicated questions. However, lurking in my mind my concern grew that Maureen would fail to ever acknowledge her opinions on many subjects could be wrong.

To everyone's delight, however, the interview went well and Maureen was successfully offered employment. Shortly after having completed her final day at school, she found herself launched into the wide world of commerce. And shortly after this another Blossom of Bloomo – Little Rita – secured employment and decided to enter the world of retail trading. Despite being fifteen, she continued to look much younger but successfully secured a position at Clays of Denman Street, hired as a shop assistant. With her interest in feminine apparel, she was delighted to obtain employment at this popular local drapery store. She found every working day a seventh heaven, for she was situated in close proximity to the ladies' outfitting department. There, every working day Rita could admire the latest fashion.

I was to remain a pupil for some time longer, continuing to study textiles until eventually I too became a wage earner. I had no desire to pursue a permanent career in the textile industry, although I had been happy to stay and finalize my academic studies. For I was given chance to attend extra classes; these intended to help pupils acquire social skills, something I realized I sadly lacked.

It was during one particular lesson when a mixed group of teenagers had been practicing the art of ballroom dancing. Suddenly the session, held at a small church hall situated on St Ann's Well Road, was interrupted. The class of ungainly dancers and their teacher were surprised when the door of the church hall abruptly flew open and a breathless member of staff rushed in. Flustered, they explained that they had come to deliver an urgent message: "The lesson is to cease immediately, gather up your belongings and go home."

We all gasped in surprise and then, following the explanation for this puzzling message, we grew silent.

"KING GEORGE VI has died – a broadcast to the nation has just announced the news of his sudden death."

Everyone was stunned, for although the King appeared frail, news of his condition during the last few months had indicated his health was improving.

No one left the building; instead, groups of students stood together in the church hall and began talking in hushed tones. I began to wonder if the teacher would ask us to pray.

As a teenage student, who had spent most of my childhood years experiencing the turmoil and hardship that war created, discomfort and shortage had been the normal way of life. More recently, however, there had been improvements and life seemed more settled. Parents now felt optimistic and looked ahead to a brighter future. For the unhappy experience of disrupted family life, threats of death from bombs and receiving bad news telegrams were becoming memories. Suddenly doubt and uncertainty returned, as we realised our King was no longer with us. During the long years of war, our patriotic feelings for King and Country had strengthened and united us as a nation. Now, a strange lost empty feeling descended. We stood together in groups, hesitating and unwilling to disband, for we needed the support of each other.

Eventually, prompted to gather up our things, one by one slowly we made our way towards the exit. Many of the novice dancers on that historic day stored away deeply etched memories of the place they had been when they heard the sad news.

Outside the building there was an air of silence. Usually this busy area of Nottingham was bustling with busy shoppers, all noisily heading towards Victoria market. Now there were groups of sombre people walking silently along the street. Across at the local bus station forlorn people were queuing; looking sombre they waited, thinking about what had occurred.

I crossed the road and walked towards the No. 39 bus stop; a trolley bus eventually arrived. As I boarded the bus the conductor made no effort to collect the fares, instead standing on the bus platform he was talking quietly to the driver. It seemed the grown ups were also at a loss as to what they were supposed to do, for the unexpected announcement had caused people to feel uneasy. We were a nation noted for a reluctance to display emotion and during the hours that followed the sad announcement, it seemed the mass silence we displayed showed clearly the depth of feelings and sorrow.

Over the next few weeks folks recognized that a new chapter in the history of our country had begun. We embraced the fact we had entered a new Elizabethan age and people began talking about the plans underway to organize a grand coronation.

About this time, a wider world anxiously was poised, waiting to enter our homes. A stranger hovered, waiting to introduce us to new ideas and customs. As if by magic, when the visitor did arrive, in the guise of a black and white flickering television screen – willingly invited into our homes – it altered our lives; for, as we adapted to this new way of communication, old habits began to change. In the past working class folk had limited knowledge of other cultures. Now the masses began to dream of so many different things. With the popularity of television growing, daily we changed. People who previously had limited experience of the wider world and had spent time locally, socializing mainly with neighbours and close friends, now seemed happy to be entertained and educated by staying at home, huddling around their small television sets. Rapidly we were entering a different type of world.

My own lifestyle was also about to change. Starting my chosen career had been put on hold, for I had not reached the required entrance age. I approached my final years of textile studies, with my ambition to study nursing at Nottingham General Hospital having to remain on the back burner. It having now become necessary for me to seek temporary employment, arrangements to be interviewed for a position as a junior clerk at a local textile warehouse on Hounds Gate were finalized.

Copestake and Crampton Textile Warehouse was situated just a stone's throw from where Maureen was employed and seemed ideally placed, as I could call after my job interview and visit my friend at work.

Meeting up with her that day at the Farmers Store had amazed me. For just like Cinderella it seemed she had undergone a dramatic transformation. Changing overnight, it seemed, from a rather untidy schoolgirl into a dignified young lady. I was astonished. Was this person in the smart outfit who confidently stood behind the large counter really Maureen?

She looked and sounded so very different. I overheard her politely speak to a prospective customer and answer their questions with authority.

Having efficiently dealt with the customer, Maureen then asked how my job interview had been. I explained it had been a nerve-wracking morning, spent in a large old-fashioned office, where two old gentlemen bombarded me with questions on the textile industry. Finally, they had concluded the interview by offering me a job as a junior ledger clerk; the wage offered was two pounds and fifteen shillings for working five days a week. I had accepted the offer. They then provided an escort to show me around the warehouse and it was agreed the following Monday I was to commence working in a small office, my task being to assist three senior female office staff.

I felt proud to tell my friend that I was joining the work force. I finally had stepped forth into the wider world!

Being a wage earner I took the responsibilities of collected my first week's wages seriously and carried it home to Dad. Once my wage packet was opened, I handed two pounds to my Dad for board and lodgings; the remaining fifteen shillings was mine to keep, this was intended to provide me with all my other needs.

I soon settled into working at Copestake and Crampton, the old established warehouse that had previously had their larger premises in London; these offices had had to be abandoned due to Hitler's bombs and they had to relocate several members of their London staff to their Nottingham Branch. Some proud Londoners found working in Nottingham rather distressing, for moving to the Midlands was not a voluntary choice.

Maureen and I continued to meet most evenings, now able to compare notes on incidents that happened during our working day. We would giggle uncontrollably over silly mistakes we made, especially if we had encountered highhanded pompous people. We became indignant sometimes at their unjust attitudes, but as we became older, we began to realize that pomposity is a shield used sometimes by people unsure of their own capabilities. However, being 16-years-of-age, we were too naïve at that point to recognize the fact. We still had a lot to learn.

Maureen when I described my first day at work was interested to know what I had worn that day. As suggested by Grandmother I had purchased a sedate outfit – a black skirt and long sleeved blouse. I primly made my way towards Hounds Gate and on arrival was directed to knock at the door of the small office where I would be working. The room was empty, so I studied the four old-fashioned desks and a large cumbersome telephone switchboard, looking at it closely. I became apprehensive, wondering if they expected me to use the complicated switchboard.

Minutes later three lady office workers arrived. They greeted me with a friendly smile and pointed to a desk near the window; these mature ladies seemed to welcome a newcomer joining their group. All went very well; my youth proved an asset, for the mature ladies' all seemed eager to ask me questions. "What's your name, age and school background?" I loved the attention and, readily answering, they probed further, asking if I had any siblings and my fathers occupation. Being eager to please I willingly replied until they questioned me about my mother; then, I then gave my standard answer to this often asked question.

"I haven't got a mother."

Then I turned away to avoid further probing. It was some months later I realized my work colleagues had jumped to the wrong conclusion. For having noted my all black attire and listening to my subdued reply, they assumed my mother had recently passed away and with loving kindness from that moment they battled each other to prove they were the most suitable person in the office to be my mother substitute. While I, in total ignorance of normal office life, assumed all junior staff received this special loving attention.

From my desk, I had a good view of the ancient almshouses bordering Friar Lane; the roofs seemed close enough to touch. I could clearly see the historic Salutation Inn. On occasions people entering the old inn would glace up and wave, especially when they realized I was staring at them from the upper window. I enjoyed their friendly contact but eventually being on public view became a matter of embarrassment. I was enjoying all that life seemed to be offering. Everything it seemed was going as planned.

Grandmother was happy I was employed and working in a respectable job. Dad, who struggled for years to deal with the trials and tribulations of rearing two motherless daughters through their childhood years, now seemed more relaxed.

Mavis was enjoying a busy social life and I, content to remain in close contact with my friends, was biding my time while waiting to start my nursing course.

Everything it seemed was working out as planned.

Much later, I had reason to remember my smug thoughts.

For as someone had wisely reminded me, "The best laid plans of mice and men."

Chapter 39

Saturday morning and Dad had already left the house to go to work. I came downstairs and noticed Cleo had made herself comfortable; happily stretched out on Dad's large wooden armchair, she appeared not to have a worry in the world.

Cleo often curled up on Dad's lap, purring happily, a truly pampered pet. The cat's lifestyle was envied by other local moggies, who given the opportunity often tried to gain access to our kitchen. When our previous well-loved pet cat Titus died, there had been a period of mourning; all the family, feeling utterly sad, had stated, "No cat will ever be able to replace our faithful old moggie."

It now seemed we were wrong, for with the arrival of an inquisitive young tortoiseshell female, once again, a feline presence was in control and the familiar smell of boiled fish heads and other aquatic delicacies wafted through the house.

I reached over to stroke Cleo and lazily she stretched out a paw. There was no sign of Mavis getting out of bed. She had arrived home late last night and I did not expect her to stir for ages.

Happily I reached out and turned on the wireless. I tuned in using the well-used knob, and the sound of music filled the room.

I smiled – what a lovely start to the day – then, picking up a loaf of bread from the table, I hacked into it and cut a thick ragged slice. The smoke-blackened kettle on the hob was already hot and before long, I was perched on a small wooden chair tightly clutching a chipped old mug and sipping a comforting familiar brew. The hot tea was well flavoured with smoky sterilized milk. As I bit into a slice of now toasted bread, liberally spread with Golden Syrup, I sighed. Ambrosia, I reasoned, could not taste any better than this.

Suddenly a voice on the wireless announced, "The next record played is a recording by MARIO LANZO. Taken from his latest film."

My idol! Eagerly I turned the volume up to its highest level, and then, overcome with emotion at the sound of his voice, I joined the chorus and began singing. How I envied the film stars Kathryn Grayson and Ann Blyth, who had been able to sing in his arms. How lucky they were, having had Mario Lanzo sing romantic arias to them.

Lost in my world of dreams, I wasn't aware the stair door was being opened until suddenly the sound of Mario's voice abruptly disappeared, replaced by an angry female voice shouting, "What do you think you are up to, playing that rubbish loud enough to wake the dead buried in Christ Church graveyard?"

My sister Mavis had woken up. Moments before she had been fast asleep in her bedroom, situated two flights of stairs away. Now having woken with a start, she had furiously raced down the stairs and turned off the wireless.

Enraged I swiftly reached the wireless knob and turned it back on; to my dismay the final notes of the song were fading away.

I was livid but before I had chance to voice my strong objections, Mavis added, "You and Maureen are obsessed with that stupid film star, it's time you grew up; he's just a tin pot singer."

Enraged I shouted, "That's all you know, he is a trained opera singer."

Mavis gave a sarcastic laugh. Then, tossing back her head, she said, "He would never get an audition to sing in the chorus of the Doyle Carte Opera Company."

Wearing a look of triumph she opened the stair door, and disappeared back upstairs.

I sat down feeling deflated. Who did she think she was, some opera expert?

Just because she went once on a school trip to the Theatre Royal to see the show *The Mikado*.

Then mockingly I began to sing, *"Willow Tit Willow Tit Willow"*.

Mario Lanzo would never want to sing those stupid words. For he sungs Italian love songs and was so romantic. I began singing again, recalling my favourite song from his last film.

As I reached the end of the song, I began inwardly muttering, "She is only jealous of my collection of Mario photos. Because she is older than I am, she thinks she knows everything. Now Maureen who works at a music shop, she really is an expert on opera; she knows that Mario was chosen to play the part of The Great Caruso because he is such a great singer. So what's your answer to that, Mavis?"

I sat down on the small wooden chair, feeling better knowing Maureen would agree with me and I could discuss the topic with her tonight. Arrangements had already been made to meet her outside the Pala`ise de Dance.

Then feeling more relaxed, I reached for the loaf of bread and generously spooned out another dollop of Golden Syrup. I turned the volume back high on the wireless and prayed the next record chosen would be sung by Mario Lanzo. For just listening to his voice helped transport me away from the dingy backstreets; It carried me far away into a glamorous romantic world.

Much later in the day, I went upstairs and began inspecting contents tucked away in a paper bag. This was the umpteenth time I had examined my latest purchases, pulling out a soft white blouse and frilly petticoat. I then reached for the artificial rose I had selected after the assistant at C&A persuaded me I needed a flower to add a soft feminine touch to my outfit. I now floundered, trying to decide where best to pin the large silk pink rose.

Mavis came into the room; touching the flower she appeared interested and began offering advice. I was pleased she offered to help, for she dressed smartly. I, not being fashion conscious, felt more comfortable throwing familiar old garments on. Recently to my own surprise, I had begun to take more interest in the frills and fineries of feminine attire.

"Are you wearing this at the Palais tonight?" Mavis asked as she picked up the white blouse.

"Yes," I replied. "I'm going out with Maureen and Rita."

"Did you buy a new underskirt as well?" Mavis asked.

I nodded and showed her the stiff three-tiered lace underskirt.

"That will look good under my black taffeta skirt, be careful not to lose it," she said, and laughing she went back up the stairs.

I glared at her and quickly gathered up my new clothes; stopping only to pick up a small wash bag hurriedly I left the room.

Standing outside Rita's front door I rattled the letterbox; glancing back I noticed Mavis appear, she was carrying a bag and heading across the street towards Grandma's house. I realized she must be planning an evening out, for she preferred to get ready at Grandma's house without anyone to interrupt her. There at Grandmother's she could dress up in style!

Rita's mother opened the door and beckoned me in.

"The tanks full of hot water, have you come for a bath?"

Before I could reply, I heard Rita calling from upstairs, "I'm in the bath."

The stair door was open. I hesitated briefly to nod a hello to Jack, Rita's dad; he was sitting reading a comic at the table.

He was a man of few words, who enjoyed the simple pleasures of life, rarely complaining about his peace being disturbed by an invasion of giggling girls. With good grace he allowed his daughter to invite me on a regular basis into his home and there he permitted me the full use of all the family facilities. It was a privilege that as a child I had accepted without question, for it seemed a perfectly normal thing to do. As I matured, I realized how lucky I had been to receive these acts of kindness. I had been blessed growing up, being made so welcome in the homes of my close friends. Rita's door was one I never doubted would always be open to me.

Rita urged again, "Come up the waters still warm."

I ran up the stairs, the familiar route to her bathroom. Having no fixed bathroom facilities at my home and it being such a chore dragging down the large tin bath from our outside back wall, what a blessing it was to be able to bathe here.

Rita tossed another large handful of pink bath salts into the water, and I climbed in the scented water. Now both of us relaxed in comfort as we talked over our plans for tonight's outing to the Palaise De Dance Hall.

Barely in our teens, it was proving something an adventure to venture into the world of grown-ups; we were novices at the sophisticated pleasures of Nottingham nightlife.

We giggled, discussing every aspect of what we had chosen to wear, hoping we had picked the right outfits and would look the part. Rita had also purchased a new outfit and anxious to show what she had chosen. Being small and dainty, she hoped the selected outfit would make her look older. For although she was earning her own wage, she continued looking like a school girl – a problem Maureen and I never encountered, for both of us were early developers, who had long ago noted physical signs indicated we were maturing.

Clutching our handbags, Rita and I made our way towards the trolley bus stop.

On Saturday nights the trolley bus service ran at frequent intervals. On the short walk to Ilkeston road, we noted others making their way to the bus stop. Saturday by tradition was the most popular night to live it up. The trolley bus was almost full when it arrived; we climbed aboard and as we ascended the upper deck the smoky atmosphere made us gasp. We secured a seat at the front and set off; from upstairs we could look down at the folk already gathering around the city streets.

Maureen had arranged to meet us outside the dance hall and as we got closer to Victoria market we anxiously peered out, hoping to spot her. Our destination in sight, we rang the bell and the bus jerked to a halt. As passengers made their way down the stairs they jostled with those trying to exit the lower deck. Everyone was pushing and elbowing their way out, until the bus conductor urged folk to be patient. Eventually we were able to join the small crowd of people waiting outside the dance hall; some were chatting together, while others anxiously were looking around waiting to spot a familiar face. We began doing the same, as there was no sign yet of Maureen. We proceeded to climb the entrance steps and stood at the top, close to the entrance door; from there we secured a good view of everyone approaching. Maureen worked all day on Saturdays and often arrived late for appointments on that day, having limited time to dress. Confident she would eventually arrive we waited, knowing Maureen never missed an outing without a good reason. From our vantage point we watched a group of giggling girls approach the doorway; many of them wore skirts similar to the ones we had selected. As they climbed the steps the rustle of starched petticoats was evident. Nottingham was noted for its abundant female population, a fact confirmed as more girls hurried past, all eager to enter the building.

Rita sighed.

"Hope Maureen comes soon, it must be getting full inside, it's getting really late."

Another group of people approached, this time a group of young men. As they drew closer I could hear they were discussing football. Then, from the middle of the noisy group, I heard a familiar female voice cry out, "What rubbish, we were been robbed of that goal, the ref needs a pair of specs."

It was Maureen. As usual, eager to voice her opinion on a football game, she had latched on to a group of visiting football supporters; they had been surprised to find themselves joined by a fanatic female local supporter. There was little chance for them or any other opponent to win this verbal battle. For Maureen was determined as ever to defend her beloved football team, and winning verbal battles was something she excelled at.

Spotting us, she waved then joined us on the steps. Grateful she had at last arrived and hurriedly opening our handbags, we pulled out our little purses and made our way in through the door. With a flourish, our entrance fee paid, we entered the building. Inside there were soft lights, carpet, and wafting towards us was a sweet exotic smell. The ballroom seemed designed to encourage romance seekers. Rita was just as impressed by the atmosphere. Maureen, however, appeared to have focused her attention on the group she earlier had encountered.

For close on our heels the group of opposing football supporters had walked in. Before we had time to leave our coats in the cloakroom, Maureen once more became engaged in another heated discussion about her favourite football player.

Rita and I stood for some time feeling superfluous. Finally, deciding to go ahead into the ballroom, we whispered to Maureen we were going to sit in the main area. Happily, she waved us on our way, then continued talking football.

We sat close to the back of the room, listening to the band and watching people gliding around the dance floor. Some couples appeared very competent; they almost floated around the floor. Seeing them display such skill, Rita and I began feeling uneasy.

We smiled, observing the dancers lightly jumping and skipping as they performed a foxtrot. This routine was quickly followed by a tango. Nudging each other, we watched in surprise as we noted one couple's amorous actions. Shortly afterwards the couple left the dance floor. It was only then we noted a group of men watching us. I suggested to Rita that we go seek Maureen out. Pushing our way through the dense crowd surrounding the bar, we spotted Maureen right in the centre of the crowd of young football supporters. Seated on a tall stool, with a glass in her hand, she was in seventh heaven, debating the same topic: football, football, football – an interest that Rita and I failed to share. I realized that any chance of persuading her to find a corner to discuss Mario's latest film seemed remote. I waved to her and she waved back; Rita drew closer, hoping to distract her. Maureen acknowledged us but after a few minutes of strained conversation it became obvious we added nothing of interest to the football discussion, so we wandered back inside the ballroom.

The room was getting crowded, and the only seats available were at the edge of the dance floor. Reluctant to sit there but having little choice we sat down. Some of the more confident girls were already up and dancing together. Other girls, invited to dance by eager young men, were now swirling around the floor. One couple waltzed by who were strangers to each other just minutes before; they were now dancing round, clinging tightly together in a familiar way. Sitting on the edge of the dance floor, we felt uncomfortable and out of our depth. We must have appeared like gauche, unsophisticated teenagers and we longed for Maureen to join us, for her presence instilled confidence in us. Although at times her forthright approach made us squirm, she did provide us with a shield against uncertainty. Having older brothers she was unfazed and could joke with members of the opposite sex, accustomed as she was to her own brothers teasing her.

We were again aware of a group of older men watching us from across the dance floor. Maureen, we thought, you better come and join us, for we have a feeling we are going to need you.

The tempo of the music changed and as a familiar tune began to play, the men appeared thankfully to have moved away. We started to relax. We both knew the song and along with the crowd began to sing, "Some enchanted evening you will meet a stranger."

Turning to Rita I began to say, "I love this song."

Before she had chance to reply a tall figure suddenly appeared; bending forward he stretched his hand out towards Rita then asked her to dance. She looking startled. Another stranger now appeared in front of me, requesting I accompany him on to the dance floor. I gasped in surprise; the man beside me I realized was one of the visitors who sometimes visited the lodging house on Bloomsgrove Street.

Nervously I stumbled around the dance floor, anxiously wondered what to reply to the searching questions that he was asking me. It was a relief when finally the music stopped. We were now situated on the opposite side of the ballroom and the tall stranger who asked Rita to dance continued holding on to her hand. I heard him enquire her name and Rita answered. It became obvious she had also recognized my partner, for she spoke to him. Soon a couple of other older men had walked over to join their friends and they all began to speak in a language we failed to understand. The tall man, his attention focused on Rita, began teasing her in a friendly way. His friend had already explained he had seen Rita many times before, for he had a friend living at the lodging house; he also had met and spoken to Rita's mother. I was still unsure about being in their company and had no idea what to expect of this dancehall adventure. Before I had chance to come to a decision, someone grabbed my arm and spun me round. It was Maureen

"I came looking for you," she reprimanded me. "I thought you were sitting over near the band."

I explained we had been on the dance floor, and the tall man hearing the discussion interrupted. He glanced at Maureen as he asked, "Are you from Bloomsgrove Street as well?"

Abruptly, Maureen answered, "No I' m not, but I am friends with both these two. None of you men come from Bloomsgrove Street, and you don't even come from Nottingham."

The tall man – who I discovered was named Paul – boldly stared at Maureen. Just as mockingly, he said, "I'm an Eskimo, I don't expect you know where Eskimo's live."

Quick thinking Maureen replied, "I know they eat bloody candles, is that what you eat?"

The tall man translated her reply to his friends, who looked at Maureen and then, nudging each other, broke into raucous laughter.

Soon after, urged away by Maureen, we left their company and, anxious to catch our bus home, made our way out of the hall.

Approaching the trolley bus stop Maureen spotted the crowd of football supporters. They shouted out to her, "Hey, are you still going to organize new glasses for the ref next week?"

Maureen did not bother verbally to reply. Our transport having just arrived, she leaned forward and firmly grabbed hold of the hand rail, climbing onto the vehicle As the trolley bus slowly pulled away she leaned forward, pointed to her red and white football scarf and gave the crowd of men the V for Victory sign.

Chapter 40

A few months passed by and as I collected my weekly wage packet I placed it in my handbag. Making my way down the stairs, I left the rambling building, my working week finished; now I was looking forward to the weekend, for plans had been made to go into town.

As rain began to fall I ran down Friar Lane; crossing the road, I hurried past the Council House, thinking again of the suggestions Maureen discussed for our Saturday night outing. My mind visualised what I would choose to wear, and I inwardly chuckled as I recalled girls parading back and forth, displaying their finery at the Palaise De Dance. Where did they shop?, I wondered. My modestly priced outfits would have to do. For glancing in the elegantly dressed windows of Toby's or Griffins stores, the price of items displayed there stunned me. Fully occupied by tomorrows plans, when I would stand on the balcony at the dance hall and hopefully view a prospective dance partner, I carelessly stepped off the pavement, narrowly avoiding being run down by a double decker trolley bus. It was full of passengers making their erratic stop and start journey heading towards Hyson Green. The No. Forty-Three bus collected many passengers as it travelled through densely populated areas, first making its way toward Trent Bridge, then returning via Arkright Street and heading through Radford on its way to Bulwell. I sometimes travelled this route but today decided to walk towards Parliament Street and travel home on the No. 39.

My chosen bus soon arrived, as I climbed on board I noticed a new neighbour who occupied No. 17 Bloomsgrove Street sitting close to the front seat. The newcomer, having noticed me, smiled and nodded her head in greeting. She then created space on the seat by moving her shopping bag on to the floor. Shyly she beckoned me to sit down. More passengers now clambered aboard; hurrying them along the conductor rang the bell, and the vehicle continued gently swaying up Derby road.

As the bus approached St Barnabus, I noticed my foreign neighbour bow her head briefly in the direction of the church and then touch a small embroidered cross-pinned to her coat. Noticing me observe her piety, she smiled and began attempting to communicate in her unusual accent. I listened carefully as she struggled to pronounce a few English words; gradually I understood more of what she was attempting to say. She had enquired if I enjoyed my job, and I smiled and nodded. By the time we reached our mutual stop, between us we had managed to have a brief conversation.

We left the bus together and made our way across Ilkeston road. Side by side, we walked up Bloomsgrove Street. As we approached the front door of her house, the neighbour reached into her bag and pulled out a package, then stretching out her hand offered me a small cake. I was surprised, for after years of strict rationing my experience of spontaneously being offered food, especially by a comparative stranger, seemed strange. The cake she held out looked delicious and the speed with which she produced it reminded me of the conjuring trick, when as if by magic a rabbit is pulled out of a hat. Half-heartedly I attempted to decline the offer; thankfully, she insisted I accept and thrust the cake into my hand. Sheepishly I thanked her, waved goodbye and crossed the street, then entered the front door of my house.

No one was home but the electric light was on and the fire in the grate burning brightly. Taking off my coat, I sat down on Dad's old wooden chair and glanced at the gift. It resembled a large flat doughnut. Hesitatingly I took a bite; its texture was similar to a doughnut but the filling inside unlike anything I had tasted before. I discovered later that it was creamed poppy seed. Having enjoyed the experience of tasting something new, I was pleased that I had accepted the gift.

Godfrey receives his degree

I had just finished eating when the door opened. Mavis had arrived, having been chatting to our older cousin Pat, who was across the street visiting Grandmother. Mavis and Pat, being close in age, got on well. Pat in the past attended Manning Grammar School. As a pupil there she visited Grandmother frequently, these days she was busy adjusting to life at a local college. Fully immersed in her studies, her sights were now set on becoming a schoolteacher and proud Grandmother looked forward to hearing her oldest granddaughter's news – as she also did about her grandson Godfrey, who was Pat's young brother.

Pat and Godfrey lived in Broxtowe. On the occasions I visited my cousins I often watched Godfrey happily play and become engrossed in the wonderful world of Meccano. Mavis and Pat meanwhile sat talking confidentially to each other in the corner. With Pat, kept busy now at college, Aunty Ivy and Uncle Lawrence began to ask if I would stay overnight and keep Godfrey Company. They were planning an evening out and felt reluctant to leave him home alone. It was a happy arrangement as Aunty Ivy provided sandwiches and homemade cakes, which Godfrey and I shared as we played snakes and ladders; then, as darkness fell, we climbed into bed and soundly slept until morning. Dad's older brother Uncle Lawrence was a gentleman and a talented artist. When younger he attended art college and intended painting to be his career. He secured work and produced many wonderful posters advertising films. The war interrupted his plans and his career, and these days he painted only for pleasure and earned a living driving a local bus.

Pat and Godfrey's parents were both proud of their children's achievements, especially Pat's grammar school admission. Aunty Ivy, a skilled dressmaker, ensured her daughter always dressed well. I was in awe of Pat, who due to her parents encouragement appeared to ooze confidence. Pat, given every chance to succeed in life and provided with elocution and piano lessons, had developed into a sophisticated young lady. The sort of grandchild any Grandmother would feel proud to introduce to the likes of Mrs Farquarson – unlike Grandmother's youngest granddaughter, whose behaviour left a lot to be desired (especially the antics she became involved in with Maureen, that caused her grandmother to despair).

However there had been a memorable occasion when it was my well-behaved cousin who stepped out of line. I had simply been an innocent witness and played no real part in the incident. However, I feared I would be the one suspected of organizing the mishap. As it turned out, no one bothered to question my involvement about what happened that cold grey day at Basford – which was fortunate, for I had decided never to disclose the truth of what occurred. For did it matter, having one extra black mark to add to my file? I knew my cousin's behaviour that day had been totally out of character, and it was only due to her foolishness that she became involved in such a dilemma.

It all began when Pat invited me to accompany her on an outing. I was surprised and flattered to receive the invitation to meet her friends; it was something that had never happened previously. I didn't question our destination, just excitedly followed my smartly-dressed older cousin. I marched happily beside Pat until we reached the spot where she had arranged to meet her friends. Within minutes of their arrival, I noticed I seemed far younger than the streetwise group of boys and girls who Pat had met at the railway crossing.

Ignored by everyone and out of place in their company, I stood aside and listened to their teenage conversation. The buzz of excitement generated seemed focused on an area of land surrounding the Basford crossing. Recent heavy rain had created havoc and a large expanse of the fields were submerged in deep muddy floodwater. The group huddled together, nosily discussing plans to build a raft; they had already collected a pile of old pieces of timber. I was both curious and disappointed at not being included in the construction of the little craft. I stood some distance away, watching as Pat and her friends hurriedly built a primitive raft. Eventually, satisfied with their handy work, they launched the rickety vessel. It wobbled as it floated on the muddy water and Pat, dressed in her smart grey school uniform, was instructed to be first to step onto the raft. I watched as her friends followed her on the craft; ceremonially, it was then launched. With growing envy, I stood by the edge of the muddy water and watched the roughly made vessel slowly floating away, carrying its passengers across the expanse of muddy water. They had not gone far when a scream rang out: the raft was sinking. Pat was the first to topple into the waters; she staggered to her feet, up to her chest in contaminated water. With great difficulty, she managed to struggle towards firmer land. Anxiously I watched as waist high my cousin waded through thick mud. The weather had turned cold and the water was freezing. I was surprised at Pats calm reaction, for despite the dramatic situation she was in Pat didn't protest –

not even when her friends who lived locally emerged from the mud and without a backward glance began swiftly to desert her, one by one disappearing to their nearby homes. Drenched in mud now abandoned to her fate, Pat watched in astonishment as they all vanished out of sight.

Pat and I, now alone, were standing in a deserted eerie field. The light, fading fast, was adding to our dilemma; Pat violently shivered. Trickles of dirty water now ran out of her shoes and wet mud dripped from her hair; she looked freezing cold. Her smart school outfit was now thickly covered in wet filthy debris and she looked a sorry spectacle. Yet she made no complaint about her friends abandoning her.

By a stroke of good luck, a local lady witnessed Pat's dilemma and being a Good Samaritan came to her aid. The lady invited both of us into her home, provided warm drinks and helped Pat get warm, by supplying her with dry clothes.

Back home everyone was worried by our absence, what with communication being difficult in those days; the family had no idea of our dilemma. Eventually when we arrived home, the family was relieved. They didn't waste time enquiring about my involvement but I became certain that Grandmother considered I had been the ringleader.

Later recalling Pat's reaction to the situation, I became impressed at how calm she had been. For until that evening, I had thought my cousin to be someone who wore smart clothes, had piano and elocution lessons, but would be unable to cope with any hazard. Although I admired her achievements in those areas, I had never wanted to emulate her lifestyle. However, this Pat, who immerged from the muddy water without complaining or blaming others, was a different person – one I really admired. She coped admirably and I felt a surge of pride and a stronger bond with my cousin from that moment. Maureen would also admire her, I felt certain.

The real story of the events that evening were never disclosed and it was to be the only time I was ever invited to share an adventure with my older cousin or her friends.

Pat, as she became older, was to visit Bloomsgrove Street less often, the reason being that college life now kept Pat bus. My oldest cousin also began courting and was preoccupied with her beau, a young student called Mike. He introduced her to the dangerous pastime of climbing to the top of the tallest peaks of the rocky mountains situated in Scotland and Wales. Pat seemed happy to join him and headed for the hills at every opportunity. They spent many romantic moments on the peaks of the Scottish mountains. Mike was still a student when Pat surprised everyone by announcing she was going to marry him. Grandmother appeared delighted to welcome him into the family. There was little time to recover from the excitement of celebrating their wedding when a newcomer arrived to join our family. For a cute baby girl named Georgina was born, her arrival heralding in a whole new generation. For other cute babies now were being born, welcome arrivals for other local families.

Maureen's parents celebrated when their first grandchild arrived. To my delight I was frequently was asked now if I would baby-sit other children. I spent many happy hours caring for young babies, an activity that encouraged me to enquire about pursuing a career nursing infants. I developed an interest in acquiring further knowledge caring for young babies. Professional training to care for newborn infants seemed to be an ideal career choice. I never seemed fazed by the fact it would require years of dedicated study.

Being too young to commence training, I was content at that time to work at Copestake and Crampton. Saturday evening however was reserved for having fun, so my life at sixteen seemed rather pleasant.

The local dancehalls were the place of choice to spend Saturday evenings. With three large dancehalls all situated within easy walking distance of the Council House you could take your pick. There was the Palaise De Dance, the Victoria Ballroom or the Astoria Ballroom. The Blossoms of Bloomo had tried them all.

Mavis however rarely discussed her Saturday evening plans with me and the entertainment destinations she chose remained a mystery. She always seemed to have something planned; her social life appeared happily busy. She would scramble away to Grandmother's house to prepare for these outings. On one occasion Mavis, dressed in a black taffeta flared skirt and shiny top, briefly returned home to collect her handbag.

I delayed her departure by firmly standing in the doorway, blocking her exit.

"Have you seen my new starched net underskirt?" I angrily enquired.

Mavis just tossed her head and ignored my question; instead, laughingly she asked a question of her own.

"Lost something again have you?"

Then grinning she made to open the door.

As she rushed to escape, I plainly could hear the rustling sound of a freshly laundered net underskirt. It was at that moment Rita entered, to hear me furiously yelling, "Give it back."

When Rita entered the room, Mavis took the opportunity of disappearing out of the door, leaving behind yet another unsolved mystery.

I grumbled loudly to Rita about how last week I lost a pair of black seamed nylon stockings. Then rambling on I exclaimed how lucky she was with no older sister living at her home. Especially a sister who rapidly applied make-up, wore long dangling earrings, then, dressed to the nines, flounced away at great speed – especially when the question of disappearing, freshly laundered undies was about to be raised. Rita, ever the diplomat, patiently listened to my tale of woe; she had heard me complain about the subject so many times. She no longer expressed an opinion on the matter, perhaps thinking it safer to stay on neutral ground. We had been friends since early childhood and our relationship was as close as any sisters, except for one big difference: I never had needed to question Rita about freshly laundered under garments disappearing.

Chapter 41

There was bustle and excitement on the street as people began to discuss the arrangements well underway now for the Queens Coronation. I felt at a disadvantage, being too old to take part in the children's street parties and too young to be included in the festivities planned by local landlords for their patrons.

Rita and I discussed how exciting it would be to travel to London and join the throngs planning to witness the Coronation procession, but realizing it impossibility for any of us to travel to London we gave up the dreaming about it. All was not however completely lost, for there was chance we would see part of the spectacle on the television. For Rita's mother, who had recently acquired a television set, was hoping to view the event, for the newspapers had recently suggested the crowning ceremony was to be fully televised and forecast that the historic occasion would be viewed by millions. Rita seemed confident her mother would allow me to view the ceremony with them. I was excited at the thought of viewing the pageant, for watching television was still a luxurious novelty, and folks who owned a television set I considered very fortunate.

I had not heard from Maureen for a while; the last time I spoke to her, she had seemed rather unsettled. I had asked her to accompany me to Trent Bridge embankment, but she declined. Her reluctance did not surprise me as I was not planning to go alone, for I had already promised to take one of the local children along to watch the swans swimming down the Trent River. Baby-sitting local children was a past time I enjoyed but Maureen didn't seem to share my pleasure and found it strange that I so frequently cared for local infants.

However my friend Pearl understood and often invited me to bathe or help feed her two little daughters. Fulvio worked long hours and Pearl seemed glad of my company. Pearl explained that Fulvio was working long hours, being determined to save a deposit that would enable him buy his dream house. The information astonished me, for the house he had in mind was one situated on the Groves. Impressed by his ambitious plan, it seemed to me an impossible dream, and I had never before known anyone with such drive and ambition.

Although I was young, I was aware that the overcrowded situation they endured was stressful. Pearl had previously mentioned some of the difficulties to my father. A recent occurrence caused wild speculation. A fierce commotion accompanied by raised angry voices had attracted attention. The voices belonged to Pearl's father, mother and brothers, who had been fighting over a wireless set. The disagreement culminated when a pair of large hands was seen opening up a window. They briefly vanished then returned to the window, now holding a bulky object: *a large wireless set*. Suddenly the object was thrust with tremendous force out of the window; it flew like a guided missile to land with an almighty crash on a dry patch of soil.

From our kitchen window I peered in amazement at the sight, for there on our neighbours garden lay a thousand bits of broken bakelite and other debris scattered about the cracked uneven path and soil.

Pearl never explained the reason behind the catapulted wireless, but it became obvious there was growing unrest in the overcrowded house and that it was causing great distress.

Fulvio's answer to the problem was to work even longer hours, taking any type of employment, however difficult or unpleasant. He was determined to raise the deposit needed and to settle his little family in their own home. Having limited knowledge of the English language, this was a brave and difficult task...

My father admired his effort and commented to me, "How strange it seems that within a few short years of the war ceasing, so many strangers have gathered together. Even past opponents are happy now to settle down and form the most unusual friendships, good luck to him."

I agreed, for no longer did it seem unusual to meet people who were born in far away places. I could well remember the first strangers who came into my life; they were the young London evacuees, who arrived in Nottingham as strangers and left us as friends.

People from strange sounding places arrived in Radford. Some had rather unusual stories to tell. Wandering freely around the streets of Nottingham, the first adults all seemed to be wearing uniforms – the Americans, Canadians and Poles; then much later came the foreign-speaking prisoners of war, walking up Ilkeston road wearing their easily identifiable jackets. The list continued to grow, for eventually civilians began arriving who hoped to settle here.

Among the strangers who became my friends was Maria, a timid Dutch woman. Her husband Herbert had been in stationed with the forces in Holland; being the wife of a British soldier Maria joined him in Nottingham, and arriving in England so soon after the war had been a stressful experience for her.

My interest in children was how Maria became my friend. She was the proprietor of a small shop on Ilkeston Road and sold dairy products to the local community. Herbert was unable to offer her assistance in the shop, as he was busy with his own job.

I visited the shop most days and Maria noticed that I was usually accompanied by young children; she asked the reason and I explained I enjoyed minding children and planned one day to be a children's nurse. Haltingly Maria asked would I consider baby-sitting her daughter Viviane. I agreed and shortly afterwards was happily dancing another cute dimpled baby on my knee. It was a boon for her parents as it gave them chance to visit Herbert's family, who were inn-keepers at Bulwell.

Little Viviane was a content baby who slept soundly, and as she slept I enjoyed the supper Maria provided me with: custard and a home-made Dutch style cake. These were simple pleasures I appreciated.

I continued working weekdays at Copestake and Crampton and my free time at the weekends just flew by.

Rita was content to work at Clay's drapery stores and Mavis now was occupied courting a new beau – a young Radford fellow that unfortunately she was nervous to inform Grandmother about, for he was the son of a local bookie, a fact that caused Mavis much anxiety.

Maureen also seemed unsettled and visited Bloomsgrove Street less often. I decided to visit her to discuss the problem

It was a warm evening as I made my way up Denman Street. On the way as I entered Boden Street and drew close to Barbara's house, I noticed the curtains drawn and I wondered why. Barbara and I had once been close companions, though lately we had drifted apart. Barbara, a shy girl, disliked changes, and perhaps feared being introduced to my new student friends. For meeting strangers unsettled her due to her suffering from a debilitating stammer. Seeing Barbara's house made me feel guilty, for it had been ages since I had been in touch. I vowed to make the effort to see her very soon.

By now, I had reached the Boden Street swimming baths, where I had so often joined the noisy children swimming. I smiled, recalling the adventures I had experienced there, especially ones that had involved Maureen. One event I experienced was not as happy. On that occasion I visited the swimming baths alone and, placing my personal items on the changing room bench, I returned later to discover my watch had disappeared. It was the first time I had owned a watch and I presumed it stolen. Immediately I reported the incident to the pool staff and sadly returned home. Hours later, a stern faced lady police officer arrived and asked to speak to my father; then she proceeded to record a formal statement. How seriously they handled petty crime in those days. However quick the response of the local police force had been, unfortunately my wristwatch never was to be located.

I walked on, now approaching Maureen's door and becoming more anxious, for I was anxious to know why she had not been visiting. As I put my hand up to rap on the door it opened. Maureen had seen me through the window.

She stood before me and I was amazed how different she now looked. Elegantly dressed, her hair styled and tinted in a gleaming shade of auburn, her lips cherry red. She was wearing a stylish cotton skirt and blouse. Maureen was also swaying uneasily as she tottered towards me. Glancing down at her feet, I noticed she was wearing brightly polished high-heeled court shoes.

"Hello Maureen," I muttered. I stared at her transformation, and continued, *"Are you OK? I was wondering why you hadn't been down to Bloomo for two weeks."*

She did not answer; pausing only to clutch her new handbag, she grabbed my arm and manoeuvred me away from the doorway. Then, as she propelled me along towards the entry, I waited anxiously to hear her explanation.

"I'm going into town," she said and continued, "I'm glad you are here; for you can come into town with me."

"Where are you going?" I muttered.

"A café on Hounds Gate," she answered.

"I'm not dressed to go to town," I feebly answered, "and I haven't got the bus fare on me."

She quickly replied, "I will pay your fare and buy you a cup of tea and a cake."

By then we had reached Alfreton Road and a trolley bus was approaching. Her urgency to get to town now compelled her to run and we had boarded the bus before she managed to explain why she was in such a rush.

She was planning to visit a café situated in the heart of Nottingham, she explained as she urged me climb up to the top deck of the bus. When we were sat down Maureen began to explain in depth her actions and I began to understand what had bought about her dramatic metamorphic change.

For it seemed my friend had met a young man at work who had bowled her over. It was clear she was smitten as she described him in glowing terms. Handsome, educated, witty, he loved classical music and that interest inspired him to learn speak Italian. A sports-lover, he was well read and a grammar school educated superstar. To sum everything up it was very clear that Maureen had fallen head over heels in love with a paragon of virtues.

Listening to her lovesick lament, I gathered that the main difficulty seemed to be that this *paragon* was not *yet* in love with Maureen. In fact, it seemed rather complicated, for Maureen declared she had rivals who also relentlessly seemed to be pursuing her *dream man* – and the horror was these girls also worked daily with him at Farmer's of Long Row.

Maureen, never one to be easily deterred, remained determined to win his heart. With that object in mind she had located the Nottingham cafés he was likely to visit and planned to be waiting there at every opportunity, in the hopes that he would arrive and notice her. Today she was heading for a café that was situated on Hounds Gate and that was the reason she was in a great hurry.

By the time Maureen related the whole story we were outside the café door and I was feeling apprehensive. Just what was it she was actually planning to do next? She grabbed my arm and firmly pulled me inside the small café. Choosing her seat to enable her to view everyone who entered, she sat down at a small table; nervously I joined her.

We waited some time before deciding to order two coffees. There were no signs of anyone who resembled the perfect man she'd vividly described, so we continued to wait.

Sipping the dark liquid, I shuddered.

"This coffee tastes terrible," I said.

Maureen gave me a peculiar look.

"It's proper coffee," she said. "Made in a real percolator; they always drink it like this in Italy."

I didn't answer, for even if Mario Lanzo himself had recommended it, I didn't fancy it. Just give me a nice sweet cup of milky tea any time.

Maureen without speaking sat still, glancing up only when someone entered the door. After half an hour I ventured to ask Maureen what time she thought he would arrive; it seemed she had no idea and wasn't certain he would pay a visit today as she realized there were other cafés he also frequented. I sighed and wondered how many venues she was planning to visit and did she expect me to drink more strong black coffee?

I sat another half an hour before I ventured to ask.

"How long are you going to wait?"

"You are so impatient," she replied.

"Well the waiter is looking at us," I ventured, and then I added, "They are wondering why we are waiting to give them an order."

She gave me a scathing look.

"They are waiters; they are paid to wait," she said.

The waiter was obviously anxious for us to place an order and hovered even closer – but knowing Maureen's reputation for a quick retort, I mulled over what she had said, and sat in silence.

Thankfully, new customers arrived and as the café began to fill up the staff became too occupied to glare at us.

Another hour dragged by, eventually a sombre Maureen decided perhaps he would not be coming today. Seeing Maureen look so downcast was unusual. Reluctantly she opened the door to leave and I trailed out of the café behind her.

I was anxious now to go home and have a meal but agreed to accompany her home; it was a new experience witnessing Maureen lose her sparkle and I was surprised at her behaviour.

Sombrely, I thought: if this is what happens when people who fall in love, it does not seem much fun.

Her mother must also have thought her behaviour seemed odd, for when at last we reached Alfred Street, Little Mabel exclaimed, "I hope you have managed to cheer her up, she has been moping around all week wearing a long face."

Then she added, "I bet her football teams losing points; she is always on about that football club she supports."

Maureen remained silent; for, strange as it would seem to her mother, her beloved football team was the last thing occupying her mind.

Chapter 42

The pomp and glories celebrations on Coronation Day were over; it had been a spectacular ceremony and an occasion to remember forever.

As Rita anticipated, her mother had agreed for me to join Rita and other friends and neighbours, who were lucky to view the televised historic pageant.

Everyone gathered in the small sitting room at Rita's home and anxiously we waited to witness the historic scene. Huddled together as close as possible to the small black and white screen, we were riveted until the final moment of transmission. Rita and I agreed that we had been transported to London. Transfixed we stared at the small screen, watching with mounting excitement as the crowds gathered inside Westminster Abbey.

Afterwards we discussed in detail the spectacular service that had unfolded before us. Watching such pageantry reinforced our belief that England was best at putting on a fine show. We felt privileged to have witnessed the new Elizabethan age begin with style, and were thrilled to have joined the vast crowd and in this strange new way shared in the ancient coronation ceremony.

Shortly afterwards, Rita's mam and her friends wandered away to join an organized celebration held at the local public house.

Rita and I sat together for a while chatting; officially too old to join the children's street parties, we decided to venture outdoors to see and enjoy the spectacle. It was a novelty seeing brightly coloured bunting and flags draped around the street, and Bloomsgrove Street alive with colour.

The celebration finally over, the bunting and flags lingered on the street for a while, but inevitably they disappeared, unlike the memories they created. For what we had seen on Coronation day remained embossed in our minds; years later we recalled the bunting as brightly as the day we celebrated the crowning of our young Queen.

Maureen's visits to Bloomsgrove Street had become rare; she was no longer keen to visit the local dancehall. She continued hoping to catch the attention of the Adonis who worked at the Long Row music shop.

I decided to pay her a visit and on the way call to see Barbara. Reaching Boden Street, I walked down the entry and opened the gate. Gently then I knocked at the small back door.

Barbara's mother, a tall and well-built lady, was a skilled dressmaker. Usually the sound of her sewing machine could be heard, but today everything was silent. Getting no reply to my gentle tapping, I knocked on the door with more force. From inside I heard a familiar voice shout out, "Who is it, what do you want?"

It was the voice of Barbara's mother.

I was puzzled. Why didn't she answer the door or glance through the window as normal and instruct me enter?

Answering her question, I shouted: "Its Bernice, I have come to see Barbara."

Barbara's mother replied, "She is out."

Then she continued, "She will be home any minute."

I was puzzled. Why she failed to open the door and come nd speak to me?

Perhaps Barbara and her Mother are annoyed that I had not called or visited for a long time. Still Barbara, knew where I lived. With the door remaining firmly closed, and I began to walk away from the house.

I had reached the corner of Boden Street when I noticed in the distance a familiar figure: it was Barbara, walking towards me.

I was relieved when she gave me a friendly wave; as she drew closer, I began explaining that bumping into her was no mere coincidence, as I had called at her home and her Mother had shouted a message to me. Barbara sadly explained that her mother had failed to open the door as she was now unable safely to negotiate around the house. For since my last visit her mother's sight had dramatically deteriorated and she was almost blind. Barbara explained that the doctors' had said the reason was diabetes.

Tragically, now her mother was unable to continue dressmaking, and it was difficult for all the family. I was stunned, unaware that these bad tidings had befallen such a gentle family. I said goodbye, promising to visit again soon. Continuing walking towards Maureen's house, I felt stunned to think how misfortune can strike so unexpectedly.

Maureen answered the door; she was dressed in an attractive outfit and her glossy hair was shining brightly, attractively displaying its recently acquired deep auburn shade. She informed me that she was just on her way out and was planning to visit her friend and ex-neighbour Jean. I had not seen Jean for a long time, but was always interested in hearing news of her activities.

Maureen often spoke of Jean and her husband. In the past Jean had given up her nursing training, deciding that marriage and babies were the career she most desired. Therefore, Jean had married and had settled down to life in a different area of Radford.

"You can come with me if you want," Maureen said.

I pondered for a while, and then replied, "Will her husband mind?"

"Cause not," Maureen said. "He will probably be out and Jean loves visitors."

I had never met Jean's husband but felt reassured Jean would give me a warm welcome – she was always friendly.

Jean opened the door and welcomed us both in. Although she was dressed in a simple summer dress, as she stood in the doorway she looked elegant, tall and slim with her dark eyes sparkling. She welcomed me in with a warm friendly smile and I noted her even white teeth. What an attractive young wife. I hoped her husband realized what a loss to the nursing profession Jean would be.

The small room, immaculately kept, had many small touches – proving how Jean was utilizing her feminine homing skills. Soon we were sipping hot tea and munching on a biscuit. Jean began enquiring about Little Mabel and other members of Maureen' family, for Jean had a close bond and interest in them all.

Maureen filled her in on Arthur and Joan's progress then began to talk about Ronnie and Young Ken; Jean chuckled at the stories. Eventually the talk got around to Maureen's problems; Jean smiled at Maureen's admission that she was smitten by a young fellow she met at work. I realized Maureen valued Jean's opinion, and she sought Jean's advice about what she should to do. They huddled together whispering softly, and Maureen listened carefully to the advice given.

After some time Jean glanced at the clock, explaining she had a meal to prepare.

I stood up to leave; it had been a pleasant way to spend a few hours. Maureen lingered on but eventually stood up to go; as she did, the door suddenly opened. Standing there was a tall handsome man: Jean's husband.

He greeted Maureen with a grin.

"Hello, you look the part with that red hair, are you still burning boiled eggs?"

Maureen giggled. Jean joined us from the kitchen; she seemed to understand the private joke and smiled.

Her husband nodded towards me; although it was the first time we had met, he appeared somehow to know who I was.

It was soon obvious he was a charmer, and with great ease he was able to chat away. Jean smiled at the clever banter developing between her husband and Maureen. As I said farewell to Jean I knew I had experienced a different view on what it is like to be married. For growing up in a one parent family had made me feel curious as to what normal married relationships were all about. There were so many questions flooding into my mind. My parent's marriage and subsequent separation had always been a mystery to me. The subject was never been discussed at home and any snippets of information were heard from whispers of local gossips. Hearing how easily Maureen could discuss her personal life with Jean encouraged me to disclose my own increasing desire to find out more about my parents; I decided to broach the subject with Maureen, knowing that long ago her father mentioned that he knew my mother. Perhaps there was a possibility he may have disclosed more information about her to Maureen. So, as we walked slowly back to Alfred Street, I asked the question: "Does your dad ever mention seeing my mother at work?"

Maureen looked at me with a strange and puzzled look. Obviously, she was still concentrating on the confidential talk she had just had with Jean.

"Your mam?" She answered, and, giving me an exasperated look, continued, "I haven't got a clue what woman he meets at work, what's made you ask me that daft question?"

"Just wondered," I replied.

Maureen muttered to herself.

"I have enough problems myself, watching the bloody girls who work with me."

I nodded, realising I had chosen a bad time to ask her such a thought-provoking question. For Maureen, who usually listened to my endless questions and willingly gave advice, was now finding it difficult to concentrate on anything but securing a desired meeting with the elusive John, and was overwhelmed with her own personal problems.

Thankfully her fruitless café stalking was about to come to an end, for the very next time she persuaded me to accompany her on a mission to town she was lucky. I was relieved, for sitting for ages in corner cafes sipping coffee had become tiresome, and seemed pointless. Now at last I was able to view the person responsible for causing Maureen to be so constantly distracted.

We had wandered into town and headed towards another café on her list. A few customers were gathered there. When we entered I proceeded to sit in the seat closest to the door; it was the one I knew Maureen would select as it afforded the best view of everyone entering or leaving the room. To my surprise Maureen walked by it and headed straight towards another table. I watched then listened with interest as in a bright tone she exclaimed, "Hello John, fancy bumping into you, have you been anywhere exciting?"

The dark haired man looked up, and in a hushed voice gave a short reply. By now Maureen had sat down and joined him at the

John

table; oblivious to anything else she continued engaging him in conversation. I rather sheepishly sat alone at the table near the door, wondering how long it would be before she decided to join me. After some time passed, it seemed there was little chance she would drag herself away from John. I wandered over to attract her attention, but Maureen failed to glance up. However, the object of her desire noticed me and attempted to draw Maureen's attention to my presence.

Barely glancing in my direction, she stated, "Oh it's my pal Bernice."

Then briefly she introduced me by pointing in my direction. John looked directly at me and nodded his head. I continued standing there, feeling uneasy – for what was the correct thing to do in the situation, I wondered? Should I walk away or sit down uninvited at John's table?

Thankfully I didn't have long to ponder, for John suddenly stood up – and, giving me a brief smile, turned towards Maureen, informing her he had to go. He added that he had no doubt he would see her at work the next day. Maureen accompanied him to the door and watched wistfully as he strode away towards Slab Square. Rejoining me, she beckoned me to sit down; then, as we sipped our warm drink, she began recalling everything John had said to her. She was excited that she had finally introduced me to the icon she had spoken about so often, and pleased that I agreed that he was a handsome figure of a man.

Maureen seemed content that I approved of John, for unlike her work mates she realized I would never be a threat. For I knew that to compete against Maureen in a love race would be futile. For when Maureen put her mind into being the victor in a competition, she was determined to carry off the prize. This particular race especially was one she had her heart set on winning. For from the first moment she met John, she had firmly placed her foot on the starting block. There was no way anyone would stop her. John and her rivals at Farmers were in for a shock. For having inherited her mam's fighting spirit, Maureen would also, if necessary, take on Goliath – and the girls at the music store did not have the remotest chance of winning. For John, it seemed, was the most important trophy Maureen ever had set out to win.

Being her loyal supporter, I would stand at her side and willingly cheer her on. I was just happy and relieved my friend had been able to introduce me to the fellow she had chosen.

Chapter 43

As I grew up on Bloomsgrove Street, I sometimes pondered why the street had such a fanciful name. For having never witnessed flowers or blooms of any variety growing on the section of the street I was born, it seemed a strange choice of name. In truth the street was typical of many in Radford with its drab grey terrace houses, cobbled roads and dim lighting provided by old gaslights (the mesh cages protecting the flame casting strange shadows). The flickering light was barely adequate to aid safe navigation across the cobbled street, and the danger was heightened in wintertime (as it was then, if you entered narrow covered entryways leading towards small backyards, the darkness engulfed you). However, this darkness also enticed courting couples to hide there from prying eyes. One such entry was situated within yards of Grandmother's domain. This entry led the way to Pearl and our backyard.

My home was attached on the opposite side to a towering factory wall, the Harts Beer Bottling Factory. From early morning the rumbling of machines were heard; sometimes human error or dysfunctional machines caused breaking glass to be heard, followed shortly afterwards by the smell of spilt alcohol, the heady fumes polluting the area.

Being Sunday the factory today was still and quiet, and I crossed over the street and noticed hopscotch numbers clumsily chalked on the road. Standing by the kerb was Sandra, Pat's younger sister, excitedly playing with her friend Bubbles. Seeing the young children playing outdoors reminded me of all the Sundays I had spent when younger. For Grandmother disapproved of playing outdoor games on a Sunday. Mavis and I, dressed in our Sunday outfits, were expected to attend both church and Sunday school. Sometimes on a Sunday afternoon we visited one of our "Great Aunties", where we were expected to sit sedately with the adults and have afternoon tea.

Since starting work and paying my board things at home had altered; Grandmother did not supervise me as diligently, although she still expected Mavis and I to behave with decorum. When Grandmother heard that I had volunteered to read scripture stories at the Sunday school to the juniors she seemed delighted. Being interested in the younger group I was glad to be helping conduct the class; however it proved a more difficult task than I expected, as I soon discovered that youngsters' have a short attention span. One bright little girl constantly interrupted to ask questions; on one occasion she demanded an explanation of "How could Jesus feed a multitude with five loaves and two fishes?"

"Where did Jesus get the extra food?" she asked.

I feebly replied, "The food appeared and there was enough to feed everyone."

M y answer did not satisfy her and she persisted.

"Who gave Jesus the extra food"?

I again attempted to explain.

"It was a miracle."

She thought about my answer, and then shaking her head replied, "My mam said if you don't have coupons, you won't get extra rations. No extras are allowed without coupons, at any shop on Denman Street."

I replied again: "This was a miracle and it all happened far away."

The little girl, determined to prove her point, continued in her high-pitched voice.

"My mam told our butcher, my dad has been far away fighting as a sergeant in the army."

Without pausing for breath, she continued her saga.

"The butcher told mam, if your husband had been a flipping captain, it would still be, no coupons no extra rations."

The little girl paused, took a deep breath, and smugly continued the story.

"The butcher told her, even a blinking miracle will not get you any extra at my shop."

The little girl, having related her story, now triumphantly sat down.

Later that day I repeated the child's story to my father.

He roared with laughter, then replied, "Her mam's right, even a miracle wouldn't work if people try shopping without coupons on Denman Street, it's harder than walking on water and it doesn't matter how many stripes you have on your tunic, for old Winston himself would be refused."

Later I heard him repeat the story to Grandmother. She shook her head and reprimanded him, saying, "Our Cyril, you shouldn't be laughing about miracles, I thought you knew better"

Dad didn't attempt to reply; being a pacifist he would never willingly look for a fight, especially with his pious mother.

As I waited outside Rita's door Sandra and Bubbles continued hopping up and down. Sandra's health problems were improving and Bubbles seemed less troubled now by rowdy scenes at home. For since the incident with the wireless set, followed by her father's swift departure from the street, life at No. 18 appeared more orderly.

The new Elizabethan age was bringing many changes as people stepped in to a different world. Recently Pat and Sandra said a tearful goodbye to their young cousin, who sailed away to Australia with her parents. Others were also leaving Mother England, for with the war years behind them people had started looking for a new start. Donald and Trevor from No. 17 had settled in Canada; their friend David missed the two brothers but being a stoic young man he was also accustomed to sad goodbyes – when a young boy he had witnessed his family's distress when his two young sisters died. Now having left school, he was proudly earning wages. David when a boy had played dobby with me on the street; it seemed now that David had disappeared and been replaced by a serious and hard working young man.

Times it seems was changing us all. The earlier years spent in

Bloomsgrove Street were becoming past memories. As childhood slipped away, waiting in the future were fresh stories and adventures to record to memory.

Chapter 44

R ita opened the door and invited me inside. I noticed her mother stretched out on the sofa; due to her failing health she rested frequently now days. Her outlook on life however was as lively as ever, and she continued embracing new discoveries with glee. Always the first to be aware of new gadgets, she happily installed each modern device into her home. New style vacuum cleaners, electric irons and the latest inventions all found their way into her home. The item that attracted the most attention and delighted all neighbours invited to view the new television. It also proved a great comfort when Lottie, due to ill health, found herself compelled to spend long evenings at home.

Leaving her to rest Rita and I went upstairs; there she explained Aunty Ivy had been admitted to a local hospital and was receiving electric treatment. It sounded rather scary but Rita assured me it was helping her recover, and she was now well enough to receive visitors. It was later that day we decided to travel to Saint Ann's Psychiatric Hospital.

As the trolley bus approached Porchester Road I began feeling apprehensive; the last time I visited Aunty Ivy she had been reluctant to talk to me. We entered the building and slowly walked into Aunty Ivy's room. I felt relieved to see her smiling; she explained that the doctors had made plans to transfer her to long-term accommodation, for she was still unable to return to live with Rita's family.

Aunty Ivy, who had for so long assumed the role of Rita's adopted aunty, was a kind generous person until illness caused her personality to change. The dramatic incidents Rita and her family had endured resulted in life becoming increasingly difficult for everyone. Thankfully, Ivy seemed to respond well to medical intervention – but for now, she continued to need expert supervision.

Visiting the efficiently run clinic prompted me to think about my plans for the future; being keen to begin my nursing training I hoped Nottingham General Hospital would contact me soon. Next year I would reach the required age to begin training and I longed to don the coveted starched cap and apron. For now, I had to be content to be a junior office clerk working at a warehouse.

My being in the employment of Copstake and Crampton, I was allowed a discount on items I purchased there. I began buying numerous goods, including smart outfits. One friendly old neighbour who noticed me wearing my latest purchase had exclaimed with surprise, "My word Bernice you do look different. It seems like you are starting to grow up at last."

I also purchased my first pair of high-heeled shoes and found it could be enjoyable to wear more feminine outfits. When I staggered for the first time into the local green grocers wearing my high-heeled court shoes, the owner raised his eyebrows in surprise.

"Bernice," he said, "have you been eating everyone's share of mushrooms? You have sprung up overnight and look like a real young lady?"

Unfortunately my growing up was not without its problems, for I was plagued by unsightly teenage spots that, to my dismay, erupted all over my forehead. I wondered why no one had ever mentioned how difficult growing up was going to be. I spent hours looking in the mirror and swabbed my skin so often with TCP that I smelt like a hospital ward but nothing seemed to help. Desperate and hoping to disguise the disinfectant odour, I set about purchasing from Woolworth's stores bottles of California Poppy and copiously splashed myself with the cheap scent – but nothing could disguise the smell of TCP or cure the spots.

Rita, who escaped teenage skin problems, would happily dress up in her finery and was keen to spend every weekend at the Palaise de Dance. We would go together, for Maureen no longer joined us. I was becoming uneasy about attending that particular dancehall, for recently there had been a group of persistent older men creating problems. At first it seemed innocent banter, but I began feeling uneasy and out of my depth and when one man suggested developing a closer friendship and insisted on walking me home. I had foolishly accepted. Usually with any problems that developed Maureen would have ploughed in and offered me her support; now, she was busy sorting out her own worries. Fortunately she could still speak to John daily at work and slowly she was discovering his every like and dislike. She was so besotted she willingly changed her image, and seemed capable of going to any length to secure his attention. When John stated he had no interest or intentions of ever attending a dancehall, Maureen lost all interest in dancing. This decision to stop going to the dancehalls left Rita and I without Maureen's protection and heightened the dangers that now seemed to lurk in the dark corners. Maureen's anguish over unrequited love was causing everyone problems; it was becoming a painful experience for us all. I began to wonder if romance was worth the pain and seriously doubted my own romantic dreams would ever come true. For what did a mixed up girl like me – with my short curly hair, teenage spots and lack of charm – have to offer the man I had so often dreamt of? For if my dream man ever did make an appearance, I doubted he would be interested in me. Finding love for plain girls was never going to be easy – not when the road to romance was not all smooth sailing for even a glamorous girl like my sister (who despite her long blonde hair, even white teeth and dainty feminine figure had seemed unhappy with her own love life recently).

For Mavis was concerned that Grandmother would discover that her latest heartthrob was the son of the local bookmaker. Grandmother disapproved of drinking and gambling. She would have been horrified if she had discovered Mavis was associating with the son of a bookmaker, so Mavis had reason to be apprehensive. Ironically, broad-minded Granddad, who enjoyed a bet on the horses, knew the young man's father – so at least he would heartily approve of Mavis's choice of boyfriends. Grandmother however had different ideas about what she thought was right and frostily condemned the type of behaviour of "girls who carry on".

Moreover, Grandmother demonstrated her determination to prevent such action by forbidding her granddaughters "to behave like that".

One dark evening Grandmother spotted a courting couple stealthily creeping into a dark entry. Thinking it was one of us, without hesitation she ran into the entry and loudly began shouting, "Come out of there at once."

The startled couple emerged; to Grandmother's surprise, it was not a wayward granddaughter. For the person who hastily scuttled away was a young married local woman who, conducting an illicit affair, had thought she would be safe hiding in the entry. When I heard of Grandmother's error my first thoughts had been feelings of relief. For on this occasion, I knew I would not be the one blamed for Grandmother reaching for her smelling salts.

The worry Mavis endured conducting a secret relationship with her boyfriend passed, for their romance ended. Mavis did not give a reason as to why they had parted, but gradually it became clear that the bookmaker's son had stopped being important to her. I was left wondering if Grandmother had discovered her secret, but Mavis did not appear too distressed and moved on to find a new love. This was unlike Maureen, who was still hoping to gain John's undivided attention, despite the café ruse failing. Her only comfort was discovering that her competitors were just as unsuccessful.

Chapter 45

Maureen's keen interest in sport helped distract her. For the cricket season was in full flow, and the cricket ground became a regular place for Maureen to visit. It also provided another topic of conversation other than the lengthy discussions about John.

Maureen, being a dedicated lover of sport, attended as many cricket or football matches as possible and expressed surprise when I showed little interest.

However, I became a dedicated listener to the special sports stories Maureen related. For she revelled in shocking me with the secret spicy stories she heard.

These were unpublished news stories that involved the private activities of several first class sportsmen. Her uncanny ability of bypassing normal rules made it possible for her to obtain this information, having access as she did to off-limit areas of local sports grounds. There she overheard the latest gossip.

People grew puzzled over her ability to achieve what others found unachievable. At times she appeared to have the ability to walk where angels fear to tread and succeed in obtaining privileges that other mortals were denied. This left the disappointed high flyers gasping at her success, wondering how a backstreet Radford girl could bend every rule in the book yet manage still to be so successful. The truth was that Maureen from early childhood had never meekly accepted a rebuff or even a forceful "no". She continued as a young adult to maintain this attitude and did not have the slightest intention of changing. She demanded explanations, especially for anything she felt unjustly denied to her. Without fear of retribution, Maureen boldly in search of justice would approach the highest authority. Using her knowledge and powers of persuasion, she challenged anyone who stood in her way. Perhaps this tenacity was what made her victorious. She fought to enter VIP areas and became skilled at introducing herself to many top sports personalities; for Maureen this seemed a natural and simple feat.

Her success often created envy among other seasoned sports fans, and puzzled, they asked, "How does a young girl like Maureen manage to obtain a front row seat at such an important event?"

They never got a satisfactory answer, for Maureen was oblivious to their comments. Happily perched on the best viewing seat at a venue, having captured the attention of experienced journalists who gathered there, she loudly expressed opinions on players, rules and game to anyone sitting alongside her. She talked with the air of authority and ease usually heard spoken by people holding senior management positions. Her comments attracted attention, perhaps even amusing the experienced journalists who listened to Maureen's youthful views on sport, and felt her bold comments introduced a breath of fresh air.

I rarely visited the sports ground and found the whole business tiring. For playing gooseberry while Maureen held court was rather boring, and listening to her views on silly mid-ons was definitely not for me. However, the gossip she later related to me was far from boring, as spicy tales of certain players proved spellbinding. These stories, gleaned from seasoned sports reporters, were never destined to reach the printing press. For in the early 1950s reporting off-field saucy tales of sporting icons was not considered the right thing to do. Decorum was the word, journalists were still discreet – and yet Maureen still managed to access information never intended for the public.

It seemed plans for the coming bank holiday would centre on Maureen being at a sporting event.

I had no idea where my long weekend would be spent now my old Saturday night haunt held so little appeal; for all I knew, I might even be spending the time alone this coming holiday. For Dad was sure to be working. On duty, dressed in his special constable uniform, he would be out preserving peace and order on Nottingham Forest recreation ground.

Mavis also had something special planned, although I had no idea what it was as she declined to discuss her arrangements with me. For since her last confidential chat about her past boyfriend I had found myself demoted to the ranks of a troublesome younger sister. Perhaps she feared any secrets she disclosed would become a topic of discussion when Maureen and I chatted together. It was a possibility she could be right, for I discussed everything with Maureen – who had been highly amused when I related the story of Grandmother's error over the occupants of the entry.

Laughing hysterically, she said, "It's lucky it wasn't one of us standing in that entry."

Then she added, "Your Grandma would have chained you down for life if she had caught you hiding in there with a fellow, that's for sure."

I smiled more with relief than amusement, for I knew Maureen was referring to my recent frightening experience and her words prompted me to recall the disturbing memory of my naïve foolishness (for I had ventured into that very same entry – and the fright it had given me!). It was an experience I did not cherish and certainly an adventure I knew Dad would never approve of. For his disapproval really would have worried me, far more so than stepping over Grandmother's strict boundaries.

Maureen's lack of interest in spending her evenings dancing and my objection to visiting the Palaise de Dance was really restricting my usual Saturday evening's entertainment. When I explained my reason to Rita I was perplexed when she firmly informed me that she intended to attend the Palaise. Previously, venturing out alone was something Rita had never done. Now she seemed bolder and was demonstrating an iron determination – a trait she never before hinted she possessed. She made her intention clear: she was going to Palaise de Dance at the weekend even if she went alone. Her determination puzzled me and it was some time before the hidden reason was revealed.

Having confessed my fears to Maureen and the reasons I had decided to stop dancing at that venue, Maureen nodded in agreement and added, "Well I told you not to trust that group of smooth talking strangers, they all strut around thinking they are Hollywood stars."

Then she giggled and recalled her own memory of some time ago when, having assumed the impression of a female film star, boldly under the light of the lamppost she had childishly flirted with one of the foreign lodgers. This was something she was never to repeat for, although she had now left school, Grandmother had secretly still been keeping us both under constant surveillance, and without warning had sternly instructed Maureen: "It's about time you went home, Maureen."

Laughing together and discussing the adventures and good times we had shared must have reminded Maureen of what she had been missing the last few weeks – for to my surprise she suddenly stated, "I think I will go dancing on Friday night with you, where do you want to go?"

Hurriedly I replied, "Let's try the Victoria ballroom and hope that group of older men won't follow us there."

Relieved I had my bank holiday entertainment settled, I didn't realize that attempting to alter ones fate is an impossibility. I discovered that destiny comes equipped with its own compass, and can track you down however much you try to change its direction.

As it was still early in the evening, having decided on our plans we went to inform Rita of our decision. We crossed the street and knocked at her door. She soon joined us outside. It was still light and felt warm; the three of us began leaning against Rita's front windowsill and chatting like magpies. Rita informed us that a friend was to join her at the dancehall.

I briefly noticed a stranger walking up the street – a small, smartly dressed woman. As she passed by she appeared to stare with interest at my front door, then she glanced across the narrow street and looked in our direction. I did not recognize her but watched as she walked a few yards further along the street until she reached the door of No. 22. She knocked and the occupant quickly opened the door; the unknown women briefly glanced back and disappeared inside the house.

We continued to discuss our holiday weekend plans, with Rita remaining adamant she would not be joining us at the Victoria Ballroom.

It was now beginning to get dark and the sound of familiar voices were to be heard coming from the direction of the Peacock Inn. It was 10 pm and turning out time at the inn; the evening revellers sounded as if they had all had a good time and were laughing as they walked up the street together.

The first to come into sight was a local man, a friendly sort of chap who always had a bright word to say. He swayed slightly as he approached, then, getting closer, he stopped smiled broadly and exclaimed in his peculiar lilting accent, "Well now look at the three of you. The Blooms of Bloomo are blossoming at last."

We smiled at his comment, for in the past he often referred to young girls on the street as the Bloomsgrove Street Blooms, but *blossoming?* Now that was something different. Did it mean we finally were no longer buds and were fast reaching our full potential?

He waved and unsteadily continued on his way. More people were making their way home; it was a pleasant evening for a gentle stroll. Wandering behind him, I noticed Rita's mam, who decided to join us. Her friend Lily, who had accompanied her, bid us farewell and continued walking on.

Rita's mother seemed happy to stand and chat with us and asked if we had made plans for the weekend. Before we could reply, across the street the door of No. 22 opened. Rita's mother glanced across the street in that direction, and then appeared startled. The occupant of the house was standing waving goodbye to a well-dressed stranger. Her visitor, without looking back, proceeded to walk slowly down the opposite side of the street, gradually making her way towards Ilkeston Road.

Glancing across at the woman Rita's mam looked hesitant, then, holding up her hand, she feebly waved. The woman noticed and briefly nodded her head in response, then, without a backward glance, she quickened her step and turning round the corner, disappeared from view.

It was only then that Lottie blurted out, "Bernice, do you know who that was?"

Before I had time to utter no, to my astonishment she said, "It was your mother."

Maureen and Rita looked at me with surprise; they explained later that they had wondered how I would react to this unexpected announcement. Both were aware that I had become more intent and curious as time passed to know what my mother looked like, and I had expressed a desire to meet her. After glancing so briefly at my mother finding the answers to so many puzzling questions seemed more urgent. I had tried asking information from non-family members, but received little response.

Maureen had asked, "Is she how you imagined?"

I found it a difficult question, for despite my curiosity after all the years of wondering, it had been an anti-climax, one that filled me with an overwhelming feeling of disbelief.

For the person who I failed to recognize was, it seemed, a total stranger – one for whom I felt no affinity or bond.

In my dreams I experienced dramatic waves of loving closeness. I now felt disappointed by reality, for I had no feelings of belonging to this stranger. She had, it seemed, merely borne me. The emotional ties I always imagined would engulf me simply failed to materialize.

Chapter 46

I had arranged to call at Maureen's house. It was getting late and I still had wet hair; it was so curly the only way I knew to make it lie flat was dampen it. I picked up the brush and cursed; I had yet to discover the art of hairdressing skills and did not earn enough money to pay for professional advice. I glanced in the mirror, sighed, and muttered to myself, "No wonder your nickname is Fuzzy Wussy."

The house was quiet, for Mavis had gone out and Dad was not yet home from work. Uninterrupted I pulled out the new pink dress I recently purchased for fifteen shillings from C&A stores. As I inspected it I began feeling uneasy that an eager shop had assistant persuaded me to choose this garment. She had been a skilled sales girl, who fluttered and flattered me into buying the garment. Now it seemed a daring choice and I was unsure I had even picked the right colour, but it was too late to change my mind. I pulled the dress on and nervously glanced in the mirror. Staring back was a young girl dressed in pink shiny taffeta, the elasticized bodice of the dress clinging tightly to her bosom and large lace trimmed frill that barely covered her bare sloping shoulders.

I gulped and thought, well at least no one knows me at Victoria Ballroom, it's just as well I'm not going to the Palaise De Dance.

Glancing at the clock, I knew I had to hurry, for Maureen was never happy if kept waiting.

Arm in arm we hurried up Mitchell Street; on reaching Alfreton Road we noticed the trolley bus arriving. We climbed aboard; as the lower deck was full, we made our way up stairs. The heavy smell of tobacco smoke filled the air. Before sitting down Maureen leaned over and attempted to open up a window. Someone at the back of the bus shouted out, "Leave the bloody window closed, I don't want to sit in a draught."

Maureen ignored the passenger and continued to wind the window fully open.

Then, turning to the woman who had shouted her protest, she said, "And I don't want to smell your bloody Woodbines."

Satisfied she had won the battle she sat down and began to talk about sport.

We decided to alight from the trolley bus at the Victoria market, for we were curious to see if Rita's friend had turned as arranged. Neither of them appeared to be standing waiting in the queue of people outside the Palaise De Dance, so we continued walking towards Victoria Ballroom. Approaching the entrance hall and locating the ticket office, we paid the entrance fee and stepped inside. We could already hear the beat of the music; Maureen eagerly pushed the inner doors open and quickly we made our way upstairs, heading towards a small balcony. From there we had a view of the dance floor; it was smaller than the Palaise De Dance and felt less intimidating. The modest ballroom just increased my fear and foolishness in choosing to wear such a fancy dress.

We wandered across to the bar and purchased a soft drink. Then we carried them back to the table, continuing our chat as we viewed the dancers below and listened to the band.

One by one the chairs around us began to fill up. We glanced at the occupants to see if we recognized anyone, but they all appeared to be strangers.

"It looks as if you picked the right place to meet somebody different," Maureen commented.

I nodded in agreement, fully understanding her hidden meaning. For previously having confided my concerns and worries to her, she had urged me to follow her advice. "Be cautious who you trust."

Now she began reminding me of the scare I experienced by going in the entry. She hoped it would make me act with greater caution and never again believe smooth talking fellows who told fancy stories.

Trying to heed her warning, I vividly recalled her past advice: "Don't be eager to believe everything a bragger tells you and never tell them where you live, or your Grandmother will find out."

Now, beginning to feel apprehensive, I was pleased she had decided to come dancing with me.

The band began to play a song Maureen knew well and Maureen, could not resist the temptation to sing. In full throttle she began to give everyone a good imitation of the Andrew Sister's, by singing "I want to be loved by you and nobody else will do."

As she sang I thought, bet the only person she would like to sing that song to never frequents dancehalls.

Soon the song began producing its magical affect, listening to its rhythm and seeing the dancers happily swaying we were encouraged to join them and step on to the dance floor. Soon we were attempting to dance in the centre of the room, clumsily shuffling in time to the music.

The hall was beginning to fill up and people gathered around the edge of the room watching the dancers floating by. This venue was popular with folk who enjoyed listening to a decent band, and the group playing were well recognized as excellent musicians. Our dancing techniques improving, we began to relax; then suddenly the band changed the mode and began to play a complicated tango. It was at that point we both beat a hasty retreat from the dance floor. As we reached the outer area of the hall, I noticed a familiar face. I whispered to Maureen, "That man standing over there watching us, I have met him before at the Palaise."

Before I had chance to explain that he was a decent sort of man and not the one I wished to avoid, she grabbed my arm and attempted to steer me away, pushing me in a different direction. We had almost reached the edge of the crowd when a hand touched my shoulder. I spun around to see a dark haired stranger leaning towards me. In a deep voice he asked if I would dance with him.

I stared at him; for a brief moment I was unable to answer. For standing in front of me and politely waiting for my response was a Mario Lanzo look alike. Black hair, brown eyes, olive skin and a strongly accented voice – my dreams had all come true. Within a minute, I was in his arms waltzing around the dance floor. Already I had forgotten Maureen's advice to avoid older men with strange accents. For here in the flesh was the man I had been dreaming of meeting. As the romantic music ended, the dancers began to exit the floor. The dark haired stranger continued to hold my hand. He informed me the friend accompanying him had explained that he knew me and had spoken to me at the Palaise. I realised his friend was the man I recognized earlier. Politely he invited me to join them both for a drink; I wanted to accept his invitation but felt I must speak to Maureen first. She had been dancing but now was no longer in view. I grew concerned that she was in the overcrowded ballroom searching for me. Explaining my problem to my dancing partner and promising to return, I hurried away to find her. When I found her and explained I had accepted the offer of a drink from a handsome foreigner, she looked shocked and vigorously did her best to dissuade me.

"Bernice are you mad? You are defeating the object of coming to this dance hall, if you intend getting involved with another older foreign man."

We took so long discussing the issue that the Mario Lanzo look alike wandered across the room to seek me out. He asked me if I would like to dance with him again and without a backward look, I sailed into his arms. As he escorted me onto the dance floor, I glanced back and noticed Maureen watching me; she was not used to my ignoring her advice and appeared totally astonished at my behaviour. As we danced around the floor the stranger now introduced himself. His name was Eddie. He enquired, "Where in Nottingham do you live?"

I panicked, perhaps he wanted to escort me home.

When I failed to reply, he continued talking, this time to ask, "Would you like to see a film at the Odeon Picture House tomorrow evening?"

Once more I failed to reply, unsure of what answer to give. Undeterred by my silence, he informed me he would wait outside the picture house at five thirty the following day. When the music ended, we left the dance floor together. I noticed Maureen standing at the edge of the dance floor, glaring. Standing close by her was Eddie's friend. To my embarrassment and Eddie's amazement, as we approached Maureen began shouting in a loud voice, "Why don't you go away and find someone else to bother?"

Eddie just looked at Maureen in astonishment and then began to smile.

Maureen continued, "My friend doesn't want to get involved with you, so leave her alone and go away."

Eddie turned to me, expecting me perhaps to speak. Feeling nervous I remained silent, my cheeks now red as he stared at me. With a hint of laughter in his dark brown eyes, he slowly winked. His puzzled friend looked at Eddie, expecting some response to Maureen's angry outburst. Eddie remained silent. His friend slowly shook his head in disbelief and then made a hand gesture, beckoning Eddie to follow him.

Hesitating for a brief moment, Eddie smiled. Then, leaning forward, he stretched out his hand. Lifting up a strand of my curly hair, he leaned over until his mouth was almost touching my ear and whispered, "Baby, be outside the Odeon at five thirty tomorrow. I will be waiting for you, so don't be late."

Then he lightly kissed my ear.

Turning to Maureen, he said, "Make sure you both get a Taxi home, it's getting late."

Maureen glared at him as she said. "Catch a taxi? Who does he think we are bloody millionaires?"

I didn't answer; I was in a mad whirl trying to decide what I should do about tomorrow. Echoing in my mind were the words he had just whispered.

I didn't want to discuss it with Maureen or listen to her well-intended advice, for I was certain I knew what she would recommend. So, hugging the secret message he had gently whispered to me and recalling the romantic way he had kissed my ear, I decided not to talk to Maureen about it tonight. I would decide tomorrow what to do.

Anyway, after the blunt words Maureen had spoken to him, I doubted he would want to meet me again. I can't blame Maureen for saying those things; for, having heard me complain of smooth-talking older foreign men, I knew she was trying to protect me. However, the type of person I wanted protecting from were the kind who made sleazy suggestions and had wandering hands. Tonight I would agree I had met an older foreign man, but he was so different; the very man I had been dreaming of. He looked, sounded and acted like my film hero Mario.

Oh what a night it had been; the kiss he placed so lightly on my ear had been so exiting.

How romantic, I sighed; then suddenly my dream was interrupted by thoughts of how Grandmother would react. *Oh Grandma, if you could read my mind tonight and discover what I have just been thinking…*

With these sobering thoughts whirling around my head, I made my way towards the exit. As I approached the entrance to the cloakroom I caught a glimpse of the young girl reflected in the large mirror. I stared and held my breath, for more thoughts of Grandmother loomed up. Certain that if she could see my reflection she would say, "What do young girls like you expect will happen, if you brazenly flaunt yourself at dance halls? You ask for trouble, going out dressed in figure hugging pink taffeta dresses with loose fitting neckline."

For a brief moment, I felt Grandmother was right. Then a defiant inner voice replied, "Yes Grandmother, the dress I am wearing is rather daring – but if I hadn't been wearing this particular dress tonight, he may never have noticed me?"

Eddie – 1948

Chapter 47

ank holiday Saturday, I had been awake for hours. I could hear Dad bustling about downstairs, getting ready to go to work. I visualized him standing at the stone sink, holding his old shaving mug of soapy water. Slowly he would begin the laborious daily task of removing his whiskers.

I heard the sound of a refined voice reading the early morning weather forecast. Dad always listened to the wireless while he shaved.

Mavis, still fast asleep, was unaware of his morning activity. Dad continued performing his usual morning routine and soon was prepared to leave the house.

He turned the wireless off, then opened the stair door and shouted farewell to both of us. Mavis still did not stir as I heard the sound of the front door close; hurriedly I climbed out of bed and, bare-footed, pattered across the grey stone floor. I leaned out of the bedroom window and waved as Dad slung his canvas bag over his shoulder and, climbing on his bike, slowly peddled away. I stayed at the window, watching until he disappeared from sight.

It was then I turned my attention to inspecting the few items of summer clothing I owned. I was hoping among the modest collection to find something suitable to wear. I pulled aside the small curtain that hid the motley of clothes from view and peeped into the alcove. The first thing to catch my attention was the pink taffeta dress I had worn the previous evening. Now viewed hanging rather limply on a large nail, it did not seem to be half as daring.

I pushed the dress aside and proceeded to inspect the other

garments hanging on the nails I had recently hammered into the wall of my bedroom alcove.

I had never owned a wardrobe and necessity inspired me to devise this primitive way of keeping my clothes in order. Sometimes, rather grandly, I referred to the tiny alcove under the sloping bedroom ceiling as my dressing room.

Considering the meagre choice of items I possessed, making a simple decision on what to wear took me a long time. For every choice now seemed difficult and the more I pondered, the more anxious I became. Last night I tossed and turned before eventually deciding that I would go into town today; I was curious to see if Eddie would be waiting as promised. I'd also decided not to reveal my plans to Maureen, for I knew my decision would not meet with her approval. No, most definitely I would keep my plan secret. I reasoned that then, if the meeting was a disaster or if Eddie failed to arrive, I would be the only one to know how foolish I had been.

The morning seemed to drag by; I tried to keep busy, hoping that by avoiding Mavis I would escape searching questions. Later in the day, I feared she would notice my damp hair, and also question why I was splashing California Poppy perfume on my neck. I placed my bag and shiny shoes close by, then, sneaking upstairs, I silently prepared for the secret meeting.

Hearing no sound from downstairs and realising Mavis must have gone to Grandmother's house, I ran downstairs. Hurriedly pushing my feet into shiny new shoes, I left the house and scurried down the street as fast as my shoes would allow. I had great difficulty controlling my feet, for being a novice wearer of high heels the ungainly wobble I displayed was obvious. I continued negotiating the uneven pavements, and it was a relief to reach the No. 39 trolley bus stop without mishap.

I boarded the bus and in record time alighted at the large Co-op stores in town. Nervously I made my way towards Angel Row, heading closer and closer towards the Odeon Picture House. I glanced across at the Council House and noticed groups of people gathering around the big stone lions. Seeing folk standing in Slab Square was a common sight, for it was a popular venue to meet, especially for courting couples. Sometimes anxious people would wait in vain for partners who never arrived. When that happened the traditional Nottingham meeting spot must have seemed a big drawback – for by standing outside Council House multitudes of folk could view your dilemma. Thinking about the consequences of being in that situation, I gained comfort knowing the place Eddie suggested we meet, which allowed me the opportunity of hiding in a shop doorway. There I could remain unnoticed. The vantage point also gave me chance to watch others approach. I am starting to doubt that I would recognize Eddie. For perhaps I only imaged he looked like Mario, for the subdued lights of a dancehall was not the perfect environment to clearly view a stranger. I doubted now he would resemble the handsome man that last night I imaged him to be.

Staying hidden in the doorway, I leaned forward to view people. They were beginning to arrive and join the queue outside the picture house. I knew the Odeon Picture House well, but this was the first time I had hid in their doorway. My memories of the Odeon were of my frequent Wednesday evening visits.

For accompanied by Dad, Mavis and Rita, I would line up to see the latest film. My only worry then was hoping I enjoyed the film. This experience was far more stressful and as the clock on the Council House began to chime, I became more agitated. I was in a dilemma, uncertain if I would feel happy or disappointed if the stranger named Eddie kept his promise to meet me. As the minutes ticked by doubts crept in: Would he come? Maybe Maureen was right: I was a fool, and it had been a silly thing to do.

What did I know about dating or sitting with an unknown escort in the dark at a picture house? Perhaps I never would know, for the appointed time had passed. Despite his whispered promise, Eddie had not arrived. At that point I felt relieved that I had kept the proposed meeting a secret. I did not have to explain the situation to anyone. Thank goodness I was not one of the people standing by the stone lions; at least my humiliation was hidden from public view.

Ten minutes passed before finally, I plucked up the courage to step out of the doorway and walk past the group of expectant picture fans lined up near the ticket office. Hoping they hadn't been aware I had been hiding in a doorway, I walked across the pavement to cross the road, intending to reach my bus stop as quickly as my high heels allowed. At first, I failed to notice the dark haired man approaching. He was wearing sunglasses, his dark hair shining and smoothly styled, dressed in a cream colour lightweight suit and sporting a wide black and gold striped tie. On his feet he wore a pair of short black socks and the *piece de resistance* – a pair of red and cream leather shoes. He resembled someone from a Hollywood musical.

I was amazed when this unusually dressed apparition waved to me and shouted, "Hello."

I jumped at the sound of his voice, reacting as a startled rabbit caught in a bright light. I did not know which way to run. For to my astonishment it was Eddie, the stranger I met the previous evening. Before I had chance to recover from the shock of his arriving and my viewing his shoes, he had firmly grabbed my arm and directed me towards the entrance door of the Odeon; then, continuing to grip my arm, he ushered me towards the ticket office. With a flourish, he paid the entrance fee; the usherette then checked our tickets and opened the door. Now guided through the entrance into the large semi-darkened picture house I was encouraged on towards two vacant seats; reaching them my escort beckoned me to sit down. The Pathe Pictorial News was already showing and straightaway Eddie seemed engrossed in the film. Settled in my seat I had a moment to compose my thoughts and gained comfort that, in the semi darkness of the picture house, it would be difficult for anyone to witness my escort's outlandish clothing. I reasoned with luck that when the film ended it would almost be dark outside and perhaps he would not be spotted. His flamboyant appearance had come as a total shock. For the previous evening, he appeared to be dressed in a conventional way. Now I began to wonder what other shocks he would spring on me. The main film had begun and once more, my escort seemed engrossed in the screen. I sat by his side feeling self-conscious; I desperately attempted to concentrate on the film but felt unusually light headed. I was being overpowered by a heavy scented smell: it surrounded me. Having believed only ladies dabbed lavender water or Californian Poppy on their skin, I was now aware the man sitting besides me smelt fragrant;

this was a new experience. I was to discover in time the pleasant odour was in fact Brilliantine, a hair cream some men chose to use.

The atmosphere inside the crowded building was beginning to feel uncomfortably warm. For the auditorium in the picture house was fully occupied and the temperature was rising. The heat feeling rather oppressive, I anxiously waited for the intermission to arrive, being too embarrassed to stand up while the film was in progress and remove my jacket.

It was at that point, to my horror, that Eddie leaned towards me. He gently stroked my arm and with his large strong hands reached out and gently squeezed my damp sweaty fingers. Shortly afterwards the film ended, and during the interval usherettes appeared carrying large trays.

People now stood up, anxiously moving forwards to buy ice cream. Without a word my escort also stood up and quickly strode towards the queue. Before long, he was back sitting besides me and now I realized he was attempting to hand me three large ice creams. As he did, he said. "You feel very warm baby, these will help I think."

I attempted to take just one packet, but ignoring my feeble protests, he insisted I accept the whole gift.

However, by the time I had unwrapped and eaten one ice cream the other two ices were melting and began dribbling blobs of milky liquid onto the floor. It was a great relief when the lights eventually dimmed and in the darkness, I could lean down and place the soggy packages on the floor under the seat. Eddie noticing my hands were free of ice cream packages spoke to me softly.

"You must feel cooler now."

Then, to my dismay, he grasped hold of my cooler but now ice-cream sticky hands.

I later learned that unlike most people I had ever encountered, Eddie never gave one gift if he could give two and frequently he overwhelmed people with his generosity, especially if the gift he offered was food. For he seemed to have a compulsion to feed anyone he cared for.

The film ended and as the lights in the room came on, the audience respectfully stood to attention as the National Anthem played. The performance had ended on time and as the crowd made their way towards the foyer, I slowly followed them. Outside it was already getting dark. I was unsure of what now to expect.

Eddie signalled me to cross the road and as we walked together towards Long Row he asked if I had enjoyed the film. I nodded, he seemed pleased but the truth was I had barely watched it; remembering the sticky ice cream mess I had left behind, I felt rather ashamed.

As we walked along together, he suddenly asked, "Do you know how to swim?"

Although puzzled by the unexpected question, it did not stop me from giving him a prompt reply.

"Yes, I learnt to swim at the local swimming baths."

He then questioned me further.

"Do you have a swimming dress?"

I smiled at his question, he must mean a swimming costume; His accent puzzled me, he sounded so different. Having proudly informed me already that he came from Poland, he had a strange way of speaking, for although his Slavic accent was evident he drawled out many American style words. When I felt confident enough to question him about it, I discovered he had improved his earlier limited knowledge of English by watching Hollywood films and thus developed an unusual Americanized–Slavic version of speaking the English language.

He now asked another question that puzzled me.

"Where is Papplewick?"

I was unsure of the location and began wondering why he asked. He explained that a friend had told him that at Papplewick there was a nice outdoor Lido, and he wanted me to join him there for a swim. He instructed me to bring a towel and swimming clothes and meet him at the local bus station the following day.

I had no time to gather my thoughts, for by then we had walked past Griffins and Spaldings department stores and reached Parliament Street; I assumed he was escorting me to the trolley bus stop and from there I could go home, but with just yards to go suddenly he stepped into the road and flagged down a taxi. As soon as the vehicle came to

249

a halt, he opened the door and ushered me inside. I was shocked to be sitting side by side with him on the back seat of the taxicab. I heard the driver ask, "Where to?"

"Where do you live," said Eddie.

I was stunned and could barely stammer, "Bloomsgrove Street on Ilkeston Road."

The taxi flew on its way.

I had never been in a taxi before and certainly had never expected to be in one tonight, accompanied by a stranger and heading towards Bloomsgrove Street.

My mind was in a turmoil; I had better be quick and find some way of stopping the vehicle before I was spotted by Dad, or worse still seen by Grandma.

Within minutes we were speeding down Ilkeston road, and somehow I found the nerve loudly to say, "We have to go that way."

The driver seemed puzzled at the change of direction, especially when I demanded he stop on Denman Street.

With a flourish, Eddie paid the driver. We climbed out of the cab and I watched as it sped away.

"Which house do you live in?" said my escort.

I failed to reply to his question, and instead began uttering, "I have to go home now. It's getting late, and Dad will be waiting for me."

He didn't question me further, but reminded me he would meet me the following day at the bus station and not to forget my swimming outfit.

I mumbled. "Thanks for the ice cream."

He smiled and said, "I will buy you another one tomorrow."

Then anxious to get home unnoticed, without a moments hesitation I hurried around the corner. Then I slipped off my high heels, held them tightly to my chest and ran away, going as swift as the wind, so fast that I doubted that on that night even Maureen would have managed to catch me.

Chapter 48

I lay in bed listening as Mavis and Dad talked together downstairs in the kitchen. When I arrived home last night Mavis was absent; it was an hour later before she returned. Dad had been sitting alone eating his supper when I arrived; he was sitting in his large wooden armchair listening to the wireless. He was not at all surprised to see me stumbling barefooted into the kitchen; because I was breathing heavily, he appeared to assume I had spent the evening with Maureen, and smilingly he asked, "Did she win again?"

Without verbally replying, I simply turned away and shook my head.

Dad, accustomed to Maureen's competitive spirit, knew of her unbroken record of champion runner – and I had long ago accepted that my defeating Maureen in a race was merely a pipe dream.

I accepted the cocoa he offered and picking up the cup said, "I'm off to bed Dad good night"

Carrying the welcome drink, I hurried up the steep narrow stairs.

Once inside my bedroom I quickly undressed, thankful to creep into the sanctuary of my bed. For now I could recall the unusual evening I had just spent and the new experiences I had discovered.

I reminisced on what had happened for it occurred to me I now had another decision to make. If Eddie assumed I would join him visiting Papplewick lido, what would he do if I failed to meet him? Would he try seeking me out and pay a visit to Bloomsgrove Street?

What a dilemma! I was in a quandary and uncertain what to do.

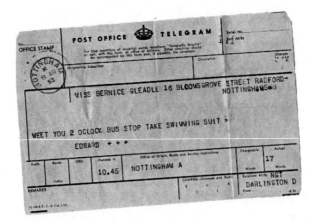

POST OFFICE TELEGRAM

OFFICE STAMP

MISS BERNICE GLEADLE 16 BLOOMSGROVE STREET RADFORD-
NOTTINGHAM=3

MEET YOU 2 OCLOCK BUS STOP TAKE SWIMMING SUIT =
EDWARD + + +

10.45   NOTTINGHAM A   17

                                    NGT
                              DARLINGTON D

Did I want to see him again or not?

Feeling confused by my own question I hesitated as I weighed up the pros and cons of the evening.

His mode of dress had been outlandish and holding my hand had been unexpected. But he seemed kind, and, apart from arriving slightly late, I had no reason to mistrust him or fear him. My greatest fear was of someone seeing me alone in his company.

I smiled, recalling the incident of the melting ice creams, imagining how Maureen would giggle if she knew of the saga. I would miss not being able to discuss my dilemma with Maureen and Rita, and wished now I had told them of my plans. For they would understand the reason I panicked at the thought of being seen in a taxis with a stranger, and the fear of being reprimanded that had prompted me to divert the puzzled taxi driver away from Bloomsgrove Street.

Rita especially would recall, as I did, a vividly imprinted memory of a few years previously, when in youthful innocence Rita and I foolishly accepted a lift from a couple of strangers. The scary event culminated in both of us hidden in the back of a vehicle being driven through the streets of Radford at break neck speed. The night it happened caused uproar, as both Dad and Rita's mother, concerned for our safety, had been out scanning the streets looking for us. Prior to accepting that lift home we were very unaware of the danger that unwittingly we had placed ourselves in. Afterwards when Dad listened to my explanation of how the situation he calmly advised me, "I hope you have more sense in the future."

Moreover, he never mentioned the incident again.

Our parents never knew the full extent of our folly for we never told them. If we had, they may not have viewed the incident so lightly.

It all started out as a fun night. Rita's mother invited us to join her and several adults at a function at the Astoria Ballroom. Both Rita and I were excited for we had never before attended such an event. Rita's mother escorted us to the ballroom and instructed us to stay close by her. As the evening wore on and the grown ups relaxed enjoying their drinks the restrictions placed on our movements were lifted, and we were informed we were permitted to join the younger folk gathered on the dance floor.

"Enjoy yourself," they merrily shouted to us and added, "You will only be young once."

Needed no further encouragement, we wandered off and were soon approached by a group of older teenagers who beckoned us to join them. They explained they were students at a local college. We listened in fascination to their stories, and impressed by their zany behaviour time passed quickly. The function almost ending, they casually asked where we lived. When we replied they offered us a lift home, explaining they lived in student lodgings at Mansfield Road and reassuring us that it would be no trouble to drive us to Ilkeston Road. At that time being a passenger in a car was a novelty and enjoying their company we were eager to prolong the experience. Hurrying to the bar where the adults were gathered, Rita sought out her mother to ask permission. Lottie seemed distracted, busily occupied with talking to her friends, and as we attempted to explain that our new young friends were offering us a lift she smiled, nodded and waved her hand. Rita and I left, assuming she had given us permission.

Without a moments hesitation we hurried out of the doors of the Astoria Ballroom.

Parked directly outside the dancehall was a battered old van. We scrambled in the back seat, the male students sitting in the front seat, and we roared away. We passed Woolworth's Stores travelling at break neck speed heading in the direction of Derby Road, the driver urged by his friend to go even faster. We sped on, heading towards Barnabus Cathedral. To our surprise the driver suddenly changed direction; we now found ourselves heading towards the direction of the Arboretum. Rita and I now shouted out in unison, "You're going the wrong way."

The driver ignored us as he continued to drive as if possessed. Eventually, his friend gave the reason for the change of directions.

"It won't take long; we have to just nip in to our lodgings."

The driver now interrupted, and continued explaining, "We promised the landlady this morning we would feed the cat and we forgot, she will go berserk if she finds out, We must put its dish out before she gets back. You will still reach home before your mother arrives."

Naively Rita and I accepted their explanation and happily continued sitting in the back of the van as it sped on towards Mansfield Road. The driver pulled into the driveway of a large house situated opposite a major cemetery. I knew this area, it was adjacent to the Forest Recreation ground where Dad worked. I had never seen the cemetery at night, it looked so eerie with the tall white gravestones and marble statues viewed in the darkness and reminded me of a horror film.

The youths jumped out the van and urged us to come inside while they fed the poor hungry cat. Glancing across the road and noting the spooky tombstones, we were glad to follow them inside the building. As soon as we stepped inside the impressive hallway they closed the door and beckoned us enter a large downstairs room. Once we entered the room, it was obvious it must house several people, for it was overflowing with furniture – a massive wardrobe and desk, a table and chairs and in the far corner of the room several unmade camp beds. The room had an air of total chaos: clothes, books and articles scattered around, everything in fact but a starving cat!

Invited now to sit down but concerned it was getting late, we meekly suggested we needed to go home. To our surprise, the room lights suddenly switched off. Plunged into darkness Rita and I began protesting we had to go home. Through the grubby lace curtained window, aided by flickering streetlights, it seemed strange shadows were moving among the grave stones. The long road that passed by the cemetery was visible. Knowing it led directly towards Alfreton Road and Bloomsgrove Street , I contemplated running home. However, having to enter the spooky lit road at night stopped me suggesting it. At that point, the two young students really began to alarm us, now acting like octopus-armed gropers. Rita and I responded by raising our voices and loudly begging to be taken home. The two young students, looking agitated, began to realise they could soon be in trouble. For having picked up a couple of silly immature girls, they realized they had no idea how to deal with the situation. Suddenly the lights came back on. Without any further explanation, they ushered us at great haste out of the house and into the back of the old van. The driver and his friend climbed in, and slamming the gears into place the driver took off with a roar, passing the cemetery as if Jacob Marley's ghost was chasing him. He drove across Alfreton Road and sped on down Mitchell Street. Approaching Bloomsgrove Street, we could see a small group of people gathered there; leaning forward in our seats Rita and I screeched out in our high-pitched immature voices.

"There's me mam," said Rita.

"There's me dad," I added.

The young driver, hearing us shout out, reacted like a person possessed and drove even faster. The small crowd to their astonishment found themselves having to jump swiftly out of the path of the speeding vehicle. The offending motor flew by them and unknown to our parents hidden in the back were the two members of their family they anxiously were seeking.

The erratically driven van eventually reached the bottom of our street and disappeared around the corner onto Ilkeston Road. Once out of sight of the crowd, the driver urged us to get out quickly. Without a backward glance, he drove away. Left to walk the few yards home we appeared, as if by magic from around the corner. Entering Bloomsgrove Street the little crowd spotted us. Their relief was obvious, and they began to inform us that they had been contemplating notifying the local bobby of our abduction! Neither Rita nor I ever confessed we had been stupid to enter a house with strangers. Nor did we reveal the tale of the poor neglected cat!

Recalling the incident and anxious to speak to someone of my latest adventure, I decided to speak to Rita the next morning. I was confident I could rely on her discretion about my decision on whether I should visit Papplewick lido.

The following day I ran across the street but to my disappointment she was not at home. Feeling unsettled at her absence and needed advice, I noticed that Pearl's door was open and decided to make my way there. I could see Pearl standing near the open door holding her baby daughter Yvonne; her other daughter Lucia was toddling around the overcrowded room, holding a hairbrush. Pearl noticed me and smiled.

"Hello stranger," she said.

Pearls remark was not intended to be unkind, however I did feel guilty. For since I'd begun working at Copestake and Crampton I hadn't visited Pearl very often. Glancing at Lucia I was surprised how quickly she seemed to have grown. Chubby, curly haired Lucia stretched out her arms and I bent down and picked her up; Lucia giggled and Pearl, smiling, said, "Do me a favour Bernice and brush her hair, she won't let me get near it."

I nodded and needed no further explanation. I had seen Pearl struggle many times, getting Lucia to sit still and have her thick blonde curls brushed. Now with Pearl having two children to cope with and Fulvio working as many hours as possible, it was becoming difficult for her to manage two young children in the tiny overcrowded room. It was a stressful situation as the living area was barely large enough to swing a cat. Pearl had somehow managed to fit in a double bed, pram cots and numerous other items. Pearl looked tired as I sat Lucia down on my knee. As I began to brush her hair and sing a familiar nursery rhyme, I untangled the obliging child's blonde hair. Lucia, a bright little child, laughed and joined in the songs chorus: "Mary had a little lamb."

Pearl sighed with relief as she watched me brush the tangled curls with ease.

"She lets you do her hair without any fuss, and it never takes you long."

I didn't reply, for my knowledge of performing this task had been learnt the painful way; I had untangled my own wild unruly curls since being young and I suppose I had now become an expert at sorting out impossible tresses.

A shadow fell across the doorway and I looked up; it was Fulvio.

In his strong Italian accent, he said, "Hello Bernice."

I watched as he patted the baby on her cheek, then reaching over he ruffled Lucia's recently brushed curls. Lucia jumped off my knee and lifting up her chubby arms, her Papa swiftly swung her up. Pearl and the children were thrilled he had arrived home early; he explained it was bank holiday so the job had finished early. Pearl and Fulvio began explaining that the house they dreamed of owning was soon to be theirs. I was fascinated by the fact that Pearl and Fulvio would soon be the owner of a house situated on the Grove. The couple excitedly described to me a place that sounded like a palace; it was a wild dream about to come true, for the young couple soon would vacate this small front room and go to live in a large three storey property. Despite the gossip when young Pearl married in such haste, their union was a great success. Noting the kindness and concern Fulvio showed for the welfare of his wife and children, it occurred to me that I could do worse than confide than Pearl, who, despite the mountain of prejudice she had suffered, seemed so happy. I was confident she would help me come to the decision of deciding if it was wise to have another secret meeting with the foreign, older man called Eddie.

Eddie with his comrades in Italy – 1945/46

Eddie, far right, preparing to sail to Britain – 1946

Ron Booth far right in Trent Bridge, Nottingham – 1949

Eddie on patrol 1946

Chapter 49

As I approached the bus depot, I could see Eddie waiting at the bus stop. Unlike the previous evening, he was now appropriately dressed. Firmly clutching my bag – one that earlier I packed with a towel, swimming costume and brush – I slowly began to walk towards him.

He looked up smiled and asked me, "Have you bought your swimming dress?"

I nodded, pointing to my bulging cloth bag, and wondered if Eddie had enquired which bus would transport us to Papplewick lido.

It relaxed when the bus conductor reassured Eddie the bus stopped directly by the lido. We climbed on board and made our way towards the rear seat. Never visiting Papplewick before, I felt curious about the direction the bus would travel. As it made its way out of the city centre and began heading towards Bestwood, I realised once it passed that point that I was venturing into unfamiliar territory. It was pleasant watching the landscape become greener and by the time we reached the outskirts of the city I began to feel more relaxed about being in Eddie's company, for we had begun to chat and exchange information about ourselves.

I discovered Eddie with other soldiers had arrived in England in 1947 on the converted Mauritania, a luxury liner adjusted to transport large numbers of military personal. The vessel had docked at Liverpool and on arrival orders had been given for the troops to disembark. Eddie had boarded the crowded ship in Italy, where he had been enlisted as a dispatch rider with a Polish unit. He seemed surprised I had so little knowledge of war time military units, until I explained that when war was declared in 1939 I was a mere toddler.

It was at that point he looked worried and, questioning the age gap that existed between the two of us, nervously asked, "How old are you?"

I confidently answered, "I'm already sixteen."

Sounding startled, he replied, "You are so young."

Then, as if it provoked disturbing memories, he sadly began to explain, "Before I reached sixteen, due to the invasion of Poland I lost contact with my family and have no chance to find them."

Then silent and lost in his own thoughts, he began staring blankly out of the bus window.

Once the bus arrived at Papplewick lido, he took hold of my arm and guided me towards the entrance gate of the pool.

It was a lovely day and the lido was alive with activity. Eddie soon demonstrated what an excellent swimmer he was and cheering up he began chatting once more. The sun shone brightly as we swam together and it was fun being in his company. Spreading out our towels, we sat at the side of the pool lazing under a blue sky. Talking for hours on many topics, I relaxed; it felt we had known each other forever. As promised, Eddie purchased copious amounts of ice cream and the time flew by. Eventually we realized it was getting late and that, although we were reluctant to leave, it was time to go.

During the journey home, Eddie asked, "Has it been fun being with me? I will take you swimming again if you are happy."

I blushed as I replied, "Yes, it is a nice lido."

With a laugh, teasingly he said, "More fun than going dancing with your friend?"

I hesitated to reply, just blushed a deeper shade.

Eddie smiled.

"Perhaps your friend is your bodyguard, do you think you need one?"

I shook my head as I replied, "I didn't have one today."

"But you did baby," he said.

Then gently, as he began stroking my hair with his strong large hand and speaking in his unusual hybrid accent, Eddie stated, "You were safe today, for I was guarding you."

That evening as I sat alone at home, I recalled the words he had spoken and began to think of Maureen. She was unaware I had agreed to meet this older foreign man and she would be baffled by my actions. For Eddie appeared to fit the description of the type of man I had firmly stated I wished to avoid.

Maureen would be shocked that her efforts to deter me in contacting him had failed. I had avoided informing her that he had accompanied me to the pictures – and now there I was, at the lido with him. What would she say when she discovered that I had also agreed to meet him next week? Or what if Grandmother discovered? Would she consider the outings as "going out courting"? It was a familiar phrase she used that had always perplexed me. For never had I understood how she defined courting. My head was in a whirl; my heart was racing – and everything that was happening was a brand new experience. Never before had a stranger escorted me to the pictures and generously treated me to ice cream. Or tenderly held my hand and laughed and talked to me with such ease as we walked openly down the street together. These were enjoyable moments and the sort of outings I didn't fear. For Eddie's actions did not appear secretive or sinister – unlike a previous unnerving experience when an arranged secret meeting had been the object.

I felt safe in Eddie's company and the only worry that could cloud my future horizon was the concern that Eddie might decide one day to meet me wearing those dreadful red and white shoes.

I hesitated for a few days before contacting Maureen, but eventually decided I had better confess I had been seeing Eddie. Prepared for her to lecture me on my stupidity, I was to be surprised at her reaction. For Maureen simply listened to me, and then speaking in a serious tone said, "Well I hope you realize if your Grandma finds out about these outings, you will be in big trouble."

I could not dispute her statement.

Maureen paused a moment, then firmly continued, "I hope you're not going to be daft enough to go wandering up a dark entry with this one."

I did not reply – it was good advice she was giving. For Maureen was aware that going into an entry was the reason I had been wary of meeting unscrupulous older foreign men.

Maureen, having issued her advice, now changed the subject and began talking about her own dilemma.

It seemed when she was at work she was able to speak to John daily, although their friendship had not moved forwards any further. She expressed annoyance regards the tough battle her besotted rivals at Farmer's were creating. For Maureen, keen to secure a date with John, despite her best efforts had not convinced her competitors to back away. I was surprised she was having these problems, for Maureen had never before found it difficult to ward off a threatening opponent. It seemed this competition was the hardest battle Maureen had ever faced. I was anxious for everyone's sake Maureen would win. For it was painfully obvious that she did not intend to give up fighting. Some weeks later, to my relief I learned John and Maureen had visited the local picture house together. Her competitors had finally admitted defeat and Maureen, having secured her first official outing with John, rejoiced; it had been the toughest battle of her life.

My friendship with Eddie was now more established. I was reluctant for him to venture near Bloomsgrove Street and had never mentioned his existence at home, but then one day Mavis informed me that she was aware I was seeing an older man and I had better inform Dad.

I decided that evening to explain to Dad. That was the weekend he was on duty; I decided to visit the Forest Park and bring my new friend to introduce to him. Dad, without asking any questions, simply nodded that it would be OK. When eventually Eddie met Dad, he was surprised to receive an invitation to visit Bloomsgrove Street and speak at length to Dad. Shortly afterwards my Polish friend became a regular visitor and could often be found sitting in our untidy old kitchen relaxing with Dad, who soon introduced Eddie to the delights of drinking mugs of steaming hot condensed milk tea. They would sit together for hours, appearing to enjoy each others company as they discussed world affairs.

Grandmother would have noted a stranger was now regularly

visiting our home but she made no comment to me. Mavis suggested that Dad might have asked Grandmother to co-operate on the subject.

Little Rita soon found it necessary to reveal her well-kept secret. The disclosure came as a big surprise to everyone when she announced she had an older boyfriend! It also explained the reason she had been so keen to continue attending the Palaise De Dance Ballroom. For months she had been developing a friendship with a Slavic man. In the beginning, he had only been her dance partner. Being an older foreign stranger he had been apprehensive about their large age gap, and had delayed asking her for a date. Paul it seemed was the same person who months before had teased Maureen by saying he was an Eskimo. In truth, he had originated from a country called the Ukraine. Hearing this information had both Maureen and I scurrying to find an atlas to discover more about this unheard of country. We discovered the winter in Ukraine could be extremely cold, with deep ice and snow. However, unlike the Eskimos, the Ukrainian people had never lived in igloos or eaten candles. Paul's beloved homeland was in fact closer to Poland than Siberia.

Rita who had been working from the age of fifteen was beginning to mature in her outlook to life, but with her hormones reluctant to spring into action, she continued to appear very young. This was the reason Paul felt uneasy. To Rita's delight eventually they became firm friends, and it was then she introduced him to her very suspicious parents.

Friends and close neighbours watched events unfolding, and saw that the homegrown buds of Bloomsgrove Street were beginning to undergo dramatic metamorphic changes. Comments were now being expressed of how quickly since the war ended everything swiftly had changed . For in spite of the young being raised in deprived harsh war time conditions, these backstreet children had developed into strong-willed individuals and, like determined sunflowers pushing forward to seek stimulating light, changes were being instigated. These buds of Bloomo stepped boldly over all the difficult obstacles and speedily reached ever upwards, the sky seeming to be their final destination.

Pearl and Fulvio were the first to show us the way; soon others were encouraged to follow their example. All it required was the conviction and courage to attempt something new. One by one this young new generation were altering the habits of a lifetime, casting the old ways aside and attempting to achieve their individual ambitious dreams and goals.

Chapter 50

Maureen had plans to visit the hairdresser and persuaded me to do the same. For me it was a rare visit, for having curly hair I never had the need for a perm or the inclination to spend time and money at hair saloons. However, Maureen, who suddenly had begun to take a real interest in her appearance, had attended this small hairdressing establishment several times before. Having booked herself another appointment at the Boden Street saloon, she encouraged me to do the same. I planned to meet her and on arriving at Alfred Street I walked down the entry that led into the overcrowded communal backyard. Knowing Little Mabel had become increasingly deaf I knocked loudly on her back door; I could hear her shouting out to enter so I walked straight into the small kitchen. Immediately I noticed a large collection of badly damaged tin cans stacked on the table, Little Mabel was admiring them as if they were the crown jewels. Peering at me through her thick lens spectacles, she exclaimed, "Look at these; I got the whole lot at the market for two bob."

I stared at the buckled tins as she had instructed, surveying her bargain collection. Set out on the old table were tins of vivid green processed peas, cans of fruit and a couple of small tins of spam. In pride of place on top of the pile was a tin of red salmon. Many of the labels were torn and the tins dented, but to Little Mabel it was a proverbial treasure trove. Picking up a tin of fruit, she urged me closely examine its battered label.

"Look at that," she exclaimed with delight. "I bet I can make three

266

fruit pies from one of these tins."

Trying to look suitably impressed I nodded my head in agreement, although I didn't have a clue how much fruit was needed to fill a pie, for sadly I lacked experience in cooking and had never made any type of pie.

The door suddenly opened and in marched Maureen. Before she had chance to speak, Little Mabel attracted her daughter's attention by waving her hands over her treasure trove; then, selecting a tin of peas, she thrust it towards Maureen, and with great enthusiasm loudly exclaimed, "Look, I got the bloody lot at the market for two bob."

Maureen glanced at the stack of peas; then, mockingly touching her nose, she simulated pinching her nostrils together as she loudly exclaimed, "Well if our Ron turns up on Sunday for his dinner, you better not put too many peas on his plate."

I smiled at Maureen's earthy actions, for accurately she had demonstrated how Ron's digestive system might react to eating a large portion of the small green vegetables.

Little Mabel turned to me.

"Did you know our Maureen's fellow is coming on Sunday for dinner?"

I nodded; Maureen had already excitedly told me John was to pay a visit. I could only hazard a guess of how he would react to eventually meeting the Booths! To me they all possessed a peculiar sense of humour and were great fun to be with, especially when they gathered as a family together. For then the repartee between them was both witty and loud. The irony was that the one who quoted the funniest lines and spoke words that usually resulted in uncontrollably roars of laughter from the rest of the gathered group was Little Mabel. Unperturbed but completely baffled at everyone falling about in mirth, she could never understand why everyone laughed so heartily. For the comments she made were not usually intended by her to be humorous. She told one classic story that became a family favourite; it was a typical example of her side-aching but unintentionally funny humour. For listening to her describe how she had persuaded a mean old market stallholder into reducing the price of a pair of rubber boots always promoted great laughter. For although the boots had been too big for Little Mabel, she felt triumphant each time she put them on. Whenever she repeated the story of her bargain buy it promoted hoots of laughter – for despite the boots being several times larger than she needed, Little Mabel celebrated securing a great victory over a mean old skinflint.

"That taught the bloody miser a lesson."

Despite having difficulty walking in the boots, she wore them with pride.

The family's sense of fun did not meet with everyone's approval, so it would be interesting to discover how John reacted when he met this enthusiastic family of jokers. For if his experience of sharing a meal with the Booth family was at all similar to when I first met the family en masse and listened amazed to their banter, then John would not forget the meeting in a hurry.

Maureen glanced at the clock and realizing it was getting late for our appointment she urged me to hurry. I entered the hairdressing saloon and was handed a garment resembling a large apron. As I perched myself on a seat, I stared at the old sepia pictures hanging on display, studying them nervously. I hoped the hairdresser didn't expect me to choose any of the hairstyles the models on the photographs were demonstrating. It seemed they all resembled old photographs of Marlene Dietrich in the 1930s. After chatting to the hairdresser, Maureen decided to have a henna rinse applied, and I watched with interest as they applied the red colour tint. Her hair now almost dry was glowing with colour and it suited her. Having been persuaded to have my hair lightened I became alarmed at the dreadful smell coming from the solution being applied. The hairdresser assured me the foul odour would disappear as it dried out. I looked at my reflection in the mirror; that cannot be me, I thought! For I lacked my mop of unruly mousy tight curls and the image I saw seemed really odd. A transformed me stared back from the mirror. I gulped at my short wavy blonde colour hair, knowing it was going to take some time to accept the new person who once was me.

Thankfully, as the hairdresser promised the smell of the peroxide rinse had completely disappeared by the time I met Eddie.

We had plans to go dancing to the Astoria dance hall, a place favoured by American service men. Although they visited in smaller numbers these days, the ones who continued to visit Nottingham were sometimes seen teaching the local girls to jive. Eddie and I entered the hall and made our way upstairs to the balcony; from a good vantage point we were able to observe everything happening on the dance floor.

The band began playing; people began crowding onto the floor. The music got louder and the dancers became wilder, making frantic and jerky movements.

Eddie and I had no desire to join them; instead, we attempted to chat and enjoyed our cool drinks. Eddie did not appear to have noticed my new hairstyle and I wondered if I should mention it. Before I had chance, he leaned forward, staring at me; he then said, "I have never noticed your ears before, why don't you wear earrings, do you own any?"

I was surprised he had noticed my ears and not my peroxide hair, then realized my sleeker hairstyle exposed my ears and now they were more prominently on view. I explained to Eddie the reason my ears were naked.

"I did once buy myself a pair of clip on earrings from the market," I said.

He listened to my explanation, while he continued to study and touch my ear lobes.

I kept talking.

"They pinched my ears so tightly I had to stop wearing them."

Eddie leaning closer to inspect my ears, then he said, "In Poland all the young girls have holes pierced in their ears; their mothers do it with a red hot needle."

Then inadvertently having reminded himself of his past memories of Polish mothers, he became sad and for a moment aimlessly stared at the dancers. He had not noticed how I had shuddered in horror at the thought of having ones ears pieced with a red-hot needle.

I was rather grateful the gory conversation had ended.

The band began to play a slow and gentle tune. Eddie and I,

having finished our drinks, made our way downstairs and headed towards the dance floor. Holding me tightly in his arms, we began slowly to waltz around the dance floor and as he pulled me closer towards his chest, he gentle lifted up a strand of my hair. Oh, I thought he has noticed my hair at last, and I wondered if he liked the style. Romantically bending his head down, he began to gentle nibble the lobe of my ear as softly he whispered.

"Tomorrow I can get a hot needle and will punch a hole in your ears, for I don't think your dad would know how to do it."

I didn't bother to answer; the very thought of having a hole bored in my ears made me feel faint, so I just waltzed on.

The following day Eddie had arranged to meet me in town. He wanted to see a western film showing at the Odeon and suggested meeting me on Parliament Street. He was waiting for me when I alighted from the trolleybus. I glanced at his feet; thank goodness, he had taken my advice and bought conventional footwear, the red and white leather shoes had now been stored away. He took my arm and hurried me along, not stopping until we reached the Theatre Royal. I began wondering if he had changed his mind and intended to visit the News Palace Picture House, for now we seemed to be heading in that direction.

To my surprise, he stopped outside an expensive jeweller shop and began to peer in through the open door. I knew Eddie was keen on wristwatches and I waited patiently as he earnestly concentrated on reading a small notice board. Without saying anything he entered the shop and approached the man standing behind the counter; the man pointed towards a display cabinet that appeared to hold a display of expensive golden items. Being Saturday the shop was busy and several customers were milling around admiring the fancy goods on display. Eddie seemed occupied studying the goods in the display cabinet so I wandered off towards the opposite side of the shop to view a selection of gold charms. Suddenly I became aware the shop assistant was attempting to catch somebody's attention; he raised his hand to beckon but no one came forward. Eventually he said, "Madam, would you come this way into the inner room?"

I glanced around; no one seemed to be taking any notice. Eddie, who was now standing near to the shop counter, was happily smiling.

The shop assistant stepped forward and in a louder voice spoke again.

"Young lady, would you follow me, the ear piercing equipment is kept in the inner office."

For a brief second I wondered, who was this young lady brave enough to submit to the ordeal of a red hot needle?. Then to my horror I realised he meant me.

Too shocked to protest, I found myself hurriedly ushered through to the inner room. To my relief there were no signs of anything resembling burning coals. A competent jeweller, smiling benevolently, speedily began to display how talented he was, for in the speed of light he thrust me into a chair, tilted back my head produced an instrument, grabbed my earlobes, pierced them, inserted earrings and helped me out of the chair. In a state of shock, I now realized I was wearing an expensive pair of golden earrings and standing outside the exclusive city shop. Eddie, now proudly smiling, held my arm as he guided me towards the Odeon Picture House.

Once in the front stalls, by the flickering light of the film I glanced at Eddie now sitting beside me, his eyes rigidly glued on the light-hearted western film. He was engrossed in watching the action. I contemplated how different he was from anyone I had met before. He was sometimes melancholy and unpredictable, yet kind and generous. Although he was far older than I was, sometimes he displayed this childlike capacity to totally immerse himself in a make-believe film world. Perhaps this trait was due to a childhood savagely having been disturbed. The horrors he experienced had made strong brave men quiver, and still affected him. I was young, yet I realized that while he was engrossed in a film, for a few short hours it seemed a blessed release for him. For having entered the world of make believe, where the good guys seemed to win, the realities of his troubles were for a while pushed aside. For many of his fellow compatriots had suffered, and he had also lost so much.

The film was about to end and as the cowboys galloped off into the sunset, Eddie took hold of my hand, squeezed it and, glancing at my golden earrings, asked if they felt OK. I nodded my reply.

"I will get you an ice cream soon."

As the lights in the auditorium came on my imagination began running wild. I wondered what other surprises might arise in the future and realized only time could answer that question.

My ear lobes were now tingling and I was feeling rather delicate . But I hesitated to complain, for his childlike enthusiasm in giving me this surprise gift made me smile. However I thanked my lucky stars he had realized that in Nottingham experts are available to perform the delicate art of ear piercing, and thankfully he hadn't needed to find a darning needle and heat it until it glowed red. I shuddered at the thought and began to feel rather queasy.

The usherette had arrived with the ice cream tray and Eddie, as predicted, made his way towards the queue. Realising how insistent he could be getting me to eat and the impossibility of refusing his ever generous offers of food, I sighed. He had dashed off happily towards the ice cream trolley and the best outcome I could hope for was that he would return with just one chocolate-coated ice cream.

Chapter 51

Rita admired my earrings and when she explained to Paul that Eddie had offered to pierce my ears with a hot needle, Paul had chuckled with glee and exclaimed, "I will be happy to do the same for you Rita."

Looking slightly pale, she declined his offer and it was several years later before she plucked up the courage have her ears professionally pierced.

Mavis looked astonished, seeing the transformation taking place. As her curly haired tomboy sister had now began to dress in sophisticated clothes and sport expensive golden earrings. The frizzy curls had gone, to be replaced by a sleek hairstyle that gleamed several shades lighter. My new image and appearance was causing rather a stir. Maureen was also taking extra pride in her appearance. Happily she was now dating John on a regular basis. It seemed that in the last few months so many changes had occurred; even Grandmother seemed to have reconsidered her position, and she no longer objected to Maureen visiting Bloomsgrove Street.

Finding ourselves untroubled by anything or anyone, Maureen and I were free to gossip for hours. We exchanged news and discussed how dramatic changes were beginning to alter our lifestyles. Although I was romantically involved with Eddie, I was also hoping to begin nursing training at the Nottingham's General Hospital, for my interest in caring for young babies had never wavered and I eventually hoped to become qualified and professionally trained in the care of babies and young children. I continued to baby-sit the neighbours' children, and to my joy the latest new arrivals at No. 17 were a delight. Katrina their mother it seemed was so busy raising them, and grateful when I offered to take her older son out to play on the local park. As her twins became older, she allowed me to help with her two baby boys and I was delighted to become involved. For since Pearl and her family left the street, I missed fussing over her two little girls, who, having vacated No. 18 Bloomsgrove Street, had made it seem a rather sad and empty place.

Having Katrina needing me was a comfort and I became involved, watching how she would snugly wrap her baby boys up and place them outdoors in their large coach built twin pram. To my delight, one day she gave me permission to take them for a stroll.

Eagerly I set off pushing the heavy pram and headed towards Radford Park. Making good progress on the downhill journey I approached the gates. I noted several people glancing with curiosity as I drew closer, then peep with interest into the depths of the tall twin pram at the two small bundles. I felt proud that their mother had trusted me to care for these two precious infants.

I paraded the pram around the park a couple of times before eventually sitting myself down on a bench opposite the seesaw. From there I watched a group of children energetically urging the playground apparatus to go higher and faster. Eventually they became bored and allowed the seesaw to gradually slow to a halt. Two daring individuals clambered up the tall iron support bar and gymnastically began to swing their feet up in the air. Hooking their legs over the bar in imitation of trapeze artists, they loosened their grip; dramatically· now they began hanging head down, suspended from a great height. Dangerously starting to swing back and forth, the urge to shout a warning overwhelmed me, for I now realised what a dangerous thing it was to do. I gulped, recalling how just a short time ago I myself often performed this dangerous feat: I vividly recalled the frustration of having grown ups interfere with my fun, so despite my being aware that childish pranks on playground gymnastics can be a risky past-time I restrained the urge to shout out. My past experience was telling me the children would return to their activity with renewed vigour once I had left. I turned away with mixed emotions, wondering if becoming mature meant that I was in danger of loosing my childhood spontaneity and spirit of adventure. For somehow we appear to lose our courage as we grow older. Perhaps a young child's failure to recognize danger is in fact Mother Nature's way of helping them discover fresh ways of conquering difficult tasks, teaching each generations ways to push ahead and discover how to conquer old restrictive barriers.

By stepping into a grown up world I had started to realise why anxious grandmothers attempt to curtail foolish young girls. For I had started to think that perhaps grandmothers were justified in worrying. For silly young girls do take such unnecessary risks. Oh well – in time more answers may be revealed, but for now it seems there are still moments I resent being restrained, even if it is done with the best intentions.

I reached the edge of the park and with the twins happily enjoying the ride I decided to continue my stroll. No plans were organised for me to see Eddie that day, but I had the urge to speak to him. I knew the location of his lodging house; it was just a short walk from the park, so I decided to walk up the hill in that direction. By the time I approached the house at Lenton, I was feeling the strain of pushing a heavy pram. Happily, the babies snugly tucked up were fast asleep.

I checked the house number and approached the door.

Tightly holding on to the pram handle I rang the doorbell. A sturdy built woman wearing a headscarf answered the door. She looked at me in astonishment and in an accented voice attempted to ask what I wanted.

"I want to speak to Eddie," I said.

She stared at me, and noted the pram that held two small babies; she looked shocked and turned away and in a strong Slavic accent called urgently to some one inside the house. A man appeared at the door and sternly looked at me and in a heavy accent curtly said, "Vot do you vont?"

"I have come to speak to Eddie," I meekly said.

He appeared to be translating my request to the woman, who began to glare at me.

Then abruptly the man spoke again.

"Vye do you vont him?"

Now feeling unwelcome, I wondered if the lodgers who lived here where not permitted visitors.

The woman had disappeared and the man silently still stood guarding the doorway. I began inwardly debating if I should walk away. Then, suddenly, I became aware I could hear Eddie' voice, he was rapidly talking to the woman. To my relief the door suddenly flew open and Eddie appeared. The man and woman both continued to sternly gaze at me, then curiously they observed Eddie greet me with a smile. Leaning forward he looked in the pram at the two little occupants. Turning towards the couple Eddie began to laugh. They looked bewildered until speaking in Polish he began to explain and reassure them he was not responsible for these two tiny infants; furthermore these babies were not mine – I was just minding them to give their mother a rest.

Eddie then translated their concern to me and I blushed, for I understood then why the couple had been shocked and unfriendly to a young girl who had unannounced turned up at their door with a large pram, containing not one but two little bundles of joy. Of course, they had feared the worst.

Politely, the couple – smiling now with relief – watched as I walked away; they waved goodbye to Eddie who, having offered to help me push the heavy pram back up the steep hill, had grasped the handle of the pram in his hand. With apparent ease he sped up the hill on his way to Ilkeston Road.

On the journey, we talked and laughed as we made our way towards Ilkeston Road. Eddie discussed how funny it was, the couple making such a mistake.

"Imagine thinking you were their mother," Eddie said and then added. "You're too young to be their mother."

I enlightened him, explaining it was not so impossible. For Pearl, whom he had met, was in fact a young mother and still in her teens. Eddie reacted with genuine surprise hearing the information, for he admired what Pearl and Fulvio had achieved and assumed them to be a much older couple. Perhaps on reflection he realized that although I was far younger than he was our friendship could happily continue;

at least, on the following day he introduced me to Stanley, his friend (who was the local Polish barber). Stanley was a married man, his wife a Nottingham girl. Having two young children as well as a husband to care for, Dorothy always seemed busy; she also had extra duties assisting Stanley with the maintenance of his barbers shop. Eddie in time introduced me to another friend Adam, an educated, distinguished gentleman. Before the war, Adam had been a Polish government representative, now he worked on a production line in a factory. Sadly, due to the political situation existing in Poland, his wife and children had to remain in Poland; he constantly worried about their survival.

Meeting Eddie had been an ongoing education, for gradually I was learning so much about the wider world. There had been few opportunities in the past of meeting strangers and the streets that surrounded my home had once been my whole world. Now listening to stories of events that occurred in places far away, an inexperienced girl from Radford soaked up this newfound knowledge. Maureen and I now had long discussions on aspects of things I had heard. After I related one harrowing story of an event occurring in war time Poland, it prompted Maureen to raise once more the subject of the mystery surrounding her maternal grandmother. For she was anxious to investigate the background of her grandmother; Jewish heritage intrigued her.

John, now recognized as Maureen's official boyfriend, also joined in our discussions. Being a widely read man he helped widen Maureen's and my own interest on many subjects. Willingly providing interesting facts and information, he proved a compelling teller of stories.

Having our view of life expanded, we looked through a wider window and developed a better understanding of world affairs.

Maureen continued her involvement with her sporting interests and keenly followed her beloved Forest football team. However, the patrons at Trent Bridge cricket ground did not see her as often.

Rita, happy and content with Paul as her companion, was gradually introduced to his friends. She continued working at Clay's drapery stores and was becoming a more confident young woman.

Mavis no longer missed Clive the bookmaker's son and seemed to be enjoying her social life to the full.

Therefore, with the year 1953 drawing to an end, 1954 seemed full of promise. The only thing continuing to cause me anxiety remained my long unanswered old question. Perhaps that particular puzzle was unsolvable, but somehow my friendship with Eddie lightened the burden. How our friendship eventually would evolve was one question I avoided thinking deeply about, for looming up on the horizon was the prospect of me going to live in the nurse's home. Perhaps when that happened Eddie would want to move on, for recently he explained he felt restless – as having no family created strong urges for him to begin searching new pastures. Anxiously I pondered if his troubled background would forever compel him to search for something he could never find. There were so many questions in his mind and heart haunting him. Strange as it seemed I understood his anguish – for, despite the difference in our age, religion, culture, education and life experiences, Eddie and I were in tune with each other more than anyone could realize. For we both were troubled and searching for answers.

Eddie, unable to return to his beloved Poland, had enquired about moving to Canada, where many of his compatriots had gone to start building a new life. My own plans – although I would be moving just a few miles away from Bloomsgrove Street – involved making changes; for me it would be a giant step, committing to living in a nurse's home. The coming months it seemed were about to bring great changes for both Eddie and me.

Chapter 52

It was hard to believe Christmas was almost here, for the year had passed by so quickly. Now as the weather became colder Eddie and I were grateful to spend our leisure time sitting around a well-stocked fire at Rita's house. Eddie and I, given an open invitation by Rita's mother to visit No. 15 Bloomsgrove, still found it a novelty to be able to watch television. We knew we were always welcome, especially when Lottie was aware that Rita and her boyfriend Paul were going to be there together. Lottie had now accepted her daughter and Paul had become an item, but still felt happier when they were chaperoned. Outings that previously Rita and I enjoyed together now included Paul and Eddie.

Rita was determined to continue courting Paul, and her mother no longer attempted to keep them apart – instead she concentrated her efforts on securing her own peace of mind by inviting Eddie and I into her home. Then, reassured all was well, Lottie would sally forth to meet her friends at the local public house, while two pairs of courting couples obediently watched a variety concert.

Pearl and Fulvio meanwhile with their two young children were settling down happily in their new home. Having made such a supreme effort to achieve what once seemed an impossible dream, they deserved all they had.

Proudly they had sent invitations to their friends to join them in celebrating New Year's Eve at their home on The Grove.

Eddie and I were delighted to accept and excited at the prospect of seeing New Year in with our friends. Paul, Rita and Maureen and John

1951 Herbert, Vivienne and Maria

Yvonne and Pearl, 1954

Bernice the baby minder

With Vivienne at Radford Rec

Left: With Lucia outside Harts Factory – 1954
Right: With baby Slawko, Woodville Place – 1951

Paul, Rita, Bernice and Eddie – 1954

Eddie and Mavis 1954

Bernice, Stan and Dorothy Slivinski,
with baby Robert

had been invited, and everyone was hoping he would accept. Being optimistic, Maureen explained that John was interested in classical opera and as recently he had studied the Italian language, it seemed an ideal opportunity for him to practice conversing with Fulvio in Italian.

It impressed and astonished me to hear so many different languages spoken, it was surprising to hear and observe the ease they switched back and forth conversing in so many tongues. I now regretted not trying harder for I had once had the opportunity of studying French. Eddie, Paul and Fulvio all made learning to speak other languages seem so easy. It was difficult for me to comprehend just how they had acquired their knowledge, knowing as I did especially how Eddie's education had so abruptly been halted due to the outbreak of war.

I had smiled when Eddie explained how his command of the English language had been improved by his frequent viewing of American films. A thought had then prompted me to ask him, "Did you also improve your knowledge of the Italian language by watching Italian films?"

Eddie roared with laughter at my question; then, leaning towards me, he extended his index finger and in his teasing way and said, "Did I watch Italian films – of course I did!"

Then puffing out his chest, he began assuming the exaggerated stance of a pompous opera singer and started to serenade me. After singing a couple of booming notes of my favourite song, he grinned widely and said, "Who knows? Perhaps I was given a part in that film by Mario Lanza's you admire so much and worked as his stand in man."

Sheepishly I smiled, for I now realized that perhaps informing Eddie of how much he reminded me of handsome Mario hadn't been such a wise move. For frequently Eddie teased me by doing Mario Lanzo impressions.

Christmas soon passed and as usual Dad had been busy working. Mavis was also away visiting friends. Grandmother and Granddad together sat in their sparsely decorated, holly-strewn home and although I was welcome to join them I didn't. Instead I spent the day wondering if Eddie would turn up on my doorstep. He had been rather surprised at the lack of celebration plans at my home, especially on Christmas Eve, but did not make any further comment. I later discovered Eddie had not spent his Christmas alone as I had, but shared the occasion with other homesick fellow compatriots. He celebrated Christmas mass at Saint Barnabus Cathedral, and then gathered later with a group of other men who also missed their Polish homeland. Joining them at the local forces club, they sang their own traditional carols and reminisced about past snowy Christmas times they had spent with their families back home.

With the end of December now fast approaching and it having been fated seventeen years before for my birth to occur at a date between Christmas Day and New Year, it was time once more for my Birthday. This was never a big event, however, as with many other celebrations taking place around that time, it tended to be rather a forgotten date. Still this year my birthday could be rather different, for I was hoping Eddie would send me a card. It was also drawing close to marking an important milestone, for I would soon be old enough to commence nursing training. Since getting to know Eddie, the prospect of living away from home was beginning to cause me some concern. For pre-nursing rules firmly stated that, because nursing was a dedicated profession, during your training courting was frowned on and getting married was simply not permitted if you wished to complete your nursing course. This rule had not bothered me at all when first I heard it. For courtship and marriage was then something I had never contemplated.

Giving up the idea of training at the general hospital or meeting the man of my dreams had then seemed impossible. Since I was young, I had planned a nursing career. Grandmother's suspicions of Eddie and his presence in my life she made obvious. She expressed so many worries about our friendship. Eddie, being older than I was, concerned her; then there was his being foreign and from a different background and culture. Last but far from least, she felt concerned Eddie did not attend her chosen church. For Grandmother had strict Victorian attitudes, especially concerning any behaviour deemed unacceptable by one particular person (whose opinion appeared vitally important for Grandmother's well-being).

I imagined Granddad saying to me,

"Don't let Mrs Farquarson find out you are courting, or Grandma will ban your boy friend from visiting Bloomsgrove Street."

Now with Eddie frequently visiting my home, I hoped Dad would speak to Grandmother on my behalf and deal with any problems that arose, but it still worried me. I knew Dad was a fair man and judged a man only on his merit. And it appeared he encouraged Eddie to visit our home, I hoped that he approved of the situation. For he seemed to be getting to know my handsome boyfriend particularly well. Dad was continuing to have long friendly chats with Eddie. As for Grandmother's silence, that seemed to indicate how much she disapproved of our relationship.

Still, other events in the family were now occupying Grandmother's attention. For recently Pat her oldest grandchild and her husband Mike had announced they were expecting a baby. Moreover, Godfrey her only grandson, who Grandmother held in high esteem, was expected soon to obtain a place at the local grammar school. Everyone hoped the arrival of the baby would not usurp him. There seemed no reason however, for the concern, for when the curly haired baby arrived, Godfrey was as besotted by baby Nina as we all were. Eventually we also celebrated Godfrey getting a place at High Pavement Grammar School.

I continued to see Eddie, especially at weekends. When escorted me home Dad would be waiting in the kitchen to welcome us. The kettle would be on the hob boiling, soon out would come the old teapot. Dad would produce a packet of biscuits; then, sitting back in his armchair, he would begin a lengthy discussion with Eddie, who also relished these chats.

It seemed the two men in my life both enjoyed sitting down and talking together for hours. Eventually as the clocked ticked by, if I felt tired, I would bid them both goodnight and depart upstairs to bed, leaving them downstairs still talking. Eddie often did not leave the house until early morning. He then headed back to the lodging house he shared with other Polish men. Both Dad and Eddie were secure in the knowledge I was safe in my bed and fast asleep.

It was following one of these late night discussions with Dad that

Eddie bluntly asked me, "Where is your mother living? Why did she leave home?"

I looked at him, wondering why he suddenly had asked. Briefly, I attempted to explain the situation, informing him I had few memories of my mother.

He appeared baffled, especially as he questioned why a mother would walk away and leave behind two young daughters to be reared by their father. For having formed a friendship with my mild mannered father, Eddie was anxious to seek out a logical answer. I was unable to help, for I had no answers to give. The snippets I had gathered as a child were chance remarks made by gossiping neighbours. These comments now bothered me more frequently and Eddie's questions prompted me to spill out hidden worries I had been suppressing for years.

Eddie listened to me relate the stories of how my unexpected arrival had caused gossip, and how there had been speculation of my pedigree. I had grown up wondering about it myself. Yet I was afraid to mention my concern to anyone in the family, so how would I ever find out the truth?

What a dilemma I was in – for not only was my mother a stranger to me, but maybe my biological father was also.

Eddie listened to me then voiced his opinion.

"It doesn't seem to make any sense," he said. When I nodded in agreement, he continued, "Why would a mother abandon a child in those circumstances. And if the rumour is true, why had your father agreed to nurture a cuckoo in his nest?"

Perhaps it was only malicious gossip, though what reason would anyone have for making up such a story?

Eddie obviously was feeling upset, as he did not want to discuss the matter further. I was surprised at the depth of emotion he was displaying.

Later I began to realise that his own father had died when Eddie was just an infant, and he now welcomed and appreciated the relationship he had with my father. The companionship and warmth was something he seemed to value. Carrying as he did the burden and horrors war had created, the harsh memories often engulfed him.

Having formed a close relationship with my easygoing father, maybe he wanted to hold on to the stability my father's calmness provided.

New Years Eve at last arrived and as Eddie and I walked slowly up Ilkeston Road towards Pearl and Fulvios house, we chatted. I began to describe how frequently in the past I had raced up this stretch of road, desperate to be the first to reach the school gate. As a young child I had often glanced across at the large impressive houses that stood opposite the school and tried to imagine what it would feel like to be rich enough to live inside such a *mansion*. It was impossible then to ever believe that one day Pearl and Fulvio would be the owner of such an impressive property. My childhood friend, Pearl, had shared many difficult experiences with me. With her living now in a Grove mansion, it was such a wonderful achievement.

The invitation to visit her home to celebrate New Year seemed incredible. And as I got closer to Pearl and Fulvio's impressive home, it struck me hard work and ambition really could help make some dreams come true...

We were welcomed at the door by Fulvio, who in typical continental way kissed us warmly on each cheek. He explained that Pearl was busy settling the children into bed, and invited us to follow him and inspect the lower floor of the property. On entering the home, I was stunned. Never before had I seen such large rooms in a private dwelling or witnessed such ornate high ceilings. We inspected an enormous sitting room, then a large dining room, a breakfast room and large kitchen followed by a pantry. The storage area appeared large enough to hold enough food for a year. As we walked around the wide corridor of the house, our footsteps echoed everywhere, for the house lacked adequate furniture or floor coverings and the size of the rooms emphasized each sound. The small amount of furniture owned by its new owners would have fitted into the pantry; the starkness of the rooms emphasized the size of the house. It seemed of little importance, for Pearl and Fulvio were young and would have plenty of time to fill these empty spaces. Over the next few years, showing great determination, they managed to achieve just that.

Soon all the guests had gathered in the sitting room and Fulvio began inviting his guests to eat and drink. Handed a tall glass, my host invited me to taste the sweet Italian wine. I had never tasted alcohol; Grandmother had always forbidden alcohol in the home. So strongly had she felt about us not drinking any alcohol that as young children Grandmother had taken Mavis and me to a tea total meeting. Bewildered we had listened as speakers told us vivid tales of all the evils awaiting anyone who touched a drop of alcohol. Everyone present urged us into signing a pledge and swearing to abstain from consuming evil drink.

Having signed the pledge and always kept the vow, I put the glass down and whispered to Maureen, "I am not going to drink this."

Maureen brightly answered, "Why not, it's nice. It tastes just like pop."

I glanced at the contents of the glass; it had bubbles like pop and did not look anything like the pints of beer I had seen local men drinking.

Eddie was busy talking and I nudged him gently,

"Fulvio has just given me this drink, do you want it?"

Eddie shook his head. "I have a drink. That's really suitable for ladies, its sweet like lemonade, why don't you try it?"

I glanced around. Everyone had a glass in their hand they were poised, ready to toast Pearl and Fulvio; it seemed rude not to join in such a special toast.

Reluctantly I lifted up the glass and took a sip.

Maureen was right, it was sweet and tasted a bit like fruit juice. It was nothing like I expected, so I took another sip.

The glass never seemed empty, for being a good host Fulvio was kept busy as he walked around up the glasses. I kept sipping. Eddie was occupied, talking happily over the far side of the room with the men, and Maureen was staying close by John's side. The time flew by and as the clock moved closer towards midnight, Fulvio and several others mentioned going to celebrate mass at the Cathedral. Soon people began saying their farewells and heading for the door. Eddie helped me into my coat and we stepped outside into the cold night air. For no apparent reason I began to giggle, then as I attempted to make my way down the front steps to my surprise I found myself wobbling and felt Eddie's hand reach out to steady me. I giggled again as I lurched forward. Eddie gripped my arm tightly and turning to Paul, who was standing close behind, spoke to him in Slavic. Paul quickly grabbed my other arm and together they guided me safely down the tall flight of steps. Once I stepped onto the pavement, I attempted to walk in the direction of the Cathedral; I wanted desperately to witness the special service.

Eddie tried to persuade me to go straight home. Not realizing that I was tipsy, I loudly began protesting, "I'm going to church."

Everyone around me then joined in a chorus of advice: "Take her home Eddie, she can't go to church like that."

Eddie tried to guide me towards my home and I burst into tears. Rita looked at me and seemed upset.

Maureen, having heard the commotion, now came forwards to find out what seemed to be the problem. When she realized what had happened, she exclaimed, "Bloody hell, what's her grandmother going to say?"

Thankfully I would never know what she would have said or done. For my friends next day assured me that I had finally been persuaded to go home and was safely put to bed before Grandmother discovered how I had heralded in the New Year. The subject was never mentioned again except by my closest friends.

The impact on Eddie of discovering how a couple of glasses of weak Italian wine had affected me gave him such a fright that from that moment he would be the first one to remind people: "Don't offer Bernice alcohol, for the smallest amount affects her in the most peculiar way!"

Chapter 53

The sound first attracted me. I looked up and hanging by a thread pinned to the old unpainted doorframe was the tattered remains of what once had been a brightly decorated poster. Fluttering in the breeze, the faded coloured paper a year ago had helped decorate Bloomsgrove Street. It seemed to be the only evidence left of such a special day. For the brightly coloured picture had demonstrated the golden coach that transported our young Queen on Coronation day towards Westminster Abbey.

I stretched out my hand and untangled the thread. As the torn remnants fell apart in my hand, I reminisced. Time had moved on and so many things seemed to have changed in Radford. It had been an eventful twelve months and although the posters and flags one by one had disappeared, I gained comfort that the captured memories of such a precious time would last forever. For it really had been a special day to remember.

The Queen's Coronation: history in the making, and I had been part of it. I hoped in the years to come that I would recall the time when I had joined a small gathering of Elizabethan subjects, all sitting around a small black and white television in Bloomsgrove Street and watching the ancient ceremony.

In the years to come, perhaps other bands of friends will also remember how they celebrated the occasion together.

Having supported and befriended each other from early childhood, I had travelled through good and bad times with the Blossoms of Bloomo.

A title given us so long ago in jest – all survivors, despite the hardships and obstacles we had flourished and blossomed.

Born in the 1930s, entering into an unsettled world of poverty and unemployment, as a world war engulfed us we battled on through the harsh years of food shortages, bombs and poor medical care. With our education and home life interrupted, somehow we had managed to stride on. Incredibly, hardships appeared to make one stronger. For life on the overcrowded terraces and backstreets it seems provided a magical ingredient that money cannot buy: a sense of belonging and the proof that man did not live by bread alone.

Grandmother's duties during the years had become easier; now she was able to sit back, her life was less stressful as she moved on at a slower pace. Mavis and I had settled in jobs and Grandmother's oldest grandchild was now a settled respectable homemaker and mother.

Dad continued with the same dedication to pace the forest recreation park, doing his best to maintain law and order. He expected little reward at the end of a busy day except the simple pleasure of enjoying coming home to Bloomsgrove Street. There, with a well fed contended cat purring happily on his lap and settled in his old armchair, he would turn the volume on his wireless up and enjoy listening to a mystery play while he drank a mug of hot tea.

Across at No. 15, Rita's mother now accepted that her daughter was becoming a spirited young woman and eventually welcomed Paul into her home. Although ill health prevented Lottie from working, she continued meeting her old friends at The Peacock Inn.

Across at No. 18, the residents there found peace had descended. For Pearl's mother was living happily there with her youngest daughter Bubbles, who almost had completed her schooling. Pearl, settled and living in her impressive new home, visited the street as often as she can.

Across at No. 21, soon a young girl would benefit from the new pharmaceutical discoveries that were leaping forth. A vivacious character, Sandra was looking forward to finishing school and despite her health problems was becoming a tough, bold individual. Her older sister Pat was in the work force, doing well and happily employed by a local solicitor.

Rita, Maureen and all the Blossoms continued enjoying life and the special friendship we have shared since early childhood. We are leaving childhood behind and now with adulthood swiftly approaching we hoped the close bond would continue.

Little Mabel's life now easier, she with great glee continued to shop for bargains at Hyson Green shops. After these shopping jaunts, often a lucky local would receive a hastily wrapped small parcel, for Little Mabel received great joy distributing food and other items to folk that she felt needed aid. Her kindness amused people and was appreciated by many. I myself was often a recipient of her generosity.

As was Eddie – who, when first he met Little Mabel, surprised her by fondly kissing her hand. They developed a good relationship despite the difficulty of her progressive deafness and Eddie's unusual accent. Eddie, however, explained he felt drawn to her side; it was obvious they had a rapport and from the beginning she made it clear that this man, who towered over her, was really just another rather large chick to be placed under her protective wing.

Saturdays always a special time for me, for that was the day I made my way into town to meet Eddie.

By now, I had developed the confidence to stand and wait outside the Nottingham Council House, there joining other courting couples who gathered around the big stone lions.

Often I declined using transport to get to Market Square, choosing instead to slowly walk up Ilkeston Road and make my way towards the town centre. Passing as I did my old school, I viewed the building where so many of early childhood memories and adventures happened. More recently, I pondered on other events. The one uppermost in my thoughts was the reason I chose the answers to questions I was asked at my recent pre-nursing interview.

One particular question prompted me to explain my choice of career more deeply.

For I was asked, "Bernice what makes you keen to pursue a career caring for children?"

Attempting to reply to such a question made me stop and recall the many kind actions shown to me by people like Little Mabel and how such kindness can affect young children. I realized then how lucky I had been to get to know her and others, recalling how Maureen was fortunate to have this tiny woman with a giant's heart as her mother. In the future any mothering skill I might display would in part have been obtained by osmosis, by observing caring people such as Little Mabel.

I walked on, now passing by the school building. It loomed down and I imagined hearing sounds echoed from the past, the laughter of children playing in the schoolyard.

Pearl's impressive house was now in sight; happy to know her childhood struggles were over, I rejoiced that she had a better life. I recalled the uncomfortable moments of years gone by. Times when Pearl, Mavis and I attempted to keep warm in a bitter, unheated bedroom. There on cold winter nights we huddled together in one bed. I never understood the reason we spent many nights together at Pearl's house, sleeping in a cold damp bedroom, for it remains a mystery.

My mother must have agreed, for at that time she was living at home. I have so little knowledge of her or memories; perhaps the reason was that she worked on night shift at the local gun factory. I also have no recollection of a responsible adult being there during those long worrying nights. Mavis, being older, mentioned that our father possibly was awaiting his medical discharge from the Army. Pearl's father was away serving in the forces and it seemed ages before he returned home. The whereabouts of Pearl's dark haired attractive mother on those cold winter nights was another unsolved mystery.

What a strange time to be growing up, yet being young had some consolation, for unlike adults we failed to understand the threat of an enemy invasion. My main worry was being an abandoned child; this created nightmares that concerned me more than anyone ever realised.

As I continued my journey towards Derby Road, I approached the Catholic Cathedral. I hoped Eddie would also be making his way into the town centre. He was not a person known for being punctual and because I was early, I walked slowly. As I neared my destination, it was a pleasant surprise seeing him waiting for me. He waved as I approached and gave me a warm smile, then stepping forward he tightly hugged me. His pleasant fresh smell that seemed so familiar now prompted sad thoughts of how deeply I would miss him if he decided to go to Canada. For a brief moment, I wanted to cry out, "Have you made a decision, are you leaving?"

Fear however prevented me doing so, for I was afraid of hearing the answer. I was too aware that if he decided to sail away, his leaving would cause me pain.

Eddie was aware that I was on the brink of taking an important step towards making nursing my career. Once my journey commenced, years of dedication, hard work and study lay ahead for me. Any other hopes and fantasies would have to be cast aside, for I knew that Eddie should also be free to seek and secure his own dreams. I was starting to realise that, in order to fulfil our long held dreams, we sometimes pay a huge emotional price.

Eddie now surprised me by suggesting we walk up Friar Lane towards the castle. He began to explain he wanted discuss something before we visited the Odeon Picture House. Feeling tense, I nodded in agreement; Eddie, sensing my discomfort, reached out and gently squeezed my hand as we walked up the hill. Now I could see the castle wall looming in the distance; hearing him promise to buy me an ice cream once we reached the castle gate, I smiled. It reminded me of our first date with all the melting ice cream. There had been numerous occasions since when generously he plied me with ices.

As we entered the gates of Nottingham Castle and climbed up the grassy sloping ground, I glanced across the lawn in the direction of Nottingham General Hospital. The nurses' living quarters were clear to see and I noted Eddie glancing in the same direction. I wondered again why he had suggested coming to this particular spot. Was it to disclose his future plans?

Pensively I vowed: whatever the future brings, I will hold on to the precious memories of the time spent with him. My teenage years had provided so many images to treasure. As had my early childhood, the times spent living with my gentle dad and long-suffering and weary Grandmother, who struggled to guide and help me. There had been so many others who befriended me, helping make my childhood journey a little smoother. They may never have realized just how much their acts of kindness supported me and brought me comfort.

Yes, saying goodbye to childhood can be a difficult (yet exciting) experience, as you plunge into an unknown adult world and take on grown up responsibility.

My sister Mavis had left childhood behind but had her own store of memories; abandoned without a mother's care she had had the extra burden of coping with her wayward younger sister.

To have memories of trusted friends and parents is something to treasure, their support and laughter is a priceless gift.

My unforgettable companions, Pearl, Rita and Maureen, the

Eddie 1948 – in Yorkshire

Blossoms of Bloomo, who had accompanied me on my early journey? We had experienced rough patches as well as madcap joyous days together.

As Eddie beckoned me to sit beside him on the bench, I felt my journey through life about to change directions. I was apprehensive about his decision, yet I realised whatever happened in the future, the time Eddie and I had spent together had given us the wonderful opportunity of adding special pages to our book of memories. I will never forget him, and hope he never forgets the moments he spent with me.

Precious memories – what gift it is that enables us turn back the pages of time and recall our earlier days.

Childhood it seems passes by so quickly. Too soon, you realise, having walked, talked, cried and laughed together with childhood friends, no longer are they children. It's then you may discover that other friendships appear, that also may become precious. Moreover, it is the reason I feel grateful I have, and am continuing to share my life with so many unforgettable people.